T0305446

Decision Making and Business Performance

NEW HORIZONS IN MANAGEMENT

Series Editor: Professor Sir Cary L. Cooper, CBE, *50th Anniversary Professor of Organizational Psychology and Health at Alliance Manchester Business School, University of Manchester, UK and President of the Chartered Institute of Personnel and Development and British Academy of Management*

This important series makes a significant contribution to the development of management thought. This field has expanded dramatically in recent years and the series provides an invaluable forum for the publication of high quality work in management science, human resource management, organizational behaviour, marketing, management information systems, operations management, business ethics, strategic management and international management.

The main emphasis of the series is on the development and application of new original ideas. International in its approach, it will include some of the best theoretical and empirical work from both well-established researchers and the new generation of scholars.

Titles in the series include:

Decision Making and Business Performance

Eric J. Bolland

Scholar-in-Residence and Visiting Professor, College of Business and Management, Cardinal Stritch University, USA

Carlos J. Lopes

Eastern Kentucky University, USA

NEW HORIZONS IN MANAGEMENT

Edward Elgar
PUBLISHING

Cheltenham, UK • Northampton, MA, USA

Published by
Edward Elgar Publishing Limited
The Lypiatts
15 Lansdown Road
Cheltenham
Glos GL50 2JA
UK

Edward Elgar Publishing, Inc.
William Pratt House
9 Dewey Court
Northampton
Massachusetts 01060
USA

A catalogue record for this book
is available from the British Library

Library of Congress Control Number: 2018931724

This book is available electronically in the **Elgar**online
Business subject collection
DOI 10.4337/9781786430168

ISBN 978 1 78643 015 1 (cased)
ISBN 978 1 78643 016 8 (eBook)

Typeset by Servis Filmsetting Ltd, Stockport, Cheshire

To: Grandchildren Joaquin, Sawyer and John-Eric Bolland
To: Children Tori, Joey, Maria and Tony-Carlos Lopes

Contents

1. Introduction

In *Hamlet*, Shakespeare wrote that the play is the thing. That is in *Hamlet* where his father's murderer would reveal himself. The drama critic would go further and say the performance is the thing too. That is our concern as well. In this book, we, the authors, examine the performance of the business organization in terms of the execution of the script, or in the case of business, the business strategy decisions. The play is what happens on the stage, something we can believe or not but the performance is what we discuss after the play in the world of the real. We know that play and performance are inextricable on the stage, but we separate the two when we consider businesses. In a cause and effect sequence, the business acts through its decisions and these decisions have detectable consequences. Unlike drama, the performance of the business occurs after the playing of the parts. Business decisions are aimed to produce future results. Decisions can be modified in their process of execution but major decisions such as strategic decisions really should not be changed in midstream. Strategic decisions are ones the organization sticks with. They are major decisions not tactical ones.

Time matters with strategic decisions. It matters because there is distance between the strategic decision and its consequences. The time between decision formulation and full execution gives the observer time to see the decision be implemented and have the organization and its people adjust to the decision. The longer the time, the more that can happen to affect performance results.

By and large, parties outside the business such as governments, communities and consumers do not act directly on business operations but after time intervals when the results of the actions have been recorded and publicized. Most of the time this is a year or so with quarterly reports of results within the year for publicly traded companies. These outside parties then act themselves with investment advice for investors, evaluations of progress and strategies that were employed as well as reviews of contracts with the businesses. There is reliance on these reports and analyses because corporate managers run things autonomously from the outsiders. The report card of firm performance is critical for outside reviewers. They hold the fate of many businesses. Invariably and repeatedly CEOs will ask, "How will this strategy affect our quarterly report?" And: "What will we have to show in our annual report?" These are not sentiments of impatience but of orientation to the future. Accountability for future results is primary the responsibility of the CEO so there is little wonder why that assignment looms daily for the CEO even if the strategic plan is not worked on every day.

In our study of decisions and results, we will trace backward from result to decision to better understand what happens. We will work from the performance results reported in our interviews with corporate leaders and case studies of both successful and unsuccessful decisions. These are also reported by the business leaders in our survey group and our findings from the cases. What is different between the successful and unsuccessful decision? What can be learned from businesses and what can be applied, if anything, to other corporate operations? A more detailed elaboration of research questions follows shortly in this chapter, but the central questions are how successful and unsuccessful strategic decisions are different and what are the connections between decisions and corporate performance?

Popular business literature abounds with stories about how good business decisions helped businesses thrive and how bad decisions caused bad results (Harnish, 2012). These decisions may not seem epic for the organization, but they are pivotal and directional. It can be a matter of hiring the right person or changing a strategic orientation but the right thing was done at the right time. A pivotal change of strategy was made.

Here are just a few decisions that had a positive effect from the book: Apple bringing back Steve Jobs, Toyota pursuing zero defects, Henry Ford doubling worker's wages and Boeing betting big on the 707 are just a few examples of course-changing strategic decisions.

On the negative side, that of bad decision making, there are also many instances of poor business decisions. There are some memorable standouts such as when Ross Perot didn't buy Microsoft, IBM letting Microsoft keep the copyright for DOS and Western Union passing on the telephone (Business Insurance, 2016). Most of these were lost opportunity decisions but there are many other business decisions which led to financial or market loss. They are exemplified by Detroit motor vehicles ignoring the Japanese motor vehicle quality control efforts, American small electronics firms ceding small electronics manufacturing to Asian firms and Exxon's failure to act quickly when Exxon Valdez spilled oil.

THE DECISION–PERFORMANCE LINK

Our purposes are to draw conclusions about the decision–performance link from an executive interview research project where CEOs, owners and key managers of American companies reported successful and unsuccessful decisions in terms of corporate performance. Over two hundred decisions, half for successful decisions and half unsuccessful decisions are included from key individuals and case studies. The survey respondents set their own criteria for successful and unsuccessful decisions.

There are six major questions we will address:

1. Is there a connection between strategic business decisions and business performance?
2. Are there business decisions that lead to successful performance?
3. Are there business decisions that lead to unsuccessful performance?
4. How strong is the linkage between decisions and successful performance?
5. How strong is the linkage between decisions and unsuccessful performance?
6. Can the decision–performance sequence be modeled?

In the language of social research, we will investigate top level decisions as the independent variable and business performance as the dependent variable. By "top level" we mean decisions that are made that affect the strategic direction of the organization. These decisions are most often done by the chief officers of the business but not necessarily so. The decisions can percolate up from other levels of the business as one sees in flat and newly formed businesses. A high technology business may have a small number of workers and the workers may themselves have considerable responsibility for product or market or both. Software developers may introduce a cloud-based application that represents a very new direction for the company and the CEO merely ratifies that direction. The decision itself truly emerged at a lower level but became the raison d'être for the whole enterprise.

WHAT IS DECISION MAKING?

Providing some definitions is a requisite launch point for research and this is no exception. Nobel laureate Herbert Simon calls decision making the process of evaluating and choosing courses of action. Decision making happens after fixing agendas, setting goals and designing actions. Decision making does not occur out of sheer fabrication or whim. It derives from the preceding problem-solving steps of setting an agenda, deciding goals and specifying what the actions should be. So, when you arrive at the decision-making stage, there should be defined and different paths that the organization can take. Simon notes that the complexity of problems in organizations necessitates cutting them down to size so that decisions can be made. Why? Because we can get bogged down in trying to cope with making big decisions like those called for in strategic management. When a company faces a large downturn in sales revenue, the problem to be solved can be broken down to explore what product lines are contributing to this, where in the country the sales decline is happening and other smaller possible contributors to the problem.

Simon is well known for demonstrating there are limits to human rationality in solving complex problems. This leads to the use of heuristics, rough modeling (simple conceptual models of depicting what is happening), and intuition when it comes to arriving at solutions. People tend to anchor on simpler and more understandable decision-making aids when facing complex decisions. They anchor on these because they may not know about more sophisticated problem-solving techniques and may not understand the methods. Simple methods may have worked well in the past too.

Another definition of decision making is that it is the thought process of making a choice from the available options (BusinessDictionary, 2016). This source advises that the decision maker weigh the positives and negatives of each option and consider all the alternatives. To be effective, the outcome of each option should be forecast. Both the Simon and the BusinessDictionary definition put a premium on choice of courses of action in their definitions.

In practice, meeting the outcome forecast of the BusinessDictionary definition is the very difficult part. This necessitates many assumptions about competitive moves, industry trends and customer preferences. Directional paths or courses of action must be converted to numbers, usually dollars in this step. Populating the alternatives with numerical specificity is more difficult than heading this way or that way is something that is commonly said by decision makers in businesses.

Behavioral decision making is a variant of decision making. As one author notes, it "attempts to understand how people make decisions and how they can make decisions more effectively" (Taylor, 1984, p. 1). In this endeavor, special attention is placed on human behaviors that affect decision making in the words of Taylor. We are clearly focused on behavioral decision making in businesses.

DECIDING OR NOT AND DECIDING WRONG

Deciding is burdensome. It takes time and consumes intellectual resources. At times, the solution developed from the decision makes the problem worse; such was the case when the British in colonial India decided to eliminate cobras by paying for their destruction. This only caused a bigger problem when cobras were bred extensively, and breeders collected their bounties. When the British stopped paying, the cobras were released thus exacerbating the original problem.

There are conditions when decisions should not be made or should be delayed, such as when a decision is unnecessarily forced, and a multitude of undesired outcomes can happen. Simply waiting it out when trapped is a choice.

Making a decision is not indicated if the alternative decision paths are direr than the present path. Then, taking a blow for the good of the business might be the best approach. If an entire industry is looking at extinction, then the best thing could be to make no decision and instead sell off all or parts of the company. Ampex faced this when digital storage took over from analog magnetic tape storage. The inevitability of sea change, like the ocean receding away from the shore as a sign of a tsunami, is a metaphor for this.

When no reliable information can be obtained to gauge the results of a change of strategic path, this too can be reason to avoid a decision. An alternative path might be beneficial, but that path might also lead to hastened doom. Pursuing a present course is a cautious but prudent choice in instances such as this. Riding it out with your corporate head above water but still breathing is an apt metaphor for this. Bob with the waves and hope you can touch the sand with your feet and get traction is the hope. If you can't touch, you can swim to shore.

Decision making is also risk taking. The decision puts the hand of humans on the process of moving the business organization through its environment. If the decision is wrong, human fingerprints are still on the act. The information technology decision making software cannot be blamed because human beings made the decision to rely on such software. The larger issue is whether any business would survive if the apex of strategic decision making was occupied by machines, not people. The idea that comes to mind is whether airline passengers would climb onboard a plane piloted solely by computers. That can be done today with navigation systems and auto-throttles but few and far between would be the intrepid souls boarding airplanes with unpeopled cockpits.

Active decision-making means risk taking. The alternative, described shortly, is to coast, go with the flow and let present inside and outside forces carry the business ahead. This passivity conflicts with what we expect from management, however. In the universally expressed term of "leadership," the expectation from top level managers is that they lead their organizations by taking reasonable risks for the sake of potential gains and not be custodians of the status quo. Corporate executive committees invariably pick CEOs who are successful and the way they are successful is in their strategic decisions. Taking on some risk with a potential but tolerable downside is the commonality of risk taking among corporate leaders. The risk is perceptible but corporate leaders can see the upside of opportunity in risk.

In the next section, the essential questions about decision making are raised in the mode of a news reporter. The who, what, when, where and how are the questions. The answers, also in this section, are based on the authors' real-life observations and participation in ten business and state government decision making efforts.

Who is the Decision Maker?

A straightforward question like this often elicits a facile but inadequate answer: the boss, the CEO of course. For all but very early stage enter-prises, the decision maker is not a party of one but a group. In some firms it is truthfully most of the organization that makes the major strategic decisions. Some cooperatives operate this way. The head of the company has the authority to make decisions, but they share responsibility for it with others. A decision maker is a choice maker.

The number of decision makers is a factor on the quality of the deci-sion. But adding numbers of decision makers complicates the process of trying to reach a consensus. It is obvious that too many people involved in decisions can slow the process of making a choice. If the culture of the company is to get consensus before making a choice, then getting that consensus can take more time than getting a choice from a fewer number of deciders. Many deciders means having differing views and a more thorough consideration of courses of action.

On the other hand, fewer decision makers means quicker decisions but the final choice of a path has not been scrutinized widely and the chances are greater for reluctant adoption of the decision or even rejection of it.

How Decisions are Made

Neither a purely autocratic, "I am the decider" George Bush kind of unitary decision making nor a totally participatory "from the ground up" type of strategic decision-making process were used. The answer was in the middle and it was a wide swath middle, so much so that none of the twenty methods could be described as typical.

The organizations involved varied much in the involvement of other people. The most constricted was an insurance company which had a chief strategy officer with a small staff of analysts. This group of five staffed almost all the process. They did the internal and external analysis and produced a set of few strategic initiatives that the executive officers discussed and adopted. In one college, the strategic plan was largely in the hands of the public relations executive who held listening sessions and then produced a shopping list of strategic actions. In another action, the executive director of a state agency produced a strategic plan and the members of the board discussed and approved the decisions recommended in the plan.

What are the Decisions?

By and large, the strategic decisions stemmed from the organization's mission, vision and goals. In every case, these were reviewed before the decision making began. The decisions were strategic in nature because they dealt with the allocation of major resources, the timing of application of the resources, considerations of competitive actions and expected outcomes. In this way, the process of strategic decisions forces the connection between decisions and performance by describing each of these two aspects.

When Strategic Decisions Happen

From the examples we were involved in, the duration of the decision scope was annual, either calendar year or fiscal year except in the case of state government when it was biennial. Interestingly, there were no long-term decision horizons of three years or more. In every instance, there was some informal accommodation of crises that would require a strategy rework though no such crises developed.

Why Strategic Decisions Happen

All the organizations were under requirement from their sponsoring organizations to do a decision-making process almost universally as a part of mandated strategic planning. All the organizations went beyond the mandates by recognizing the limitations of tactical planning, the value of analyzing their external environments and the desire to at least set some directional vectors for their organizations.

EVOLUTIONARY AND HISTORIC ROOTS OF DECISION MAKING

Decision making has always been a component in humanity's evolution. The ascension of human needs from the most basic, those Maslow labeled physiological up through to self-actualization, have always been accompanied by choice. The land we inhabit, the shelter we build, the food we eat, the societies we create are all functions of choice. That choice may not be entirely free choice, such as when matters of disease, war and scarcity drive us elsewhere and force choice, but our inherent mobility and drive for something better is the spark that ignites human progress. Decisions are driven by available choices for us as individuals and in collective actions. We will address collective actions on decisions as they occur in businesses in this study.

Creation of businesses is relatively recent in human history and choices within the world of business stem from formulations of social order that well predate business organizations. Humans have spent almost all their time making choices and decisions in non-business environments. The artificial creation of business entities emanate from king's charters. They are not creations from the natural order of things. These charters made the early business organizations legitimate. Territories of their operation, both literal and actual, were carved out for companies. Increasingly sophisticated legal systems defined the limits and the privileges of corporate activity. The legal system has a heavy influence over business decision making. That system provides the rules for decision making between businesses and within businesses as far as civil and criminal law is concerned.

A long social tradition predates business decision making. Even the traditions of law do not supersede social tradition. Factors like the drive for individual power as articulated by David McClelland explain the social context of business decision making. Individuals want their decision preferences done. That happens at the supervisor to employee level and up through interactions between work groups. In business settings, we also have the matter of responses to decision making. This takes many forms: resistance, compliance and compromise exist but the added factor of the group adds other choices: sabotage and passive resistance among them. Since most business organizations need the consent of others to get things done, reaction to decisions is a critical factor because it extends decision making consequences as the decision works its way through the organization.

The process of group decision making is well known by management theorists and experimenters. Individuals may use their power to influence the group's decision. They may use other devices to have an outcome they want to be the group decision. We will consider group decision making and implementation as we move along with our subject.

Many management practitioners have devised ways to better-optimize group decision making. Some ideas involve the composition of the group, the process used in decision making, the structure of the group to achieve effective group functioning. The effort to improve group decision making serves to reinforce the notion that decision making is important in business organizations, either individually or in group settings.

At the highest level of the organization, its chief officers engage in strategy-setting decisions. These decisions have occurred in increasing layers of public scrutiny as concepts like sustainability play a part in corporate decision making. Corporate accountability has also been heightened as well through SOX and other laws. Strategic decisions, to be effective, require broad commitment on the part of employees. In a way, employees should decide whether to commit themselves to a strategic decision or not.

This approach of including reactions to decision making is a rarity for most practical businesses studies especially those of large, well established businesses. There the key decisions about what product to offer, what markets to be in, what resources are allocated and how to competitively position the firm are matters for senior executives. They concern themselves with core decisions which nudge and even, linebacker-like, shoulder the organization into new commercial worlds. This includes consideration of what to do, when to do it and the anticipated results. These kinds of decisions are tectonic in nature and decisions which we can properly designate as strategic decisions.

IMPORTANCE OF TOPIC

The subject of business decisions and performance of the firm is important for several reasons.

1. Decisions are done by people. The people in the organization through their decisions affect the results of the decisions. Accordingly, if the decision process changes then the results of decisions change. Not all business decisions are done by people all the time. Minor decisions are done by people but codified in policies and procedures. Increasingly, minor decisions are done by decision support programs. These routine decisions are imperceptible, but they do occur.

2. On a daily basis, thousands of decisions are made by larger businesses and hundreds of decisions are made by smaller businesses. It is important to sort out these many different types of decisions to know

which decisions are most consequential to the business and which are less consequential.

3. Decisions are made about investments by outside investors based on the decisions that led to certain results by the business. Effective decisions with results lead to more investment from investors.

4. Sound decision making is a source of competitive advantage for businesses. Businesses with a record of such decisions can differentiate themselves from organizations without sound decision making.

5. Results of business decisions are based on hard facts. The facts cannot be distorted and so, the performance results are definitive and do not require another round of verification. The proof is in the pudding so to speak.

6. Overall, not much is known about how business decisions affect performance. Studies of the subject have been narrowly defined. It is important to know more about what decisions lead to specific results so that speculation is reduced.

7. Little is known too about aggregated performance results although that is important for managing the whole enterprise. The decision–performance continuum has been studied more on the basis of single decisions and single or few performance parameters and not on multiple strategy dimensions and multiple performance measures. This book will add to this understanding.

8. Major corporate decisions are game changers. They can have the effect of restructuring industries. Some of these instances are when King Gillette changed the way people shave by deciding to produce disposable razors to replace blades that required constant sharpening. Another was when Pan Am decided to embark on international air travel. Other carriers quickly followed. When Sam Walton revolutionized the distribution system by deciding to explore neglected trade areas by large scale retailers like Sears and Penney's, retail distribution itself changed.

LEVELS OF BUSINESS DECISIONS

Starting with the individual and proceeding to the corporate level, we can and will further delineate decision making.

At the individual level, decisions at large, established organizations are very often preferences for courses of action which are not specified by policies or procedures or by embedded information technology systems. An individual can sometimes decide how they will do the work, what the sequence of actions will be and when the work will be done. Think of work of an artist as an example of this. Individual-level decision making happens more in emerging businesses where there are fewer policies and procedures.

At the next level, a work team, work group or small department level a few individuals can make decisions about work they are responsible for.

In ascending the organization, the functional level is where business decisions can occur. Hofer and Schendel have expanded on this (Hofer and Schendel, 1978). This level is where most day-to-day decisions happen so the scope of the functional level is quite broad. By functional level, what is included is the maximization of resource productivity. A focus on distinctive competencies rather than large scope initiatives is a mark of this level. When considering structure, the functional level decision making happens in business units such as finance, marketing, production and purchasing. Fit is also a major component of decision making. Decisions made need to fit with upper level business purposes. Coordination across other functional units is also important.

The next highest level for decision making is the business level. This can be a single line of business. At this level, there is attention to environmental factors outside the immediate business. How environmental factors affect the business operations along with internal operations are the scope of business level decisions. An example of a single line business is Victor mouse traps.

At the apex of decision making is the corporate level. Here we find decisions about the formulation of strategies which are aimed at meeting the purposes of the organization. The corporate level is the broadest level possible. It deals with the entire universe of decision making, from survival to balancing the separate businesses that a holding company might own to global operations of many individual businesses. An example of a corporate level decision base is General Electric which owns single businesses in broadcasting (NBC), medical imaging and aircraft engines.

Our treatment of decisions will include the corporate, business and functional levels with most emphasis on the corporate and business level where we can find strategic decisions being made. At the individual and workgroup level, strategic decisions are largely absent except in very small and venture stage businesses.

STRATEGIC AND TACTICAL LEVEL DECISIONS

To further clarify the nature of the decision that is in the scope of this study, a distinction between strategic and tactical decisions is made. Our interest is in strategic decisions.

A strategic decision is a determination by the business of when considerable resources are directed to non-short-term objectives. It is directional or re-directional for the organization. Many if not all the work units are affected. A strategic decision cannot easily be reversed. A strategic decision is usually formulated after a serious analysis of options and its implementation often involves challenges and more individual commitment than tactical decisions. Strategic decisions are most often made by the top corporate executives. Strategic decisions look more at the outer organization than do tactical decisions.

Strategic decisions are very apparent while tactical decisions are less obvious. Strategic decisions are known to competitors because they require visible resource movements, add or subtract from the workforce, alter product markets and initiate or retract from major markets. Competitors can see and react to this. Tactics, on the other hand, are smaller and quicker moves which are more difficult to decipher as patterns. Most times, tactical decisions remain internal and are not visible outside the organization.

A tactical decision involves fewer resources and the objectives are more short term, frequently within a year's time. Its domain is within a division or department or work unit. The consequences of the decision are also more evident within the division, department or work unit. A tactical decision can be more easily reversed. Tactical decisions are made in cases when an organization may want to test market a product or may want to try a sales approach. It may also mean trying a marketing message to provoke a competitor's reaction. It can be thought of as a foray instead of a strategic advance. Tactics that fail are less consequential than strategies that fail. Tactical decisions are made by vice presidents, directors, managers and supervisors. Implementation of tactical decisions is easier than strategic decisions though tactical decisions are reviewed for fit with strategic decisions. Strategic decisions are not as subject to conformance with tactical decisions.

Strategic and tactical decisions are not entirely separate, however. A strategic decision to introduce a new product in a new market may have a whole series of tactical level decisions which stem from the strategic decision. Tactical decisions about distribution channels might be: how many? This tactical level decision follows from the strategic decision of having distribution channels in the first place. Corporate or independent and the like are very consequential and can involve complex and interdependent subsidiary decisions that, especially for those involved, may seem strategic in nature because they consume time and require organizational change. Overall then, the difference between tactical and strategic decisions is one of degree. That leads to the idea that businesses themselves, depending on at least their size and complexity, should sort out the two forms for their purposes. Our approach is to use the aforementioned descriptors as a guide for distinguishing between the two.

Tactical decisions are largely outside the scope of this book because these kinds of decisions are quite varied, and they tend to be isolated to the specific circumstances of the company. What kind of load weighing equipment for coal extraction is a specific tactical question for coal companies that is irrelevant for natural gas production companies. Strategic decisions, our focus, are common to most types of companies and this approach thus becomes more useful for most business organizations.

Strategic decisions will have more impact on the overall business organization than tactical decisions. Each is important and when they are coordinated with each other, the overall strategic direction of the organization is a force of nature.

PROBLEMS WITH MAKING BUSINESS DECISIONS

The sequence of making the decision and then measuring performance is syntactically simple but in actuality it is complex. That complexity manifests itself in different but important ways as enumerated.

1. The performance that is measured has changed over time. As described shortly in the chapter, the measurement of corporate performance has shifted from the collection of financial measures used in the 1950s through the 1970s in U.S. businesses to more customer focused measures, cross-industry measures, and an array of nonfinancial methods perhaps best exemplified by balanced scorecard techniques.
2. Establishing a causal relationship between the decision and the performance has always been difficult but it is increasingly difficult in contemporary times where corporations have encountered more governmental scrutiny, a circumspect public, rising expectations from the financing communities, review and regulation by foreign governments and more intense competition in many industries. Executives can intelligently speculate about the causes of performance but certainty about decision cause and performance results is far from certain.
3. Strategic decisions do not have immediate impacts. They are more gradual unless they occur in a crisis. Strategy managers often use the expression of "turning battleships" when referring to the directional sets or resets that strategic decisions cause.

   If strategic decisions were quickly measured for their effects, then many other intervening variables explaining performance could be eliminated. Instead, strategic decisions take time – as well they should so the decisions can be digested by the business as a whole.

4. Implementation of strategic decisions is not direct. Formulators of strategy are not direct supervisors of the front-line troops. The front-line troops are led by managers and directors who interpret the strategic decision. Conformance of this to original strategy can vary greatly with some managers and directors paying lip service to the strategy, others actually opposing, and others truly committed to it.

5. Another problem with linking the decision to the performance is that the performance measure may not validly measure what is supposed to be measured. Market share will serve as an example. Market share information is often modeled and based upon a sample of potential customers. A very difficult part of this is that new customers may come into the market who are undetected in the model.

6. Still another problem is filtering of measurement, both intended and unintended may occur. Enron concealed information about its true financial condition in order to meet investor expectations.

7. The reliance on past information to make predictions about the future faced by the business can also be a difficulty as Kurt Christensen observes in assessing the impact of market disruption on corporate strategy.

8. Each company has variations in the way they measure performance. In the world of accounting, there has been some uniformity through the use of generally accepted accounting practices (GAAP) and accountability with the implementation of the Sarbanes–Oxley Law.

9. The presentation and communication of performance information can skew interpretation. CEOs want to constantly paint rosy pictures about the status of their organizations. The temptation exists (and is sometimes succumbed to) for highlighting modest, minor and temporary good news in annual reports while downplaying bad news.

10. The measures of performance may be changed by upper level managers if they do not meet internal organization objectives or outside market expectations. The restatement of financial results is one way this is done. The timing of cash inflows is another. Tax law allows deferment of revenues as a way of deferring or reporting revenues in one year or another.

11. Strategic business decisions are the handiwork of the people who set strategy for the organization. There is no other aspect of business which is more closely connected to people as this. Strategic management and strategic planning do use information gathering and analysis tools, but these actions are evaluated by strategy crafters, not by computer-based decision-making programs.

12. Indecisiveness is a problem with business decision making as it is with the human condition itself. Indecisiveness can cause the elimination of available choice as time precludes available choice. That makes worse decisions possible. It may be reason to try stopgap measures or workarounds so frequently found in information technology activities.

This is not a complete listing of the problems inherent in business decision performance measurement. They may be formidable in some instances, but they are not insurmountable. The reason for their listing is to identify how they may raise their ugly heads. For each of these problems, there are ways the problems can be mitigated or even eliminated. The role of people is immense and touches most of the problems.

The listed problems would appear to affect larger businesses more than smaller businesses mainly because change to solve the problems is more difficult for larger organizations. Smaller companies are nimbler in this respect

It would be essential for the strategy managers to address each of the problems (and add other problems that would be relevant) and determine which must be addressed.

The work of managers, of scientists, of engineers, of lawyers – the work that steers the course of society and its economic and governmental organization – is largely the work of making decisions and solving problems, which is a paraphrase of Herbert Simon.

STEPS OF DECISION MAKING

Simon has also contributed to an understanding of organizational decision making by proposing that decision making happens in stages not in one fell swoop. Commonly, an attribute of decision making is to say that one is decisive. This connotes rapid decision making. Simon, however, states that decision making happens in three phases: Finding reasons to make a decision, finding courses of action and picking a course of action (Simon, 1960). There are two respects in which this is important. The first is that snap decisions are not advocated by this leading management theorist and the second is the implication that the decision involves others in the organization. Strategic decisions involve others to a greater degree.

The time element also comes into play in a phased approach to decision making. The time between when the reason for making a decision happens and when the decision is implemented can be a time for uncertainty and change to come into the decision equation. Uncertainty can emerge if new environmental factors, unforeseen at the first phase, come in to challenge assumptions made. The recession of 2008 did just that for the American automobile industry. Unanticipated change can also happen. The people who were expected to implement the decision might leave for outside jobs. A natural event like a hurricane could disrupt a supplier chain.

DECISIONS AND PLANNING

Two authors have delineated the roles of decision making and planning (Mankins and Steele, 2006). They argue that strategic planning isn't about making decisions, but it is about documenting choices that have already been made. Strategic planning is still a very popular tool among corporate leaders. These authors take a skeptical look at the *process* of strategic planning. They assert that strategic planning inhibits decision making. It takes too long and does not focus on making decisions. They state executives plan 66 percent periodically but decide 100 percent continuously. Unit by unit planning is done but decisions are made issue by issue. An antidote for this is continuous, decision-oriented planning which begins with identifying strategic priorities, then through executive committee dialogues as many decisions are made on issues faced by the company. Alternative actions are devised, and a decision is made to resolve the issue. Budgets follow the decisions rather than lead the decision process. This means budgets and strategic planning are better integrated.

THE PROBLEMS WITH MEASURING PERFORMANCE

In this section, the problems and issues about measuring performance are discussed. This review will demonstrate just how varied these problems are.

1. Deciding just what is to be measured can be a problem. In our times, the ways of measuring performance are legion in number, and many can be used in business settings. The mere act of screening out inappropriate measurement tools is time consuming for the organization. Screening might also result in the elimination of very appropriate methods of measuring performance. In considering the broad measures of business performance, economic (macroeconomic, GDP, etc.), financial (profitability, earnings), market (market share, market position), innovation (patents, research and development new product introductions), customers (satisfaction, loyalty), social

responsibility (sustainability measures, value of charitable contributions), employees (satisfaction, tenures): there are dozens of measures embedded within each of the categories. This leads to hundreds of measurement tools.

2. There may be a problem with standardization of performance. This problem can happen internally or externally. Internally, it may be discovered that performance criteria are no longer useful and should be replaced. Externally, the business may not be measuring performance using methods employed by other businesses in the same industry. It may also be true that the business is holding businesses in multiple industries each with different performance standards.

3. Another problem could be that the performance measurement chosen does not fit the outcome that it is supposed to measure. The Total Quality Measurement movement unveiled the notion of root causes in which fundamental or root problems were identified in the fishbone diagram which pointed the way to controllable causes and not symptoms of those causes.

4. Still another problem is the Heisenberg effect which is a very loose derivation from the physics phenomenon of measurement distortion. If an objective measurement is taken at a certain time and position, mass and energy, the process itself distorts measurement in such a way that not all elements of the interaction can be measured accurately. Applying this to the world of management, if employees know that something they are doing is being measured, they react in unnatural ways to distort the result if it affects assessment of their personal performance. That is the very basis of the Hawthorne experiments of Elton Mayo that reshaped management thought.

5. In addition to the measurement validity issue described above, there is the possibility of a measurement reliability problem. Reliability means consistency in repeated uses of the measurement in producing consistent results.

6. Calibration of instruments to measure performance results may be another cause for concern. Very famously, the Hubble Space Telescope had a primary mirror with a very slight amount of spherical aberration that was not caught on Earth because the instrumentation used was incorrectly calibrated in the first place. Once in space, the fuzzy images caused an initial failure for Hubble and it was not until astronaut Story Musgrave inserted a corrective lens into the imaging path that Hubble was fixed. For management, measurement calibration of performance parameters is essential for reliable calculations. Using standardized instruments which take accurate performance does this. People build trust in performance measures as a consequence.

7. Informal versus precise measurement is yet another issue. Casual observation of work is in fact a level of measurement. Management-by-walking-around is a management practice in which a manager visits different work areas, watches and sometimes interacts with workers and makes judgments about how satisfied they are about what they see. At the other end of the spectrum, objective measurement of time spent on projects, computer monitoring and the like are numerically based. The numerical base identifies them as being objective. The numerically-based measures can easily conflict with casual measurement. Managers may trust their direct observation more than the numbers produced by another source.

There are solutions to these problems and issues of performance measurement. For standardization, the measurer can investigate if there are established measurement practices within their industry grouping for single industry businesses. If there are not, then they can determine if there are trends favoring certain measures.

If there is doubt about whether the right way is being used for performance measurement, the fishbone diagram of total quality measurement can be employed. Also checking assumptions about the appropriateness of a particular tool can be evaluated by using a designated devil's advocate who is assigned the task of critiquing the measurement technique.

The problem of individuals responding to research scrutiny by changing their performance can be corrected by non-intrusive measuring. It can also be neutralized by the myriad of experimental designs which compare the measurements of studied participants with non-studied participants.

Reliability can be improved by employing proven performance measures. Reliability is also better served by increasing the number of repeated measurements.

Calibration of measurement instrumentation can be enhanced by more frequent calibration and by calibration against more widely accepted standards. An example is measuring a meter by wavelength of light instead of a physical rod a meter long.

PERSPECTIVE ON PERFORMANCE

We take performance to be a consequence on decision making. As such, we are obliged to present a cautionary tale. That follows.

A perspective on business performance is offered by Robert Eccles (1991). He tracks the evolution of performance measurement from financial terms to a much broader set of measures that include market share, customer satisfaction and other non-financial indicators. Eccles notes that purely financial measures have had a long history of dissatisfaction among practitioners and academics. Offering many products in many markets and encountering competitive reaction are more of a fact of life for the modern business organization. These factors make the old accounting measures obsolete. Numbers like quarterly earnings and profits serve investors' concerns more than strategic direction concerns of the business leaders. Eccles adds that financial measures depict the consequences of past decisions, a further limitation. He observes that the quality movement and customer satisfaction measurement have challenged the old financial measures. Benchmarking against industry leaders and information technology has further challenged the old systems of measurement.

To further the effort for better performance assessment, new information architecture is the needed first step. It must be directed to produce the data that the business needs to pursue its strategy. This can lead to what Eccles calls a common grammar within the organization so all know the terms and concepts of an expanded sphere of performance.

How the business generates the performance data is a second step. It incorporates established financial performance with a softer element of innovation, quality, human resources and customer satisfaction. While the company's grammar may be stable, organizations experiment with methods to measure what is important to them. Firms can adopt their own performance measures but should be prepared to modify their structures to get a performance management system that works. Eccles cautions that it is more difficult. If formulas are developed to measure incentives, these rarely work. Thus, there are limits to wholescale incentive-based performance.

Additional information about business performance information is plentiful. It emerges from both practice and academic research. Eccles points out that this needed shift to more expanded performance measurement is a revolution and consequently difficult for all involved.

Though the article is decades old, the issues described remain current. For our purposes, we can use this as an identifying factor for our own look at performance. That is the changing nature of performance management itself.

To a considerable extent, the academic investigation of business decisions and business performance has been confined to building taxonomies of the types of business decisions or describing the many processes of business decisions. Both these efforts have led to a rich development of typologies and processes but there are far fewer and much narrower casual studies that connect performance with decisions despite its promising outcomes for researchers and practitioners alike. The overall aim of this book is to fill the gap between decisions and performance with a sounder understanding of that relationship. This effort will begin with an examination of decisions and then business performance from the point of view of theorists and researchers. What follows is a description of the interviews and cases which are the basis for the research part of the book. Research findings are then presented. Interpretation of research results by executives are offered and finally implications and recommendations along with predictions about the future for corporate decision making and performance.

What follows immediately are briefly presented objectives of each chapter.

PLAN OF THE BOOK

In this chapter, the basics of business decisions and performance were outlined. The objective of explaining performance based on business decisions was set. The importance of the topic was introduced. Problems and issues of decisions were raised as well. Research questions were also posed.

In Chapter 2, much more detail will be presented on business decisions. Literature on business decision making is described and implications are drawn for the present study. The evolution of business decisions is included, and a model of business decision making is described. The circumstances of differing approaches to making business decisions are offered. Different types of business decisions are described including programmed decisions, decision making under uncertainty, data-based decision-making, and intuitive decision making are explained.

Chapter 3 is dedicated to business performance. Literature on the subject is covered and theory and empirical findings from leading management investigators are explained. The various methods of measuring performance are presented and issues about performance are revealed. Each method will be evaluated and a performance measurement system for use in this study is introduced.

In Chapter 4, the focus is on modeling decisions and performance collection. The interview process is described including the purposes for each of the research questions. A model of the decision–performance is presented. That model will be reevaluated in Chapter 8. Finally, interviews with individual CEOs will be conducted to provide elaboration on some of the open-ended comments in the interviews.

Chapter 5 concerns details on the first round findings from the research.

Chapter 6 presents key findings of the research. The key findings will be presented and discussed.

Chapter 7 offers the focused findings through using research techniques aimed at discovering underlying patterns and associations among performance factors. The intent is to fully explore these possible relationships for some of the less obvious findings.

For Chapter 8, overall conclusions are made. Points of difference between perceptions of practitioners and academic investigators are done. Also, through feedback contacts after interviews with some survey participants, the matter of what they believe about performance results from business decisions is explored and possible explanations are reported. A revised conceptual model of decisions and performance is provided.

In Chapter 9, recommendations by business size and other factors are offered. Recommendations for optimizing business decisions is a topic of the chapter. The recommendations will be based on the business leader interviews and separate feedback from individual leaders.

In Chapter 10, the future of business organization performance and decision making will be forecast. Decision making future and performance measuring future will be separately and jointly addressed. Projective speculation by the authors will be done with respect to decision risk reduction, computer-based decision making, inclusion and exclusion of certain performance measures, composition of strategic decision-making groups are among the topics.

REFERENCES

BusinessDictionary (2016) retrieved October 22, 2016 from www. businessdiction ary.com/definition/decision-making. html.

Business Insurance (2016) retrieved October 21, 2016 from http://www.businessin surance.org/10-worst-business-decisions-in-history.

Eccles, R. (1991) The Performance Measurement Manifesto, *Harvard Business Review*, 69(1, January–February), 131–137.

Harnish, V. (2012) *Greatest Business Decisions of All Time*, New York: Fortune Books.

Hofer, C. and Schendel, D. (1978) *Strategy Formulation: Analytical Concepts*, St. Paul, MN: West Publishing.

Mankins M. and Steele, R. (2006) Stop Making Plans; Start Making Decisions, *Harvard Business Review*, 84(1, January), 76–94 retrieved January 24, 2018 from https://hbr.org/2006/01/stop-making-plans-start-making-decisions.

Simon, H. (1960) in Taylor, R. (ed.) *Behavioral Decision Making*, Glenview, IL: Scott Foresman and Company.

Taylor, R. (1984) *Behavioral Decision Making*, Glenview, IL: Scott Foresman and Company.

2. Decisions

Decisions are our independent variable in this study. They are the "what we decide to do" side of the sequence of the action yields results equation. Decisions are what we want to carefully define in this chapter and treat as the input variable in the research. The extent to which performance is affected by strategic business decisions is the primary goal of this effort. Consequently, it is essential to define the business decision with more depth and scope than in Chapter 1 where it was discussed and put in the cause and effect continuum that is our interest. This chapter is mainly devoted to the subject of strategic business decisions. A framework for our study of decisions is provided here along with findings on the subject of business decisions.

A decision is a making up of one's mind for the individual in common dictionary terms. To that we would add that a business decision is determining a course of action on business matters to the exclusion of other choices. The exclusion of other choices may not be permanent, but the definition needs to involve some kind of change in the present course of action or it is not truly a decision. It is especially not a strategic decision.

What may seem as a semantic nuance is something quite important in business operations. Choices are not the same as decisions. Choice is an act of choosing or selecting. A decision is the making up of one's mind. While seemingly sounding similar, when put in a grammatical context, they are different. As examples, a Hobbesian choice is not the same as most business decisions. A Hobbesian choice is a simple take-it-or-leave-it proposition while a business decision is often conditional with satisfaction guarantees, varied payment terms and performance incentives. Common usage of these words implies that decision is more powerful than choice. Decisions suggest to us a deeper level of analysis and a resolution of an action than choices. Decisions appeal to our need to solve things while choices seem constant and without endpoints. President Obama, a maker of many decisions is known to have avoided choices over what to have the White House kitchen staff prepare when he instructed staff to make the choices themselves.

In the world of business and in our private lives, there are many other variants of choice other than take-it-or-leave it. Bargaining on terms of acceptance is certainly commonplace for durable goods and services for businesses and individuals alike. We can take it in part. We can take it later.

We can use it but not own it. Choices can be as simple as Hobbesian or as complex as decision trees for equity futures trades.

Decisions follow a process even if it is rapid fire process. Choices are the end points of the decision process. Decisions can be difficult as they are when outcomes are unclear and unpleasant. They are usually the result of a consensus process of a decision team where choice is often in the mind of an individual. Decisions are frequently combined with choice for important operations. The choice is the course chosen by the authority or sponsor of the decision process. The responsibility for making the decision work may be in the hands of others. The buck stops not only at President Truman's desk but at the desk of the decision authority. Decisions made without authority have no meaning in contemporary business because accountability must be assigned for things to work.

Business decisions are those made in the process of business. More specifically, they are decisions made by those in business. The effect of these decisions may be felt outside the firm, but they are decisions made by the men and women of the business. The human side of decision making brings in rationality as well as emotion. Humans bring color to decision making so much so that deciding executives have profiles in their decision-making characteristics. In government, the fast decision making of President Trump contrasts with the slower, contemplative decision making of President Obama.

Choices dominate in business as in our non-business realms. They are frequent, perhaps in the order of hundreds a day compared with strategic businesses which we believe are far less frequent, perhaps in the order of one every ten to ninety business days depending on the size and nature of businesses. Choices occur with such rapidity that they are not even fully conscious activities. From what is known about human cognitive processes, we fall into routine patterns of choices on such things as the colors of office carpeting, the kind of music played in elevators, the arrangements of furniture in our offices or cubicles and the many other frequent and mostly inconsequential choices at work.

Decisions also summon accountabilities not happening with choices. Business organizations have review processes for major decisions. The decisions must be justified. Business choices do not have the same level of accountability nor are the choice-making processes recorded.

STEPS OF DECIDING AND CHOOSING

We say that choosing and deciding can and are combined in business operations. Choice can and does stand alone in less consequential operations.

The rational problem-solving model. A stalwart of management course work is the basis for the following depiction.

The process of deciding and choosing can be depicted as the following steps:

BOX 2.1   DECIDING AND CHOOSING

1. Recognition of Need for Decision > 2. Decision Making > 3. Choice > 4. Implementation > 5. Evaluation and Feedback

---

The diagram expands in both directions from the decision–choice nexus to make it more complete and loop the entire process back to step 1. The first step is sometimes not acknowledged but is important. There may not be a need for a decision if the conditions seemingly indicating a need disappear. For example, the federal government may put a regulation in place requiring manufacturers to meet certain tire tread depth minimum rubber depths when the original decision might have been: What is the minimum tread depth that our tires need because consumer groups are asking for that? The regulation obviates the decision. The standard is imposed by government and requires compliance.

It might also be that any solution to the decision might be worse than the original problem or issue that needed to be addressed. A massive retooling of the tire manufacturing process that adds considerable cost but not much additional safety while also introducing new possible safety risks (from unproven new manufacturing processes) is probably not worth doing.

The decision-making process happens next and it has been described. This step is loaded at the front end with analysis of the decisions. Many organizations in the private and public sector do the development of alternatives as part of the decision process but then clearly indicate what the alternatives are in forms of different choices. The authors have seen decision making reports, especially in the public sector, describing not only the choice but the expected consequences from that choice. In the public sector, these reports usually have revenue impact from the choice and other descriptions on how that choice differs from the others.

In step 5, the choice is implemented, and the results are collected for the feedback stage where the results of the decision are fed into the decision–choice cycle again.

The depiction in Box 2.1 exhibits most of the elements of the rational decision-making process which is itself an idealized version of optimized decision making. That model falls apart if there are power factors at work which influence the choices. If the choice is forced by power players in the organization, there may be few choices or even one choice other than retaining the present way of doing things. Feasible choices might be eliminated by a report author being influenced by a manager who wants the decision to go in their direction. A manager wanting to set the path to favor their preferred choice might also attack the assumptions behind an unfavored alternative of the power-playing manager.

MANAGER ROLES IN DECISIONS: ACADEMIC VIEWS

Accounts of the roles of managers in decision making are plentiful. In his book, *The Nature of Managerial Work*, Henry Mintzberg cites three major categories of roles the manager plays (Mintzberg, 1973). All stem from formal authority and status of the manager's position. The first of the three are the interpersonal roles of figurehead, leader and liaison with other work groups. The second group is informational roles which includes monitoring of information which affects the organization, dissemination of information and acting as a spokesman. The third category is comprised of decisional roles. This includes acting as an entrepreneur, as a disturbance handler, a resource allocator and as a negotiator. Mintzberg calls this role as making significant decisions such as requests for authorization, scheduling their own time, holding meetings on strategies and problems and negotiating with other organizations. He remarks that "the manager takes full charge of his organization's strategy making system . . . the manager is substantially involved in every significant decision made by his organization" (Mintzberg, 1973, p. 77). This comes from the manager's formal authority, their position as being a nerve center of the organization and the fact that one person can be more easily integrated by having a single person in control.

In the entrepreneurial decision role, the manager acts as an initiator and designer of change in their company according to Mintzberg. This aspect of deciding requires that the manager look ahead and see conditions which might cause change for the company. In the disturbance handler mode, the manager must make decisions in which they are only partially in control. When direct reports cannot agree on a course of action and functions are or could be harmed, the manager-as-decider steps in and rectifies the situation. The manager as resource allocator is also a decisional role. This ties closely to the strategy creation function. Almost all managers have some level of direct resource allocation; they can use their influence to guide resource allocation at a higher level. Also, general managers are in promotion paths to higher levels of the business, so their organizational impact grows for successful managers. Finally, we arrive at the manager-as-negotiator. In this stage, non-routine negotiations between other parties and individuals occur. This can be observed in supplier negotiations, customer negotiations and the like. Very obviously, negotiations about mergers and acquisitions involve strategic decision making.

It would be difficult not to recognize that managers of businesses are the crux of decision making. Time after time, the authors have heard managers talk about how they have improved their decision making by repeated use of their own judgment. Practice makes performance, in a manner of speaking. Mintzberg shows just how much time managers spend on decision making roles, so it is manifestly important that decision making is a fundamental aspect of modern management.

STRATEGIC PLANS AND DECISIONS

Ostensibly, many major corporate decisions are found in the strategic plan. However, there are practitioners and academics who see a disconnect between decision making and planning. For one practitioner pair strategic planning and decision making are at odds. Writing in the *Harvard Business Review*, practitioners and authors Michael Mankins and Richard Steele write that strategic planning is not about making decisions. Instead it is about documenting decisions that have already been made (Mankins and Steele, 2006). The authors offer several cases in which traditional off-site, annual, multiple day strategic planning events encounter problems such as infrequent scheduling of annual events, inability to respond to decisions that need to be made, opportunities that may suddenly spring up such as acquisition opportunities, and a focus on business unit planning not issue planning. The suggested antidote is to switch decision making to a continuous basis. Also, decisions should be made by issues rather than by business unit, because issues in business cross business units and are felt by the entire organization.

The critique of strategic planning and its deciding component is echoed by Henry Mintzberg (1994) in *The Rise and Fall of Strategic Planning*. Making strategic decisions is a part of strategic planning and Mintzberg argues that strategic planning is neither strategic or planning. He traces strategic planning back to its roots and asserts that flawed methodologies and bias prevent strategic planning endeavors from attaining their purposes. Despite this criticism, strategic planning retains its popularity as a decision-making tool according to Bain and Company.

NUMBER OF STRATEGIC BUSINESS DECISIONS AND OTHER BUSINESS DECISIONS

Regarding the number of other, non-strategic decisions, the number of decisions is quite high. American consumers make about 35,000 conscious decisions every day. Most of these decisions are minor (what to eat, wear, watch on cable and the like) but they are decisions.

The number of non-business decisions appears to greatly exceed the number of daily business decisions. This following information provides a basis for showing the magnitudes of difference between personal and business decisions. It also serves to demonstrate how the many personal decisions precondition us to make business decisions. In other words, we learn decision making from our private lives.

Turning to business decisions, one estimate is that people make 500 business decisions a day (Major, 2015). That can total 10 million decisions a year in a 100-person decision making employee base. From the same source but by a different author (Martin, 2015) the estimate is that business leaders make dozens of business decisions that have an impact on company success, employees, customers or markets. Referring to dozens of business decisions per day almost certainly means operational decisions for the most part in which daily issues of how to do things are handled, but true strategic decisions occur with far less frequency.

The number of key or strategic business decisions as opposed to non-strategic decisions made drops considerably. As part of the *Harvard Business Review* article by Michael Mankins and Richard Steele (2006) they separate annual strategic business plans focused on business as being 2.5 decisions per year while those focused on business issues were 3.5 decisions per year. Those business decisions with continuous reviews focused on business units were 4.1. Those business decisions focused on issues which were continuously reviewed were 6.1 per year. Their point is that issue and continuous review yield more and more meaningful decisions.

The number of strategic business decisions varies by size of the organization as well. Scope strategic decisions for multinational businesses exceed scope decisions for single country operations. The paucity of studies on this subject makes it very much of a guessing game in terms of the number of decisions, but tactical level decisions are far more than strategic decisions. Part of the point of strategic decisions is, in fact, to reduce the number of decisions overall.

TYPES OF BUSINESS DECISIONS

The vast number of business decisions prompts efforts at classifications of types of decisions often for the sheer sake of making sense of the myriad of numbers.

For a long time, simple classification of business decisions has been to place the decisions of either being programmed or non-programmed decisions. For programmed decisions, these are frequently occurring and not unexpected. They can be handled usually by having processes and procedures in place. Certain functions within the production line are not in alignment and backlogs are building up, stalling the throughput. The source of the problem is clear and on page 1005 of the production line manual, a pinpoint solution is found and executed. The solution to the problem has been proven and it doesn't work then some alternative solutions are found on pages 1006–10. This is an example of a programmed decision solution.

For a non-programmed decision, the solutions are not found in a handy procedures manual and that is because it is a new problem for which there is no existing solution. It is novel enough a problem so that possible solutions are not defined, or they are ill-defined. There is not any guarantee that any alternative decisions will work. A non-programmed decision criterion is clearer about what is expected but less clear about how it will be addressed. Those trying to fix the problem are strangers in a strange land and the expectations are heavy on the shoulders of those who are trying to do so. These decisions are non-programmed because they do not fit in the former example. Solvers must think broadly and deeply. An example of a non-programmed decision might be that a competitor has found a way to increase production line throughput using an undisclosed process that reduces net cost for the production of unit costs for something very comparable to what the company being outdone by the competitor does. Here, there is little information that can be acquired to solve the problem.

Strategic decisions are characteristically non-programmed decisions. There is time available to make the decisions and the resources and talents are also available. The rational model of decision making applies for strategic decisions.

Intuition plays a role in both programmed and non-programmed decision making. A chief executive or other corporate leader can set up a non-programmed decision-making process by speculating on possible decision choice which they have experience with. A caution here is that the speculations need to be objectively evaluated by a non-programmed process and that the power of the executive does not sway the process one way or another. This is similar to using focus groups for initial investigations but also allowing for systematic and rigorous marketing research for the actionable courses of action in new product development processes.

DECISION MAKING LEVELS

The categories of types of decision making have been expanded by decision theorists. These types occur at different structural levels of the business organization.

At the highest point on business decisions which are most likely to be encountered in the real world, business decisions are defined by the level of the decision and the nature of the decision. For level, the highest level is the corporate level followed by tactical and then by operational levels. Tactical and operational level decisions are for the shorter term and corporate level decisions are for the longer term. At the highest level, corporate decisions are more directed to and formulated as goals and not as objectives. Goals are not strictly defined but objectives are. There are fewer resources allocated to decisions at this level and the decision-making process is not as formalized for tactical and operational levels.

Achievement of tactical decisions is very frequently sought within a year or a couple of years and it is even shorter for operational decisions which are made in a day for an effective duration of days or weeks.

Whatever the classifications, a rose is still a rose and decisions permeate businesses so much so that the well-run business pulses with decisions at every level, up and down the organization and horizontally that it is difficult to fixate on a single aspect of decision making occurring at any one place and time. The vibrancy of decision making is what gives the organization its hum, and its perception as electric. The caution here is not to rely on classification systems but causes and effects to understand corporate decision making.

In making strategic decisions, one writer has stressed the significance of considering the type of decision made (Rosenzweig, 2013). Rosenzweig states that the four different types of business decisions are:

1. Making routine choices and judgments which are frequent and highly individualized.
2. Influencing outcomes which is exerting some control of collective decisions.
3. Placing competitive bets which involves competitor analysis and possibly game theory. It considers competitor moves and reactions to those moves.

4.   Decisions in the fourth field which brings together active influence of decisions and success in doing better than competitors. This type of decision is the most strategic in nature.

Rosenzweig advises managers to consider both the nature of the decision at hand and responding with an appropriate choice for the nature of the decision. The implication is that a decision choice for a routine choice such as a replacement tool for a minor production function need not involve placing competitive bets since the ramifications for competition are not consequential.

FROM PRACTICE: TIPS ON BUSINESS DECISIONS

The Small Business Administration has the responsibility of aiding small businesses in many planning areas. In making business decisions, they offer practical advice on how to optimize decisions (U.S. Small Business Administration, 2017). Their suggestions stem from the rational decision-making model but with an emphasis on small businesses. Tips are:

- Define what the decision is, if it needs to be made, who decides and when.
- Brainstorm alternatives using your friends and associates as sources.
- Visualize the outcomes of the alternatives. Are any more satisfying than others?
- Do a reality check by crossing off unlikely alternatives.
- Move on the decision.

Decision making mistakes include relying too much on expert advice and overestimating the value of information provided by individuals having status in the field. At the other end, underestimating the value of others who may not have status but may have insight is something to be avoided. Only hearing what you want to hear is another mistake. Discounting your intuition can also limit your search for answers to a decision. While consistently relying on intuition as a sole means to a decision obliterates rationality, the fear of using intuition at times is not advisable. Intuition has been described to author Eric Bolland as a "super-fast" deductive process which the user of intuition is not even aware of. This company manager simply used it to make fast decisions which he felt were logical but could not articulate how they were logical decisions and frankly admitted that he did not know how they were logical. But he was right most of the time.

EXAMPLES OF STRATEGIC NON-PROGRAMMED DECISIONS IN SMALL COMPANIES

We have put together a list of typical decisions faced by small firms and ventures. This results from our interviews with owners:

1. What are the roles and responsibilities of the business owner and the business manager?
2. What should change about these roles and when?
3. What is the initial basis for financing operations and how might that change as the business grows?
4. What is our structure and what should it be?
5. Should we grow and how?
6. How do we attract and keep talent?
7. What are our responsibilities to external stakeholders?

For newly formed businesses, there are a set of strategic decisions that must also be addressed. They are:

1. Initial funding sources. To what extent is the venture self-funded by the founder and to what extent is it funded by banks, venture capital and grants.
2. What equity should be retained and what equity should be shared? Granting equity to lenders can lead to loss of control by the founder.
3. Partnering or sole ownership. Sometimes ventures work in partnerships when one partner is the "idea monkey" – the generator of creative, possible but unproven business ideas and the other partner is the regulator – reality checker and modifier of schemes. The combination of the two partners produces inventive yet feasible business concepts.
4. How can this venture become feasible? What benchmarks are in place to make progress to successful commercialization? Founders want to make sure that their standards of success meet the standards of investors and stakeholders.
5. Should the venture grow or remain the same? Not all ventures seek to become Microsoft or Apple. Some seek to operate within a niche that sustains and remunerates founders. Resolution of this is a strategic decision.
6. What should initial pricing be? The strategic decision here is: what should our pricing strategy be? Choices for the decision may be skimming pricing, penetration pricing, market pricing, everyday low pricing, product line pricing or others.

7. Fitting the type of business to the entrepreneur. The decision is: is there a fit or not? If there is not, then the founder may lose commitment to the venture concept. If there is commitment, then the issue is the matter if the commitment is backed by the requisite skills to make the venture work.

8. Staffing issues: internal hiring, contracting or a mix? Staffing costs are a variable expense. Staffing costs can be managed and for ventures especially, cash flows in the venture inception period can be problematic. The decision with this is a trade-off between the less flexible costs of having full time staff and the costs of having a possibly less committed workforce.

9. What are supplier and distribution issues of consequence for the venture? Supplier and distribution issues affect business organizations at any point in their life cycle. With ventures, the path to excellent supplier and distributor relations is bumpier. Fundamental issues of types of suppliers and distribution routes arise and force basic decisions such as: Company owned distributors? Number of channels? Management of channels? Number of suppliers? Terms of supplier operations?

10. Should and when should the venture be turned over to professional managers? This is often a very difficult decision for the venture owner. In many ways, the venture is the founder's baby and much of the owner is invested in the thriving of the business.

11. Should the venture be abandoned? Under what circumstances? Ventures cannot be willed into success. Their success depends on many factors: the efforts of people, the timing of the venture, luck, planning and, of course, decisions. Casting a cold eye, in Yeat's grave, on the existence of the venture itself is difficult but necessary. The mortality rate of new companies heavily favors death, not prosperity so painful decisions must happen. The circumstances of extinction also need to be looked at and decisions made about allocation of assets, the payment of debt and the future of the people who vitiated the venture.

12. Should the venture be acquired? Should the venture acquire other firms? These decisions apply to the venture in trouble while the acquisition decision normally is raised if the venture grows.

EXAMPLES OF STRATEGIC NON-PROGRAMMED DECISIONS IN MEDIUM AND LARGE COMPANIES

1. What is our business?
2. Who are our customers?

3. What markets are we in: Domestic, regional and international?
4. What products/services do we offer?
5. What is our core strategy?
6. For public firms, what are our investment, debt, dividend and equity decisions?
7. Who are our competitors and what do we do about them?
8. How do we attract and keep talent?
9. Do we grow our own innovation or acquire it?
10. What are our responsibilities to outside stakeholders?

PROCESS OF MAKING BUSINESS DECISIONS: SOME CONSIDERATIONS

From the side of making business decisions have come ideas about the who and scope of business decisions. From one source (Decision Confidence, 2016) the advice is to consider who is making the business decision, how many people will be affected by it and if the decision is aligned with organizational values and principles. These are all ways of saying the business decision should conform to business purposes and the scope of who is affected by the decision should be accounted for. Decisions about procedures that only affect one work unit should not overreach other units.

Decision making processes differ greatly by company. In many cases the processes are legacy ways of doing things that are preserved simply because they have been there for a long time and seem to be working without dragging on efficiency. Other times they may impede efficiency but are still in place because nobody in the organization wants to go through the task of revising procedures manuals.

Your authors have observed that considerations of business decision making have been directed toward the avoidance of harm and not the optimization of decision making. CEOs we know want to avoid unintended consequences such as creating an incentive for producing things that are not profitable (see the incentivizing of Cobra production in colonial India). They also want to avoid a loss of commitment for the strategic decision that was made. Let the opponents of a decision have a chance to speak their minds is one piece of advice we were given. CEOs have also told us of their concerns about a strategic decision that was far short of being strategic and was in fact more tactical in nature.

Further distinction of strategic decisions and the problems stemming from them is found in a *McKinsey Quarterly* article (Lovallo and Sibony, 2006) that is relevant here. These authors assert there are two forms of problems that happen in strategy decisions. The first fall into the category of distortions of reality and the second are deceptions done in the decision process.

Within the distortions category, there can be the commonly occurring spirit of optimism over what the decisions can accomplish. This is associated with an underestimation of challenges, especially technical challenges. The second distortions category is loss aversion and inaction to even acceptable risks. This is associated with the result of having a scarcity of investment propensity.

For the deceptions category, a deception condition might be a misaligned time horizon which is evidenced by a focus solely on the time horizon for a current company position. The result is a focus on incremental innovation with strategic impact instead of more enduring and more positive impacts. A second deception is called misaligned risk aversion profiles which can be translated into managers not wanting to risk their careers on risky ventures. The result is that, as expected, managers will avoid risky projects. A third deception is named champion bias, which is demonstrated by the acceptance of evaluation from a trusted associate than from someone without that quality. The result takes the form of CEO reliance on biased advice. The last of the deception categories is what the authors call sunflower management. This is when a collective consensus forms around a senior person's presumed opinion about a decision. The result of this is an absence of dissent in decision making.

The bulk of practitioner-oriented literature on business decision making has to do with improving decision making and less on analysis of decision making practices.

THEMES OF PRACTICAL AND RESEARCH-BASED DECISION-MAKING LITERATURE

There is consensus on the steps of business decision making in the practitioner literature. These steps are problem identification, the development of possible solutions, the evaluation of these solutions, the making of a decision and the implementation of the decision, which includes a judgment about whether it works or not. A further commonality of the practical literature is to have a well-defined process of making the decision. The pitfalls of poor decision making are identified in practitioner articles and how to reverse the course of a bad decision is discussed. This body of literature uses examples of firms making poor choices to illustrate what can happen if your business follows the same path. Opinion about decision making abounds on the practical side but it is based on far fewer examples as done in the field of decision research. The opinions of business leaders on decision making are as prominent as the business leader themselves. As in most cases of practitioner versus researcher articles, the tests for validity and reliability are far fewer and less rigorous on the practitioner-based articles. The practitioner articles focus more on the individuals than on process.

Practical articles often offer advice in simple checklist terms. These articles contain generalized advice without exploring reasons for the advice.

On the research side, consensus is not as apparent on rules about decision making. The empirical studies tend to be much narrower in scope and research streams are fewer. Implications for decision managers are not as apparent as found on the side of decision practice. The research articles place findings in the context of prior significant research and they lay the groundwork for discovery by defining terms and justifying methodologies.

CHALLENGES TO RATIONAL DECISION MAKING

The presumption of decision making in the business arena is that it is fundamentally a rational-based model. A problem is identified, alternative solutions are developed and analyzed, and a decision is made to employ the optimal solution. The challenge to this has come from Malcolm Gladwell as a best-selling author and from psychologists and economists. In particular, Economics Nobel Laureate Daniel Kahneman explores the complexity of decision making and, at the same time, reveals the errors of decision making in a book that derives from his lifelong study of human choice and decision making (Kahneman, 2011). His book has many applications for business decision making though that is not the explicit intent of his work.

Kahneman poses that there are two ways of thinking. One is called system 1 which is fast, intuitive and involves emotions. The second is called system 2 which is something different. It is slower in the time dimension. It is more "rational" in the sense of following the rational decision-making model. It is also more logical.

One might expect all business decisions to be system 2 decisions. After all, there are millions (and, at times billions) of dollars at stake, but that is not the case. Our extrapolation from this is that system 1 decisions happen in business crises such as the Exxon Valdez oil spill, the Dai Ichi nuclear power plant and other instances where corporate reactions had to be sudden and correct or there would be extraordinarily serious consequences.

Other examples might be a hostile takeover, executive criminality, natural disasters and other unforeseen events. Then, snap decisions must be made by those in charge.

The mainstay of business decisions are system 2 decisions though. Kahneman finds flaws on the irrational side too.

In Chapter 3, performance of the firm is the subject. There several sources pose that luck is not a prominent a factor in accounting for business success. Kahneman's take on success is the form of an equation where success = talent + luck and that great success = a little more talent + a lot of luck.

Kahneman is more direct when he considers the question of: do better CEOs lead more successful companies? Kahneman's answer is that stronger CEOs lead stronger firms 60 percent of the time, only 10 percent more than would be expected than randomly (Kahneman, 2011, p. 205). Yet powerful CEOs get more credit than they deserve. What's more troubling is the halo effect that develops around successive performances by CEOs.

As a final note on Kahneman, he comments on planning and says that planning goals tend to be far too optimistic and not very realistic about the chances of dire events or impacts happening which were never raised in the planning development phase. He comments that many CEOs are very optimistic in their attitudes about potential success. That optimism may be reason to be cautious about the entire company accepting that position.

EVOLUTION OF CORPORATE DECISION MAKING

Corporate decision making has existed as long as business corporations have existed. This is certainly no new news to anyone, but it does let us track a several-century lineage of corporate decision making. Since corporations are legally endowed to independently pursue goals and because they incur risk in making fundamental choices about how they make their own futures, they can make their own choices via the humans in the organization.

The decisions that were made became more complex with time. Markets became more organized far beyond the road to market systems of agricultural societies. Ways were invented to keep inventories through canning. Advertising on a mass scale, especially catalogs like Sears Roebuck, spread the messages through mail about goods that could be purchased. The education system, nationwide by the Civil War, created a consuming class and so production and consumption spread across the continent.

Population growth and the growth of cities, the marks of the Industrial Revolution, flourished. Financial markets boomed and companies were able to incur debt to expand. It was a perfect time to build corporate power from the 1870s to the 1950s.

Something that also grew was the practice of business decision making.

Gilded Age corporatism with its excesses was tempered by the emergence of unions and the concentration of wealth in the hands of a few was blunted by the Progressive Movement. New laws prevented monopolies and the regulation of corporation practices in labor exploitation, safety and food handling were put in place at the federal and state level.

Such a sweeping review of corporate history would not be complete without mention of changes in the way work was done and its impact on decision making. The factory system emerged in the early part of the twentieth century making it possible to produce mass standardized goods and vehicles. What that meant was an improvement in the speed of manufacturing to fill needs of a growing population. Associated with the speeding up of production was the advent of management. Formerly, owners ran companies themselves, but the scale of production was such that a management class was needed to make decisions about the entire company, not just production.

Chester Barnard contributed to defining the functions of the executive as playing a part in the managing of the organization and not managing the people of the organization. His vision of a business was a cooperative structure in which the executive orchestrated organizational purpose with the consent of the workforce (Barnard, 1938). One of the functions was the formulation of purpose which occurred with decision making, which itself was comprised of analysis of factors which created a system of achieving goals and a synthesis of the interrelationships between and among the parts of the organization. Barnard's concepts on decision making and executive functions took hold and drew fans, one of which was Herbert Simon who enlarged upon Barnard's work.

With World War II, the complexity of making weapons of war brought the advent of systems analysis. This method integrated statistics and other methods of data analysis together to coordinate bombing runs, maneuver fleets and execute invasions. Systems analysis is the manifestation of the successful use of the rational problem-solving method and large firms with professional managers delighted with its inception. In the post-war era, systems analysis became popular in many industries. Systems analysis enabled managers to make data-based decisions.

Systems theorists combined the stalwart elements of classical economics in the form of utility and choice with economics to produce models of how organizations worked. Executives used this approach to optimize operations of their companies.

Around the early 1960s, Herbert Simon did considerable work on decision making and won a Nobel Prize in Economics for work on decision theory. Simon spent a half century on the study of organizational decision making. From his various writings, some key ideas have emerged which are very relevant to business decision making. One is that decision making is a major part of management. Decision making cannot be avoided by administrators and it takes its place alongside actions as being the essence of management. There are problems with decision making though. One is the bias that managers have toward their own departments in determining which decisions are most urgent. For bettering decisions Simon identifies the decision condition for human actions. The condition acknowledges the context for decisions by stating that "economic man" is the orientation when rational decision making happens. The assumption under this idea is that the decision maker has knowledge of conditions in the environment and that the person has analytical skills. That economic man can see and understand alternative actions which will lend themselves to an optimal choice by the decider.

Delving into psychological elements of being human, Simon asserts that rationality is not utter but bounded. We are rational in our decisions to the extent we can be and when the conditions of the decision go well into the unknown of speculation, pure rationality cannot be employed. Decision makers try to make simple models for their decisions but often cannot do so. At this point, Simon's concept of satisficing comes into play. This approach does not aim for optimization of decision results but instead goes for sufficiency of a decision solution. The solution must meet predetermined and feasible outcomes but need not go beyond these. Improvements may not be financially justified. They may be in the area of diminishing returns with greater resource commitments or they may be simply too abstract to be attainable. The idea of satisficing can be understood as the low bar of organizational performance with ideal performance being the high (and in actuality too high) bar. There is therefore a range of performance outcomes that can be set for the organization.

The difference between the two levels again shows the difference between the high level of "hard" science where everything goes to truths about the universe down to the lower level of sufficiency of "it is truthful enough" which is also where most of social science dwells. The cost of absolute truth or idealization is too much for business pursuits so it is not attainable for businesses, being their study falls within social sciences.

The importance of Simon's work for our study is that he not only introduces the limitations of rationality in business decisions, he proposes solutions (satisficing) as a way of alleviating the difficulties of business decision making. Satisficing is used to produce business decisions even though business deciders may not know its name or its origin.

Another significant study of decision making was done by Charles Lindblom (1961 and 1968). Though he is a political scientist and deals with the public policy-making process in the main, the decision processes of government must deal with the limitations of rationality that the private sector has. Lindblom's response is to advance incrementalism in decision making. That is to gradually move towards a solution but not take giant leaps to it. The process is to move away from the present state of affairs to a better state of affairs without too dramatic a single step. Under incrementalism, decision makers can work with a smaller set of better-understood alternative solutions. To this we would add that time may accord its own solutions with self-healing solutions such as a disease cure so that drastic public policy changes are avoided.

An incrementalist approach to decision making in the private sector might be to take a large problem such as a decline in sales for a particular product and subdivide the problem into demographic segments. The segments most critical for sales volume would be addressed first and investigated such as the 18–25-year-old segment for a gaming product. If this segment is cured as far as restoring demand by way of new game features, then other segments can be investigated.

Later still, in the 1980s, the thrust toward total quality management especially necessitated by the Japanese import auto challenge, push the entire U.S. auto industry to even more process analysis and informed decision making. Managers had to be more sensitive to quality issues as the Japanese manufacturers cut deeply into the domestic vehicle share, a phenomenon well documented in David Halberstam's book, *The Reckoning* (1986).

Systems analysis was only a start in the direction of incorporating digital computers into the world of business. Managers found support for their decisions to take actions through computer-based decision support systems, expert systems and artificial intelligence though the latter method is still in a protracted development phase.

Computer-based functions in the decision-making process have expanded the involvement of others within and among associated businesses. Shared applications, when supported by company information technology systems have enabled engineering units located in different geographic areas to share detailed engineering diagrams and let engineers make modifications jointly to see what happens if something is changed in the diagram. Better decisions can be made based on collegial agreement with shared applications.

In another area, information technology has supplanted individual decision making in programmed decisions. This has swept through industries and is particularly prevalent in medicine, vehicle diagnostics and finance. Though humans have a final say, there are an abundance of programs that aid in decision making.

It can also be said that there has not been as much displacement of human decision making for non-programmed decisions than there has been for programmed decisions. Non-programmed decisions deal with more uncertainty and the implantation of decision rules for corporate strategic decisions is not at the point where executives fully embrace it.

The last level of corporate decision making affected by computers or more appropriately database management has been the putting together of separate and large databases. This has greatly affected Customer Relationship Management (CRM) practices. Companies now know much more about customer preferences and behavior than ever before.

The Internet and the World Wide Web are related developments which have enabled more rapid communications of strategy decisions. Intranet connections within organizations have facilitated the communications of strategy. Corporate decision making about competitors has been enhanced as considerable information about competitor strategy can be found for decision making about what competitors intend to do.

THE CARNEGIE DECISION MODEL

One influential model of how corporate decision making actually happens and which was either formally or informally adopted was the Carnegie Model (Cyert, Simon, and March, 1958). The model contrasts with the prevailing notion that corporate decisions are made at the top level of the organization. The need for decisions flows from lower levels but the decision is made by upper level executives. Then the decision is pushed down through the organization.

However, in practice, the researchers found that many managers are involved in organizational decisions. The managers influence the decision in rational and non-rational ways. An example of a non-rational way comes from the universe of politics where managers will use organizational coalitions to support one decision or another. It is similar to legislative logrolling. A strong coalition is built around support for a clear idea and it eventually wins top executive support. That executive support is not automatic. The managers may then argue for a problemistic search in which a sufficient but not necessarily ideal decision will be formulated and approved. That search reflects the idea that a social science exercise like business does not have the time and resources for the absolute correct answer as does science by a workable decision that is sufficiently correct. The Carnegie Model remains viable in management science.

HOW BUSINESS DECISIONS ARE MADE IN PRACTICE

In the everyday world of business, decisions are made constantly. Most are tactical decisions, but some are strategic. The characterization of these decisions and the subject of how companies make good business decisions is the subject of a past McKinsey & Company survey (Garbuio, Lovallo, and Viguerie, 2009). The survey of 2,327 respondents provides a real-world assessment of decision practices of capital or human resource decisions made in the course of doing business. The financial results of the decisions were also discussed. The decisions involved ranged from new product expansion to maintaining infrastructure. Overall, the business benefits of increased profits and rapid implementation were attained by having the people with the right skills together with making decisions with transparent criteria and a fact base, as well as including the person responsible for implementation in the decision process were keys for success.

The researchers found that more than three-quarters of investment decisions were aimed at revenue growth. The majority of decisions were done at the request of the CEO and executives. Very interestingly, more of the decisions were made apart from annual planning processes and only about a quarter of decisions were the results of an immediate threat.

Nearly two-thirds of participants expected to realize decision results within two years. The goals of strategic decision making were expansion of products, services or geographies at 34 percent and organizational change for other reasons at 21 percent. These two reasons amounted to the majority of responses in the corporate decision category. Lesser goals were existing product or market investment, building new infrastructure, maintenance of that infrastructure or mergers and acquisitions. The majority of human resource decisions (57 percent) were to improve efficiency or productivity.

Most of the decisions were apart from the annual planning process (30 percent). External factors caused 28 percent of decisions and 24 percent of decisions happened because they were not the kind that were part of annual planning. Presumably that includes personnel decisions which are not normally part of strategic planning. Nine percent of decisions were outside annual planning because there was no process for them and another 3 percent were outside annual planning because they happened as budget cycles were closed or closing and funds needed to be sent or they would be lost.

In about two-thirds of decisions with known results, performance met or exceeded executive expectations for revenue growth and cost savings.

The worst financial results were when decisions were initiated and approved by the same person. Successful decisions (in the minds of respondents) involved the use of tools and techniques such as:

- Financial model of decision, net present value, internal rate of return as examples,
- Comparable situations from experience,
- Risk examinations, and
- Sensitivity analysis and financial models of risk.

The authors take a more positive view about the politics of decision making in which individuals or groups influence decision making. They comment that politics can be helpful by including alliance building and horse trading. These are often the results of broader discussions before the decision is made.

The McKinsey study answers many of the questions about how decisions are made in business organizations, but it does not answer all of them. From the observations of this book's authors, we can confirm that not all decisions happen at annual planning meetings. Other decisions happen as situations and opportunities arise. A telecommunications CEO we know kept his ears open to rumors of retiring independent local phone company chief executives. These retirements happened throughout the year every year. When word came out about the retirement he asked his staff to evaluate the value of the phone company as an acquisition target. If the potential acquisition fit the bill as far as being a revenue contributor to the expanded company, he made an offer. Put another way, the same process for potential acquisition was used outside the planning period as was used in the planning period.

In the many cases we observed, the method we saw that was used in making decisions was essentially the same. These strategic decisions were not unilateral by the CEO. They were decisions which were not spontaneous or done on the basis of "having a feeling" or "my gut instinct is." There was involvement on the part of second-order executives which took the form of consultation at a minimum and debate and decision at a maximum. In no cases were there instant decisions. All the CEOs gathered facts and did analysis before the decision was made and the question was asked and answered about the repercussions of making the decisions among customers, suppliers and stakeholders. CEOs kept their boards informed about the decision, but direct consultation with board members unless the member had some specific knowledge that might be useful for the decision is inadvisable.

One technique about getting acceptance of the potential decision was to socialize it. This meant informally suggesting an action to influential executives to get their reaction before a more formal presentation of the decision. The reaction to the socialization was part of the chief executive's decision about the decision. Lee Iacocca (1984) used a method of making decisions through key party acceptance before he would advance the decision through the rest of the Ford Motor Company. Iacocca would get buy-in from the finance department at the early stage of a project such as the Ford Mustang to make sure he and the department were in agreement with numbers and assumptions behind the numbers.

Our CEO observations lead us to say that invariably CEOs also did a risk assessment of the decision consequences before making the decision. This may be a consensus-based risk assessment or a mathematical risk assessment but it happened. Also, a fallback state was speculated on in which executives envisioned what failure would produce.

Like the scenes of mission control in so many manned and unmanned space missions, there was frequently a final check-in from the involved departments for go or no-go on the decision.

As far as intensity of activity during decision making, we have observed that the phases which are most intense are the analysis of potential decisions and the formulation of the decision. There was lesser intensity with implementation and communication of decisions. By intensity, it is meant the relative level of intellectual investment in an aspect of the decision-making process and implementation of it. In the implementation phase, the key executives typically turned over the responsibility to lower level executives. In the communications phase, there was activity in the messages that came out from the CEO on the decisions within the strategic plan. Outside the strategic, CEOs were similarly highly engaged about dissemination to the larger organization the reasons for the decisions.

It appeared to us that almost all the CEOs were very involved in launching the decision-making processes in both the strategic planning context and separately as issues came up requiring decisions. They also were aware of the pitfalls of making best decisions. They reminded themselves and their executives and directors of the impact of individual bias on decision making. "I want you all to hang your departmental biases up on the wall when you come in here to make company decisions" was the paraphrase of one CEO.

A McKinsey & Company article assesses the role of biases on decision making (Lovallo and Sibony, 2010). The article warns that subconscious biases undermine strategic decision making. The nature of these decisions and the processes used are described in the article. The authors surveyed executives who made 1,048 decisions; 41 percent of the decisions were expansions into new markets, products or services followed by 18 percent involving organizational change, 17 percent mergers and acquisitions, 14 percent investments in current markets, current products and services and 10 percent in infrastructures. These are collectively strategic decisions and they are varied by types of decision which address either internal or external conditions. Turning to the influence of the decision process, analysis and industry variables on decision-making effectiveness, they found that the quality of the process to exploit analysis and reach decisions (inclusion of perspective opposing senior leader opinion and allowing discussion by those with skill and experience rather than rank) accounted in 53 percent of performance. Industry/company variables (number of investment opportunities, capital availability, predictability of consumer tastes and availability of resources to implement decisions) amounted to 39 percent of performance. The quantity and detail of analysis that was performed amounted to a much smaller 8 percent. Process matters more than analysis in explaining performance, the authors conclude.

The CEOs of our observations could be considered to be in agreement that a regular process for making decisions was desirable and productive in making decisions. That adds to a summative observation that decision making within and outside the formal process continues to be employed as a management tool by CEOs.

REFERENCES

Barnard, C. (1938) *The Functions of the Executive*, Cambridge: Harvard University Press.

Cyert, R. Simon, H. and March, J. (1963) *A Behavioral Theory of the Firm*, Englewood Cliffs, NJ: Prentice Hall.

Decision Confidence (2016) Some Important Aspects of the Business Decision Making Process, retrieved November 17, 2016 from http://www.decision-making-confidence.com.

Garbuio, M., Lovallo, D. and Viguerie, P. (2009) How Companies Make Good Decisions: McKinsey Global Survey Results, McKinsey & Company, January.

Halberstam, D. (1986) *The Reckoning*, New York: William Morrow and Company.

Iacocca, L. (1984) *Iacocca: An Autobiography*, New York: Bantam Books.

Kahneman, D. (2011) *Thinking Fast and Slow*, New York: Farrar, Straus and Giroux.

Lindblom, C. (1961) *The Intelligence of Democracy: Decision Making through Mutual Adjustment*, New York: The Free Press.

Lindblom, C. (1968) *The Policy Making Process*, Englewood Hills, NJ: Prentice Hall.

Lovallo, D. and Sibony, O. (2006) Distortions and Deceptions in Strategic Decisions, *McKinsey Quarterly*, February, retrieved November 17, 2016 from http:// www.mckinsey.com/business.functions/strategy.

Lovallo, D. and Sibony, O. (2010) The Case for Behavioral Strategy, *McKinsey Quarterly*, March.

Major, R. (2015) How to Make Effective Business Decisions, *Business News Daily*, October 12. Retrieved November 28, 2016 from http://businessnewsdaily. com/71-how-to-make-effective-business-decisions.

Mankins, M. and Steele, R. (2015) Turning Great Strategy into Great Performance, *Harvard Business Review*, July–August.

Mankins, M. and Steele, R. (2006) Stop Making Plans; Start Making Decisions, *Harvard Business Review*, January.

Martin, M. (2015) How to Make Effective Business Decisions, *Business News Daily*, October 12.

Mintzberg, H. (1973) *The Nature of Managerial Work*, New York: Harper & Row Publishers.

Mintzberg, H. (1994) *The Rise and Fall of Strategic Planning*, New York: Free Press.

Rosenzweig, P. (2013) What Makes Strategic Decisions Different, *Harvard Business Review*, November.

U.S. Small Business Administration (2017) Starting and Managing Business, retrieved on January 3, 2017 from https://www.sba.gov/managing business/lead ing -your-business/making/decisions.

3. Performance

This chapter is dedicated to an exploration of business performance, the chief dependent variable of our study. We will develop the characteristics of performance, elaborate on the various ways performance is defined and used by business as well as review the research literature regarding the matter of if certain decisions are connected with performance. CEOs will speak to us in their own words about what performance means to them and the issue of pay and performance is introduced. A comparison will be made between the CEO perspectives on causes of performances and the research-based findings. This chapter will set the stage for the next chapter on the design of the survey for our own findings on decisions and performance.

Working first from the general issues of performance to the more specific issues, we begin with some operating generalizations about performance and then move to more details on how they will be used for our purposes. The generalizations offer a framework for understanding what we mean by business performance. These are not intended to be inclusive of all the characteristics of performance but at least indicative of the scope and depth of what business performance is.

For our purposes, business performance in general has these characteristics:

1. It occurs as a result of business decisions. Hence it is the dependent variable of this study.
2. Performance happens after a business decision. There is a time separation between the decision and its results. For the kinds of business decisions, we are investigating, strategic decisions, the time is usually a year. The duration of the effects of the decision can be brief or they may be prolonged over several years.
3. Business performance results from the implementation of business decisions. Decisions do not enact themselves. The decisions mobilize the organization's resources to head a certain direction.
4. People in the organization are largely responsible for implementing business decisions. Boards of directors are included as part of the organization as far as decisions are concerned though they usually ratify CEO decisions rather than originate them.

5. Performance happens because of controllable circumstances but it also occurs because of non-controllable business events. Performance can be enhanced by favorable macroeconomic conditions such as low interest rates and industry deregulation as examples of non-controllable effects.
6. Performance gets measured. Performance is mainly expressed in numerical terms. These terms of performance are well understood and accepted as comparators by those in the industry. Performance is score keeping that ranks different businesses in an industry.
7. Performance is usually not demonstrated as a single factor but as a multiple factor or an index of several factors. Executives do not look at a sole factor in assessing performance but at a number of factors, some financial, some not.
8. The audience for performance is both within and outside the organization. Business performance is followed by the business media and general media. Outside measures are often couched in terms of community responsibility and ethical behavior.
9. Business performance is not an individual but a collective consequence of business operations. It is achieved by people working together in the business for common ends and it is unmet by people of the business not cooperating for a common purpose.

To return to the formulation of our study, we say performance is the consequence of business actions. It is what happens at the end of the day and at the end of the decision time scope when all the daily decisions take effect. Without decisions, there are no results to look at. With decisions, there are. Performance is what lures investment in the business organization. It is an objective measure of how well the business is doing in comparison to other similar businesses and other business members of the industry. In aggregate, business performance demonstrates which industries are attractive and which are not. It affects industry input factors such as cost of capital and ease of entry to the industry.

STANDARDS FOR BUSINESS PERFORMANCE

What kind of performance should be expected from business performance? In addition to characterizing business performance, the expectations of what performance measurement entails should be established. Here are some general guidelines from your authors:

1. The business performance measures should be meaningful. Measures such as cost–benefit analysis are more meaningful than profits because

profits are highly distortable by tax law while cost–benefit analysis is far less so.

2. The measures should be understandable. Performance measurement is only useful if those who are accountable for it understand what it means to achieve performance. The measure of a specific dollar amount in new sales is more understandable that a compounded net present dollar amount of sales divided by employee numbers. The latter is more difficult to understand.

3. The measures should be transferable. For comparisons of different businesses, it is helpful to have measures which many businesses use.

4. The measures should be well established over time. Some businesses such as health insurance have used long-standing measures such as waiting times as measures even though new measures have emerged that more directly measure the impact of waiting times of patients. By adopting a new measure, the insurance companies would have to start new baselines of analysis and long-term trend analysis could no longer be done. There is good reason to hold on to legacy methods sometimes.

5. The measures should be directly attributable to decisions. The idea here is that if there are other variables that are between the cause and the effect, their explanatory value may distort or even replace the direct cause and effect connection that is being sought. Irrelevant variables need to be reduced to the extent possible.

6. The measures should be discrete. The measures should stand by themselves and not be mixed with other measures. If a chosen measure is return on investment, then it should not be accompanied by another measure such as return on new investment.

7. The measure should be controllable by those responsible for it. By this, the measure used should be something like labor productivity and not labor productivity compared to aggregated national labor productivity which cannot be affected by single businesses.

One of the problems faced in performance is the conflict between specific measures for individual companies versus generally accepted measures transferred across wide industry groups. The former is desirable because it makes the measures controllable and relevant and the latter is desirable because it eases performance measurement comparisons among the separate businesses.

ISSUES WITH PERFORMANCE

One of the issues with performance is simply the matter of getting it. CEOs and owners of businesses sometimes do not want to report performance to outside parties. There are reasons for this. Competitors may use this information to cast a competitor as an organization in a weak financial situation. Rare is the organization that is doing well in all dimensions of performance.

Another problem is that the performance of an organization may be inaccurately reported by senior officials. In other instances, performance may be inaccurately reported in order to deceive the inquirer or it may be inadvertently reported with errors that have to be corrected.

Still another way that it is a problem is that the CEO may not know what performance is. We have observed many CEOs who have not been able to respond when asked: What is your ROI or ROE? Yet they seemed to be able to readily report employee numbers and growth as well as revenue.

These problems with performance that were cited are really performance communications problems which inhabit all levels of the organization. They are identified here to pose a caution to anyone investigating corporate performance. At a minimum, the issues just described should be used as a basis for establishing the quality of performance data. Publicly-held firms report performance information more openly and to a wider variety of publics than privately held organizations. For verification of private firms, Dun and Bradstreet reports help discover and report accurate financial information outside performance that parties can use.

The general problems of measuring business performance are identified in an article in the *Harvard Business Review* (Sherman and Young, 2016). The article itself applies to financial reporting in general but there is application to financial reporting of performance. The first problem is universal standards. There are, in fact, no universal standards. Generally Accepted Accounting Standards (GAAP) are predominant in the United States while European countries use International Financial Reporting Standards.

The second problem is revenue recognition. When the revenues are actually accounted for makes a difference in financial reporting. They may be accounted for immediately or later as revenues continue to come in over the years.

A third problem is unofficial earnings measures. To the authors this was evident in the dot com era as high tech companies counted some unofficial earnings and perhaps good will as earnings.

A fourth problem was fair value accounting and that occurs when accounting practices assign dollar value to proxies for revenues and not actual dollar amounts.

The fifth problem is when the decisions by the organizations are put in place but do not show up in the books. There may be hidden reserves for major strategic project decisions made but the dollars associated with the decisions do not show up in the company books.

The financial reporting practices used by corporations do not reveal strategic decisions in and of themselves. They also do not measure true performance because of ways that financial reporting can distort financial performance. This is not a trivial problem and should lead to caution in using financial reporting alone as a definitive statement of corporate performance.

There has been research on the measurement of performance in privately held businesses and one article in particular elaborates on this. Dess and Robinson's (1984) articles observes that strategic management researchers experience problems obtaining objective measures of business performance. With consideration of privately held organizations, such data may not even be available. In the case of conglomerate business units, performance data is often mixed together with company level data. These authors studied how useful subjective performance measurement data is for such situations when problems occur in getting accurate performance information. Twenty-six manufacturers were involved in the study. The researchers did on site CEO interviews, additional responses were collected on some fourteen potential strategic decisions for the top management team. This was used to devise and administer a questionnaire which identified several key issues of performance. Lastly, a follow-up questionnaire was sent for CEO reactions. The results were that there was a strong positive correlation between objective and subjective measures of return on assets. There was an even stronger correlation between objective and subjective measures of sales growth. There was a strong correlation found between subjective and objective measures of sales growth and return on assets and the global measures of performance by the organization's members. While the researchers do not claim that subjective measures are better than objective measures, the top management team's subjective measurements of performance correlated well with objective measurement.

One researcher who has studied business performance in a series of articles is Phil Rosenzweig. In one article in the *Financial Times* (Rosenzweig, 2006) he asserts that companies can learn from experience by looking at three issues: clearly defining success and failure, avoiding judgmental biases and avoiding the halo effect. There are no commonly used definitions of success and failure and the definition of the terms differs from study to study. Though many acquisitions do not achieve initial goals, with stock price dips occurring, there may be other benefits that happened. Hewlett Packard might have been worse off by not acquiring Compaq.

The other factor is judgmental bias which is overconfidence in producing results because of an overestimation of skills and abilities by the parties to business transactions such as acquisitions. The confidence of executives who have a history of successful business transactions in the past blinds them to expect more success in the future. The last factor is the halo effect which has it that people make general conclusions about an individual based on impressionistic hunches than more objective appraisals about the actual chances of success or failure.

The same themes are echoed in another article by Rosenzweig in the *McKinsey Quarterly* (Rosenzweig, 2007a). Rosenzweig expands on the theme of human hubris in performance expectations with other examples, namely Cisco systems which was both criticized and celebrated even though not much had changed in its internal operations. He cites the halo effect at work in perceptions about performance that don't match actual performance. He states that no formula can guarantee a company's success. Companies that outperform peers will often lag at other points in time. This idea need not be a source of dismay though, since gathering and using data will improve the probability of better performance even if it does not guarantee success.

In the last in the series of articles on the subject, Rosenzweig take issue with the formulistic explanations of business performance as expressed in popular literature (Rosenzweig, 2007b). Two examples are the books *In Search of Excellence* (Peters and Waterman, 2004) and *Good to Great* (Collins, 2001). Rosenzweig argues these authors base their conclusions that there are clear paths to success on questionable data. Strategic decisions are made under conditions of uncertainty. The fact that the decisions turned out badly does not, in and of itself mean they were bad decisions. The formulators of the decisions did the best they could with what they had but circumstances changed that could not be readily determined to be consequential as the strategy was unfolding. He finally advises business people to be aware of the halo factor and the other false attributions made in an effort to explain the often inexplicable.

PERSPECTIVES ON PERFORMANCE

As in the case of decision making, there has been a body of research and theory on business performance. This part of the chapter offers some of the thinking on business performance. Both academic and executive perspectives are included here.

Chief executive also marks the modern CEO and is inextricable from them. Performance is how they become CEOs and is how they stay CEOs.

There is not a single CEO of the hundreds we know who is not concerned about their organization's business performance. "It is what keeps me up at night," remarked one CEO while another said, "I am the only one totally responsible for my company's performance. Our customers don't care about our performance or problems. They want things that work, that help them do the job. Performance consumes me though, all the time."

The sentiment of seeking something elusive permeates executive consciousness with respect to performance. "There is no secret sauce that produces performance, no amount of dial twiddling that gets your organization to peak performance," commented one CEO. While others spoke more affirmatively about how they could influence the organization to get it to perform better, none ever claimed absolute control over performance from among the fifty executives commenting on the matter.

As Jack Welch of General Electric remarked:

> There are only three measures that tell you everything you need to know about your organization's overall performance: employee engagement, customer satisfaction and cash flow. It goes without saying that no company, small or large, can win over the long run without energized employees who believe in the mission and understands how to achieve it. (Windust, 2016)

In this statement Welch ties corporate performance to its organizational sources.

A familiar strain about employee satisfaction and profitability is echoed by Anne Mulcahy of Xerox. "Employees who believe that management is concerned about them as a whole person – not just an employee   are more productive, more satisfied, more fulfilled. Satisfied employees mean satisfied customers which leads to profitability," states Mulcahy (Daisyme, 2015). The same source cites Ben Horowitz of Andreessen-Horowitz who links executive decisions to success, "Every time you make a hard correct decision you become a bit more courageous and every time you make the easy wrong decision, you become a bit more cowardly. If you are a CEO these choices will lead to a courageous or cowardly company."

Performance as the sole pursuit of business is downplayed by executives. "Just as people cannot live without eating, so a business cannot live without profits. But most people don't live to eat and neither must businesses live to make profits," remarks John Mackey of Whole Foods (Pontefract, 2016). There is also the endorsement of a higher purpose other than sheer profits. From the same source, Punit Renjen of Deloitte Consulting, "An organization's culture of purpose answers the critical questions of who it is and why it exists. They have a culture of purpose beyond making a profit."

What we have in the statements of business success and performance from these CEOs and most others the authors know is the sentiment that performance is to be measured in and by the people of the organization. This is what endures after CEO tenures and CEOs want to mention this frequently as something they want to accomplish. The dollar measurements are all uniform and, frankly, boring because corporate gains and losses do not translate well to how an employee feels about working in the organization.

What about time effects on CEO tenure? Do CEOs enjoy increasing company performance over their tenures or does company performance decline or does something else happen? This is the topic of a trio of researchers (Limbach, Schmid, and Scholz, 2016). The researchers found that over time, CEO's tenure was associated with increased performance but performance decreased over time as the fit became less ideal. The authors referred to this as a hump-shaped relation between the CEO tenure and firm value. They report that for the average Standard and Poors 1500, the hump-shaped relationship holds. There is a 4.5 percent increase in firm value in the early years of CEO tenure and a 4.2 percent decrease over later year tenures. They suggest that replacement of an initial CEO becomes more difficult for companies. In dynamic industries, company value increases more rapidly than with less dynamic industries. Adaptable CEOs were found to have quicker positive company value climbs as opposed to less adaptable CEOs.

If organizational performance is not up to investor expectations, then it is the CEO who becomes the focal point for criticism as did David Taylor, CEO of Procter & Gamble (Terlep, 2016). The article describes years of tepid growth by P&G and reports that Taylor faced critical questions from investor groups during an industry conference. He acknowledged the problem and said P&G has not been delivering and that the company needed to bring standards up. He planned double across the board cost reductions. Taylor was surprised during a visit to China to learn that competitors had stolen market share. China is a huge market for P&G but the company is plagued by perceptions of low quality compared to competitors.

This brief set of opinions and exhortations from CEOs that corporate performance is attributable to factors other than the CEOs themselves. They suggest in general that a shared mission and employees who are valued are causes for performance. Stated another way, the CEOs do not point to themselves as the reasons why their companies do well.

Like the coach of almost any sports team, the CEO takes the blame being as they are the lightning rod for criticism. This example is another demonstration of how CEOs are constantly concerned with the performance of their business. It is they who hold the reins of change to improve or retard success, a situation that Taylor was immersed in.

Do CEOs matter more or less in their firm's performance? Walter Frick of the *Harvard Business Review* responds affirmatively to the question (Frick, 2014). The impact of CEOs on organizational performance has risen considerably claims Frick in citing work of strategy researchers. This is generally referred to as the CEO effect. That effect has increased from about 8 percent in 1950 to 20 percent in 2009. CEOs simply matter more than they used to, the author states. There are more opportunities to make international investments, utilize technology and financing to produce results now compared to mid-century when businesses were simpler. The results vary by industry though, and high-growth industry CEOs are hobbled by more inability to predict future performance outcomes.

CHARACTERISTICS OF HIGH PERFORMANCE COMPANIES

Popular business media has covered the characteristics of high performance companies (CEO Advisor, 2014). The five critical traits are: a 100 percent sales culture, a focus on their own people, tracking, measurement and metrics, diligent customer service and accountability. Although this is not an empirical article, it does offer themes that resound in the field of practice.

Performance of the organization is part of the compensation package for CEOs so that is a reason why organizational performance is a top-of-mind concern for CEOs. But is there a relation between business performance and pay? Research suggests that is not the case at all (Cooper, Gulen, and Rau, 2016). They examined 1,500 companies and found that CEO excess compensation is negatively related to future firm returns and operating performance. This effect is even stronger for CEOs who are overconfident and have weaker governance structure. The authors speculate that CEO overconfidence leads to overinvestment and value destroying merger and acquisition activity.

CEOs individually or as a group will argue that this research is incorrect or immaterial for them but there has been no body of rigorous research that has produced contrary findings. CEOs would say that the findings do not apply to them which in itself may be a sign of overconfidence. They are also likely to claim that truly effective CEOs are few in number and that the few and the proud should be able to earn the salaries and compensation packages they do. Their total compensation is negotiated individually with their boards and to a considerable extent is based on their recent and past success.

From the observations of your authors, the issue of corporate performance being reflected in compensation packages, the compensation packages are not sufficient to explain motivations of CEOs to succeed. A more significant component can be found in executive competition with one another. It is a very exclusive club that the CEOs belong to. They want to excel even within their own membership ranks. Money seems to be a way of keeping score, but it does not fully explain the drive to achieve or, in David McClelland's terms, the need to achieve. Success in that effort does. Chief executives measure themselves against one another. All one has to do is to ask them who they compare themselves to. They may be living peers or historic figures but all CEOs we have known are continuously measuring themselves against others. That can be a matter of personal ego or the need for esteem in Maslow's conception of the hierarchy of needs. Either way it is there. Neglecting the element of a CEO's personality is a mistake in understanding the impetus of performance.

The subject of CEO characteristics and company performance has been reviewed by the Stanford Business Corporate Governance Research Initiative. Two researchers there looked at the research in the field (Larcker and Tagan, 2016). These researchers conclude that it is not clear what influence CEOs have on firm outcomes. One study of twelve British companies reported that CEOs were responsible for 3.9 percent to 7 percent of firm performance. The CEOs had no significant impact in this study. In another study of 92 CEOs, the CEOs accounted for 29.2 percent of unexplained performance variance which the Stanford University researchers believed was a significant impact. Yet another study of 830 companies concluded that CEOs have a 35 percent influence over firm outcomes expressed as return on assets. The Stanford researchers called this a significant impact. They reach an overall conclusion that there is modest evidence from the research that personal and professional attributes that CEOs previously experienced and work style are predictors of performance. The safe of performance causes has yet to be cracked.

From the other side of popular business media, a contrary view of CEO impact on business can be found. Luck affects performance more than one might think. W. Yakowicz writes about that in a blog (Yakowicz, 2015). Yakowicz begins by noting that *Harvard Business Review*'s 2015 best performing CEO Lars Sorenson says that luck was the single most important force in attaining that ranking. Yakowicz writes that a Harvard Business School study found that CEO impact on company success ranges from 2 percent to 22 percent, depending in the industry. Also reported is a Texas A&M study which says that the range is between 4 percent and 5 percent.

As a summary of CEO influence on organizational performance, there is a very clear division of opinion ranging from a hearty yes to a robust no and everything in between. Even limiting the answer to empirical work, there is still no dominant opinion with both sides producing some empirical evidence.

FACTORS AFFECTING PERFORMANCE

The primary question addressed in this section is what factors affect business performance? This question pries open a Pandora's Box of answers. For our purposes, we will confine our consideration to empirical work.

The first research to be considered is the impact of powerful CEOs on corporate performance (Adams, Almeida, and Ferreira, 2005). The conclusion of the researchers is that it does. They test the idea that CEOs who have more decision-making power should have more variability in firm performance. The authors focus on the power CEOs have over their boards and company executives. They examined 336 Fortune 500 firms. They report that stock returns are more variable in companies where the CEO has greater power to influence decisions. Similar findings are reported for return on assets and Tobin's Q (another measure of performance). The results are particularly evident when the CEO is also the founder.

The forms of power discussed are ownership power (which is often manifest as founder power, expert power, prestige power and structural power). Firm performance is more variable as decision making power becomes more centralized in the hands of the CEO. In all, this research helps establish the CEO and their exercise of power does influence corporate performance.

The subject of middle management involvement and organizational performance was explored by two researchers (Wooldridge and Floyd, 1990). Wooldridge and Floyd depart from the view that top level management is the domain of strategy. They cite authors who assign middle level a crucial role in strategy. Though the study does not explicitly treat decisions as the independent variable, the fact that strategic moves are effectuated by strategic decisions seems highly plausible. These researchers theorize that two paths, both involving middle management participation in strategy, lead to organizational performance. One path is through higher strategic consensus to improved implementation and the other path is through improved decision making which leads to superior strategies. They tested these two paths in the form of research hypotheses on eleven banks and nine manufacturers. In addition, qualitative data on strategic processes was collected from structured interviews with top level managers in the sample. "The results suggest that middle level management involvement in strategy formulation is associated with improved organizational performance

(Wooldridge and Floyd, 1990, p. 231). Though the sample size is low in this study, the proposition that middle management's role in strategy can be explanatory in performance and may also be beneficial.

The roles of CEOs and middle managers have been addressed in these two studies but much more needs to be investigated. In the next set of explorations, other factors are introduced and evaluated in the decision and performance causal stream.

The next study on performance considered the speed of strategic decisions and firm performance. Two researchers looked at the effects of environmental and organizational factors on firm performance (Baum and Wally, 2003). These researchers surveyed 318 CEOs over a four-year period from 1996 to 2000. The organizational and organizational factors included environmental dynamism which was defined as unpredictability, munificence which was defined as environmental capacity for organizational growth, centralization of strategic management, decentralization of operations management, formalization of routines and informalization of non-routines. Growth and profitability were the performance measures. They found that "fast strategic decision making predicts subsequent firm growth and profit and also mediates the relation of dynamism, munificence, centralization and formalization with firm performance" (Baum and Wally, 2003, p. 1107). They also found "that the direct effects of the influences of dynamism, munificence, centralization and formalization reduced when the indirect effects of these factors through decision making speed are included in the total effects model" (Baum and Wally, 2003, p. 1114). That finding can be construed as a managerial decision-making balancing of dominating factors to smooth out the influence of the research model. Baum and Wally have added decision speed as a performance factor.

What could be a more definitive approach to the decision speed factor would be to contrast rapid speed strategic decisions with slower speed decisions in two different groups to discern the performance differences between two demarked-by-speed groups.

Team effectiveness is another theme of corporate performance undertaken by researchers. An example is one study of 210 Fortune 1,000 companies (Payne, Benson, and Finegold, 2009). The main finding here was that team effectiveness was associated with higher levels of board effectiveness (as defined by the board) and that was significantly related to corporate performance. This study presents an indirect route to corporate performance involving teams through the board to performance but it does support a team role in performance.

Other researchers have produced mixed results on the relationship between board composition and firm performance (Bhagat and Black, 1999), with the appointment of new directors and stock price reactions to that event. Reporting on research by others, the authors note that when companies appoint outside directors, stock process increase by 0.2 percent on average. While this is statistically significant, it is financially small. When an insider is added to the board, stock prices neither increase or decrease in other cited research.

Board size is not tied to performance differences. These authors say that the results are mixed on the matter of a direct correlation between performance and board composition. Most studies find little correlation but a few report a negative correlation between the proportion of independent directors and performance of the firm. Doing their own research, the authors found a negative relationship between the degree of board independence from independent directors and performance.

Taken as a whole, very little can be said about the connection between board composition and firm performance.

Another approach to explaining performance was undertaken by H. Kurt Christensen and Cynthia Montgomery (1981). These authors built upon work of Richard Rumelt's 1974 study. They took a subsample of 128 firms and analyzed the possibility that market structure variables might account for performance differences. They found that performance differences could be found in some of Rumelt's categories of types of diversification. These included market concentration and market share strategies, but across the range of categories performance differences were not found in the survey of research the authors conducted. The authors also believe their study helps clarify and explain Rumelt's original classification scheme.

Another study of boards of directors and financial performance, earlier than the previous study of boards and performance but related to boards and performance provides a more skeptical view of any connection between these factors (Dalton et al., 1998). This team of writers conducted a meta-analysis of 54 empirical studies of board composition and 31 empirical studies of board leadership. They found "little evidence of systematic governance structure/financial performance relationships" (Dalton et al., 1998, p. 269). Other research has established that effective boards are made up of board members outside the firm but the relevancy of outside membership and strong financial performance has not been a consensus point among researchers.

Researchers Lawrence Brown and Marcus Caylor (2004) studied corporate governance and firm performance. The authors created a 51-factor governance measure. This score was related to operating performance, valuation, and shareholder practices for 2,327 firms. They found that better governed firms are relatively more profitable, more valuable, and pay more cash to shareholders. They found that good governance (as associated with executive and director compensation) is most highly associated with good performance. Good governance when measured by using charter and bylaws is most highly associated with bad performance. Brown and Caylor's use of a large dataset and comparing conditions for both good and bad performance makes this study more comprehensive than most.

The Organisation for Economic Co-operation and Development produced an older but still relevant summary of the effects of corporate governance on firm performance and economic growth (Maher and Anderson, 1999). They take an international perspective on the governance issue and highlight differences among countries in governance laws and practices. They write, "The vast majority of empirical studies, it turns out, do seem to favor the beneficial effects of enhanced monitoring as a result of higher ownership concentration" (Maher and Anderson, 1999, p. 31). Firms with owner-controlled operations as opposed to firms with manager-controlled operations do better when enhanced monitoring happens. Direct shareholder monitoring of firms helps boost overall profitability. These authors also report that owner-controlled firms are more profitable than manager-controlled firms. The presence of large shareholders improves firm performance because it increases supervision of managers. That is another finding from other research that was reported in this study. Evidence that firm performance is tied to board ownership is mixed. "The vast majority of studies find no significant improvement in firm performance following a merger" (Maher and Anderson, 1999, p. 38). For hostile takeovers, the same decline in performance does not happen but it is not as pronounced either that takeovers improve performance. Regarding the impact of executive pay for performance being tied to overall performance, "Excluding stock options, current evidence that sensitivities of pay to performance are quite small" (Maher and Anderson, 1999, p. 41).

Much of the literature on corporate performance is directed to governance and board/ CEO interactions. Far less is directed to the operational level of business organizations.

Inside director representation on a board's investment committee correlates with better firm performance. That is a conclusion of one researcher (Klein, 1998).

Departing from the higher corporate level of strategy decisions and down to the strategic business unit level, there has been some research on business unit level performance. A study of the connections between strategy, control systems and resource sharing on business unit performance has led to some insight on the matter (Govindarajan and Fisher, 1990). Data was collected from 24 firms. The results of the study supported the idea that strategy, resource sharing and control systems have an interactive impact on SBU (strategic business unit) effectiveness. Output control of the SBU and high resource sharing with other units are associated with higher effectiveness for a low-cost strategy (from Michael Porter's strategy typologies) and high resource sharing are associated with higher effectiveness for a differentiation strategy (also from Michael Porter).

While these are limited findings, they are associated with strategy decisions albeit at the SBU level, not the corporate level. These researchers provide evidence that SBU strategies, not solely corporate level strategies, may have an effect of corporate effectiveness.

The contribution of boards of directors to the success of their firms has also been a research topic. According to three authors (VanNess, Miesing and Kang, 2010), there are positive effects due to board actions. They discovered that board membership heterogeneity was related to growth. However, board members with more education and financial expertise yielded a negative performance result. A duality of CEO and Chair of the board and higher average board tenure had a positive effect on return on assets. There was no significant impact of outside directors, gender or board member age on financial performance.

On the same theme of CEO and board interactions and corporate performance, other positive results were found (Pearce and Zahra, 1991). The authors typify boards as being caretakers, statutory, proactive and participative. A sample of Fortune 500 and service companies was drawn. They found there were significant differences between how the different board types acted. They also found that powerful boards had superior corporate financial performance.

From these two research projects, we can add CEO decision making as a factor explaining organizational financial performance.

Based on a sample of 126 South African companies, two researchers considered the factor of board structure on financial performance (Meyer and de Wet, 2013). They found that the proportion of independent, non-executive directors had a significant effect on earnings per share and enterprise value but not on Tobin's Q ratio. Board ownership had a significant negative correlation with performance as measured by earnings per share enterprise value and Tobin's Q ratio. The number of directors serving on the corporate board had a significant positive effect on earnings per share, enterprise value and Tobin's Q ratio. Overall, the researchers say their study suggests that greater independent non-executive director representation, lower board share-ownership and larger board sizes should be encouraged to enhance board performance.

A link to corporate performance and a strong commitment to ethics was found by an author Verschoor (1999). This study was aimed at discovering if there was a link between large corporation's financial and non-financial performance and a public commitment by management to follow a code of ethical corporate conduct. The investigation included Businessweek's 500 largest public U.S. companies, Fortune's 200 largest U.S. industrial non-regulated utility and non-financial services companies, other "Most Admired" Fortune companies and 100 additional companies using market value added for performance. Verschoor found that companies committing to follow an ethics code as an internal control strategy obtained significantly higher performance in financial and non-financial dimensions using the measures of market value added (2.5 times greater than firms not mention codes of ethics or conduct), Businessweek rankings of 500 largest companies by financial performance (13.8 percentiles higher than those with no ethics emphasis), Fortune rankings of most admired companies had reputation scores 4.7 percent higher for public commitment to ethics than those without commitment. This author speculates that ethical commitment is not a strong determinant of superior corporate performance but there is an association between these factors. Instead, Verschoor speculates that top management has set an ethical tone and these values permeate through the organization.

Extending the study of ethics and performance to the residual effects of ethics, the reputation of the firm, there has been some research. One example is from a team of practitioner and academic writers (Hammond and Slocum, 1994). Their study connected corporate reputation as identified in Fortune 500's Most Admired Companies list with financial performance. A sample of 149 firms was used and seven measures of financial risk and return were collected at two different points in time. The mean scores from four attributes from the 1993 Fortune list were subjected to regression analysis. Two of the variables, standard deviation of the market return of the firm and return on sales explained 12 percent and 14 percent of the subsequent reputation. An implication for management is that they can affect reputation by lowering financial risk and controlling costs.

Endorsement of the idea that innovation can lead to better firm performance is examined in a *Strategic Management Journal* article (Hill and Snell, 1988). The authors argue that managers prefer strategies that maximize their utility. When managers dominate in research-intensive industries, diversification strategies are favored over innovation strategies. Innovation is presented as having an association with greater firm profitability though. The theory was tested on 94 research intensive Fortune 500 firms and the theory was largely confirmed.

What can be said of the impact of human resource management practices on corporate financial performance? A partial answer is found in an article by Mark Huselid (1995). This study considered formal systems of High Performance Work Practices and firm performances. A 1,000-firm sample established an economically and statistically significant positive result on short- and long-term measures of corporate financial performance.

A related question to human resource management practices and their impact on performance is the matter of corporate culture and its impact on performance. The authors summarize their findings in paraphrase as: Consistent with previous studies, these results suggest that corporate culture, as assessed by employees, helps predict subsequent firm performance. The findings provide empirical support for recent theories of the firm that model employees as the key corporate asset (Chamberlain, 2015). The research team examined 100,000 Glassdoor employee reviews. The measures of performance were the company's current market value and return on assets. Chamberlain reported the researchers found a statistically significant and causal link between employee satisfaction and the market value of companies. That translates to a 7.9 percent average increase in the company value from a one star (from 1- to 4-star scale) increase in employee satisfaction.

A very different examination of a relationship between a factor of management and performance was presented in an *Administrative Sciences Quarterly* article (Straw and Epstein, 2000). Starting with the question most directly related to this book: Do popular management techniques affect corporate performance?; the answer is that they do not have a higher economic impact. However, popular management tools such as involving quality, empowerment and teams were more admired, seen to be innovative and rated higher in management quality. Their CEOs were given higher pay when these management tools were used.

The performance of business organizations has been a subject of interest among strategic management researchers for quite some time. Among the early wave researchers was Richard Rumelt (1974). He studied the connections between diversification strategy, organizational structure and economic performance in large American industrial firms. Bearing in mind that the businesses of study were large firms and that they were industrial companies and that diversification activity was a further condition, Rumelt discovered that related business firms (those with non-vertically integrated firms that are diversified with low specialization ratios where diversification has been done by relating new activities to old) have higher profitability, higher rates of growth and higher price–earnings ratios than other categories of firms. He also established that related-constrained firms (those firms diversifying by relating the new business to a specific central skill or resource which is related to almost all of the other business activities) outperform related-linked firms (those which are diversified by relating new businesses to some strength or skill already possesses, but not always the same strength or skill). These firms are active in widely disparate businesses. Unrelated-passive firms (those unrelated businesses which do not have aggressive acquisition programs) had low performance results.

BUSINESS PERFORMANCE: A MYRIAD OF MEASURES

The large number of business performance measures has been the subject of inquiry by many. One article is an example (Van Looy and Shafagotva, 2016). The authors recognize that the performance of business processes has become a central issue in academia and business because organizations are expected to perform. Performance measurement models align with business strategies. That implies a choice of organization-dependent performance indicators according to the authors. Nonetheless, there is not much guidance on what performance measures to use in practice. The authors conducted a literature review to uncover patterns or trends in the research on business process performance measurement. What was discovered was 140 process related performance indicators and that they could be categorized into eleven performance perspectives.

The main implication of this review is that there is choice in performance measurement. An organization makes a decision from available choices of performance. Consequently, these authors note that businesses make their choices from the many measures manifested.

There are certainly some performance measures that are formally or informally mandated so the range of choices is not solely dependent on executives in the business itself.

A REASON FOR TRADITION

Strong is the bond between tradition and practice with performance measurement. When performance measurement tools have been in practice for an extended time, it is baked in an organization's DNA. That is because trend analysis is so important in businesses. The creation of new forms of measuring performance interrupts the use of older forms, even if they are supplements to older measurement forms.

OBSERVATIONS ON BUSINESS PERFORMANCE

Discovering what and how decisions lead to better business performance means finding the key to the kingdom, so to speak. But the keys have been elusive and only an edge of the cut has been revealed here and there. In this section, the research on business performance will be reviewed with an eye toward discoveries which have shown some support for causes of performance.

One step in that direction has been research done on data-driven decision making (Brynjolfsson, Hitt, and Heekyung, 2011). The authors review research suggesting that more precise information should facilitate greater use of information in decision making and accordingly lead to higher firm performance. Though this applies to specific situations and there is little independent empirical evidence to confirm the relationship, the authors set out to find out if relationships exist between performance and productivity, financial performance and market value. They found that data-based decision making is associated with a 5–6 percent increase in their output and productivity above what could be explained by traditional inputs and information technology inputs. The research was done on 179 publicly traded firms in the United States. Their overall conclusion is that data-based decision making is associated with higher productivity and market value and that there is at least some evidence that this form of decision making is associated with return on equity and asset utilization.

The modern theories of strategic management incorporate the element of competition in planning and executing strategy. Most notably, Porter's Five Forces Model poses that competition affects the current rivalry among firms in the competitive arena and the threat of competitive entry is a major factor for a company when it does it strategizing. This theme is followed by strategy theorists and Porter's model has been modified but has not been discarded.

What of the evidence about competition and performance? An example is found in an article in the *Journal of Political Economy* (Nickell, 1996). Nickell takes on the question of whether competition improves corporate performance. Theory would expect that competition improves efficiencies and hence performance of firms in competitive conditions. Competition puts a downward pressure on costs and produces other efficiency effects. The author believes this to be true but overwhelming support for such a hypothesis is not present. Additionally, empirical evidence is weak for that hypothesis. Nickell found in his analysis of 670 firms in the United Kingdom that there is support for that view. He provides evidence that competition as defined by increased numbers of competitors or by lower levels of rents is associated with a significantly higher rate of total factor productivity growth.

One of the primary difficulties in discerning overall findings from this review of pertinent research on performance is that there is absolutely no uniformity in the measurement of performance. This cripples any grand design of a decisions and performance bond. Researchers have not answered even the most basic of questions (see Table 3.1).

Table 3.1   Performance literature summary

Main Author, Publication Date	Subject	Findings
Hammond, S. 1994	Impact of prior performance on subsequent reputation	Market return and return on sales explains subsequent reputation
Verschoor, C. 1999	Commitment to ethics and performance	Firms committed to ethics statements as internal control strategy had significantly higher financial and non-financial performance
Govindarajan, V. 1990	Strategy, control systems, resource sharing and business unit performance	Strategy, control systems and resource sharing have impact on business unit performance
Hill, C. 1988	Innovation and performance	Innovation associated with greater firm profitability
Huselid, M. 1995	Human resource management and firm performance	Economic performance related to corporate culture
Chamberlain, A. 2015	Employee satisfaction and firm performance	Greater employee satisfaction associated with greater market value
Straw, B. 2000	Popular management techniques and financial performance	Use of techniques does not lead to better performance, some techniques (e.g. TQM) associated with higher management quality
Rumelt, R. 1974	Strategy, structure and strategic performance	In diversification, related business firms have higher profits, growth and price/earnings ratios
Nickell, S. 1996	Competition effects on firm performance	No overall finding of a link between performance and competition but some weak evidence of a link
Brynjolfsson, E. 2011	Data-driven decision-making and firm performance	Data driven decision making associated with increase in output and productivity as well as market value, some evidence of positive ROE and asset utilization
Christensen, H. 1981	Diversification vs. market structure and firm performance	Performance difference in some but not all diversification strategies

Table 3.1   (continued)

Main Author, Publication Date	Subject	Findings
Maher, M. 1999	Corporate governance and firm performance	For owner control, enhanced monitoring no evidence that mergers lead to performance improvement
Cooper, M. 2016	CEO – Incentive compensation and corporate performance	No relationship found
Adams, R. 2005	CEO – Impact of powerful CEO on performance	Firms with CEOs having more decision-making power experience more variability in firm performance, stock returns greater
Pearce, J. 1991	CEO – Relative power of CEO and boards on corporate performance	Combined CEO plus Chair has positive effect on ROA, Differences found in 4 types of boards, powerful boards had superior performance
Limbach, 2016	CEO – Tenure and firm performance	Better firm performance in early tenure compared to late tenure
Wooldridge, B. 1990	Middle management in strategy and organizational performance results	Middle management involvement in strategic management associated with improved performance
Baum, J. 2003	Speed of strategic decisions and performance	Fast strategic decision making predicts firm growth and profits
Payne, G. 2009	Team effectiveness and firm performance	Team effectiveness associated with board effectiveness and that is related to corporate performance
Bhagat, S. 1999	Boards – Composition and firm performance	Undetermined association
Dalton, D. 1998	Boards – Composition, leadership and financial performance	Little evidence of board and performance relationships
Brown, L. 2004	Boards – Corporate governance and financial performance	Better governed firms more profitable, valuable and pay more to shareholders. Good governance (via compensation) associated with good performance

Table 3.1 (continued)

Main Author, Publication Date	Subject	Findings
Klein, A. 1998	Boards – Inside directors' representation on board investment committee and firm performance	Better firm performance with more inside director representation
VanNess, R. 2010	Boards – Composition and financial performance post SOX	Board member heterogeneity related to growth
Meyer, E. 2013	Boards – Structure impacts on financial performance	The proportion of independent, non-executive directors had significant impact on earnings-per-share and enterprise value.

SUMMARY OF PERFORMANCE LITERATURE

The two most prominent aspects of the performance literature that was reviewed concentrate on what happens at the top of the organization. The CEO and boards are the most investigated subjects. Governance which is associated with these two factors is also a popular theme. Strategy and structure have several articles devoted to these themes.

Other than the structure theme, there is little in the way of streams of research and this is surprising. Even more surprising is what has not been the subject of study. That includes industry life cycle, industry itself as well as size of the organization. Scant attention has been given to competition though this is certainly a major force in company analysis. More recent developments such as disruptions are absent too. Global impacts on performance are not described here though they too are consequential.

While the literature review on performance was directed to the decision–performance nexus, it is remarkable how many of the factors which could be considered dependent variables are not addressed in the literature.

Departing from purely academic studies of decisions and performance, there is a gap between this research and practice. The views of CEOs are important, but they are mainly based on individual experiences of the CEOs and not on research. For as much as executives emphasize data driven decision making in strategy decisions, they do not follow that practice in their analysis of what makes business decisions successful.

CEOs are not likely to go into depth on their analysis of corporate performance. For one, they do not want to give away secret formulas for success to competitors. For another, they may not be sure of any of the reasons they propose accounts for success. Recall how "luck" has been cited for performance success. Luck represents such a range of possible explanations that the real reason or reasons is closer to unknowable than it is to knowable. CEOs are also primed to respond by their own record of success, not just in a single firm but more often in the series of companies they succeeded in before advancing to their current CEO-ship. "Do as I did" might be their paraphrased answer to the question of what they did to improve corporate performance.

The CEO is only as good as their last success. Once they lead an underperforming firm, their currency as a Midas man or woman no longer gleams. And big businesses still fail or decline.

So, the gap between practice and research remains. On the research side, the problem of performance is the infinitesimal progress being made to produce a general theory or even a standard model as has occurred in the sciences.

On the side of research, the problems are varied but substantial. The sample sizes used to draw conclusions are often small, sometimes as low as twelve companies. Another problem is that the ideas tested percolate from academic questions instead of questions posed by business executives and managers. An example is testing popular management techniques deriving from academic studies. Another problem is the varied use of different performance measures. Each author devises their own performance measurement or an indexed method. When this happens, it becomes very difficult to determine if the decisions are producing apples, oranges, bananas or the many other fruits of work.

Very little of the research has gone beyond top levels of corporate decision making. The middle management levels are largely absent of research on their roles of initiating, influencing and implementing decisions.

As a whole, the research streams of decision making and performance have diverged, not converged. These absences have made the task of understanding our initial question about decisions and performance daunting but not insurmountable.

Though it is beyond the scope of this book to conjoin practice and research on decision making and performance, there will be an effort to bring research and practice closer together. That will be to have practitioners reflect on research findings about decision making and performance. Surveyed practitioners will be asked to rank order from a selected list of what researchers have found to be reasons for corporate performance.

REFERENCES

Adams, R., Almeida, H., and Ferreira, D. (2005) Powerful CEOs and Their Impact on Corporate Performance, *The Review of Financial Studies*, 18(4, Winter), 1403–1432.

Baum, J. and Wally, S. (2003) Decision Speed and Firm Performance, *Strategic Management Journal*, 24(11, November), 1107–1129.

Bhagat, S. and Black, B. (1999) The Uncertain Relationship Between Board Composition and Firm Performance, *The Business Lawyer*, 54(3, May), 921–963.

Brown, L. and Kaylor, M. (2004) Corporate Governance and Firm Performance SSRN December 7, retrieved December 12, 2016 from SSRN: https://ssrn.com/abstract=586423.

Brynjolfsson, E., Hitt, L., and Heekyung, K. (2011) Strength in Numbers: How Does Data Driven Decision-making Affect Firm Performance? SSRN New York, April 22.

CEO Advisor (2014) Five Critical Traits of High Performance Companies (November 7), retrieved on December 18, 2016 from http://www.ceoadvisor.com/?p=340.

Chamberlain, A. (2015) What is the Causal Link Between Employee Satisfaction and Company Performance?, Glassdoor and based on Huang, M., Li, P., Meschke, F. and Guthrie, J., Family Firms, Employee Satisfaction and Corporate Performance, *Journal of Corporate Financing*, p. 3 retrieved on December 16, 2016 from https://www.glassdoor.com/research/u-kansas-study/.

Christensen, H.K. and Montgomery, C. (1981) Corporate Economic Performance: Diversification Strategy Versus Market Structure, *Strategic Management Journal*, 2(4, October–December), 327–343.

Collins, J. (2001) *Good to Great*, New York: Random House Business.

Cooper, M., Gulen, H., and Rau P. (2016) Pay for Performance: The Relation between CEO Incentive Compensation and Future Stock Price Performance, SSRN retrieved on December 8, 2016 from https:// ssrn.com/abstract=1572085.

Daisyme, P. (2015) July 21, 25 Insightful Quotes from Legendary CEOs, retrieved December 20, 2016 from https://www.entrepreneur.com/article/248627.

Dalton, D., Daily, C., Ellstrand, A., and Johnson, J. (1998) Meta-Analytic Reviews of Board Composition, Leadership Structure and Financial Performance, *Strategic Management Journal*, 19, 269–290.

Dess, G. and Robinson Jr. R. (1984) Measuring Organizational Performance in the Absence of Objective Measures: The Case of the Privately-held Firm and Conglomerate Business Unit, *Strategic Management Journal*, 5, 265–273.

Frick, W. (2014) Research: CEOs Matter More Today Than Ever at Least in America (March 2) retrieved December 18, 2016 from https://hbr.org/2014/03/research-ceos-matter-more.

Govindarajan, V. and Fisher, J. (1990) Strategy, Control Systems and Resource Sharing: Effects on Business Unit Performance, *Academy of Management Journal*, 33(2), 259–285.

Hammond, S. and Slocum, J. (1994) The Impact of Prior Firm Financial Performance on Subsequent Corporate Reputation, SMU Working Papers 172 January retrieved on December 15, 2016 from http://digitalrepository.smu.edu/business_workingpapers/172.

Hill, C. and Snell, S. (1988) External Control, Corporate Strategy and Firm

Performance in Research-Intensive Industries, *Strategic Management Journal*, 9, 577–590.

Huselid, M. (1995) The Impact of Human Resource Management Practices on Turnover, Productivity and Corporate Financial Performance, *Academy of Management Journal*, June 1, 38(3), 635–672.

Klein, A. (1998) Firm Performance and Board Committee Structure, *Journal of Law and Economics*, 41, 275.

Larcker, D. and Tagan, B. (2016) CEO Attributes and Firm Performance, Research Spotlight, retrieved on December 8, 2016 from gsb.stanford.edu/cgri-research.

Limbach, P., Schmid, M., and Scholz, M. (2016) Do CEOs Matter? Corporate Performance and the CEO Life Cycle, Draft Paper, November 30, retrieved on December 21, 2016 from https://ssm.com/abstract=2626340.

Maher, M. and Anderson, T. (1999) Corporate Governance: Effects on Firm Performance and Economic Growth, Paris: Organisation for Economic Co-operation and Development.

Meyer, E. and de Wet, J. (2013) The Impact of Board Structure on the Financial Performance of Listed South African Companies, *Corporate Board, Role, Duties and Composition*, 9(3), 18–31.

Nickell, S. (1996) Competition and Corporate Performance, *Journal of Political Economy*, 104(4), 724–746.

Payne, G., Benson, G., and Finegold, D. (2009) Corporate Board Attributes, Team Effectiveness and Financial Performance, *Journal of Management Studies*, 46(4), 704–731.

Pearce, J. and Zahra, S. (1991) The Relative Power of CEOs and Boards of Directors: Associations with Corporate Performance, *Strategic Management Journal*, 12(2, February), 135–153.

Peters, T. and Waterman, R. (2004) *In Search of Excellence*, New York: Harper Collins.

Pontefract, D. (2016) The Top 15 CEO Quotes About Operating with a Higher Purpose (2016), Forbes Leadership #Like A Boss retrieved December 20, 2016 from http://www.forbes.com/sites/danpontefract/2016/05/03/ the-top-15-ceo-quotes.

Rosenzweig. P. (2006). *Financial Times*, September 29.

Rosenzweig, P. (2007a) The Halo Effect and Other Managerial Delusions, *McKinsey Quarterly*, 1, 76–85.

Rosenzweig, P. (2007b) Misunderstanding the Nature of Company Performance: The Halo Effect and Other Business Delusions, *California Management Review*, 49(4), 6–20.

Rumelt, R. (1974) *Strategy Structure and Economic Performance*, Cambridge: Harvard University Press.

Sherman, D. and Young, S. (2016) Where Financial Reporting Still Falls Short, *Harvard Business Review* July–August, 94(7/8), 76–84.

Straw, B. and Epstein, L. (2000) What Bandwagons Bring: Effects of Popular Management Techniques on Corporate Performance, Reputation and CEO Pay, *Administrative Science Quarterly*, 45(3, September), 523–556.

Terlep, S. (2016) P&G CEO Says Company Hasn't Been Delivering, *Wall Street Journal*, February 18.

Van Looy, A. and Shafagotva, A. (2016) Business Process Performance Measurement: A Structured Literature Review of Indicators, Measures and Metrics, *SpringerPlus*, 5(1), 1–24.

VanNess, R., Miesing, P., and Kang, J. (2010) Board of Director Composition and Financial Performance in a Sarbanes–Oxley World, *Academy of Business and Economics Journal*, 10(5), 56–74.

Verschoor, C. (1999) Corporate Performance is Closely Linked to a Strong Ethical Commitment, *Business and Society Review*, 104(4), 407–415.

Windust, J. (2016) Cognology, retrieved on December 9, 2016 from http://cognol ogy .com.au.

Wooldridge, B. and Floyd, S. (1990) The Strategy Process, Middle Management Involvement and Organizational Performance, *Strategic Management Journal*, 11(3 March–April), 231–241.

Yakowicz, W. (2015) How Much Does Luck Affect a CEO's Performance? More Than You Think, November 17, retrieved on December 19, 2016 from http:www.//inc.com/will-yankowicz/study-luck-looking-the-part.

4. Modeling performance and research approach

Putting together business decisions and business performance is much like mixing oil and water. For good reason, they don't mix well and they should not mix because they are separated by time and are intrinsically different. Decisions happen first and performance follows. Decisions happen in the mind and performance happens in the motion.

There are other reasons for differences; human decision making is an imprecise activity. How the decisions are made vary quite a bit in the business world. Some organizations are quite methodical about it while others just play their hunches. Why the decisions are made is also the stuff of mystery. A business may simply say it is time to decide about purpose, mission and vision while other businesses may hold true to a course of action until it is no longer feasible to do so. Performance is a more complete idea. It is not precise but it comes closer to being more systematic than does human decision making. There are shared standards for what and how performance measurement is done in organizations. In decision making, there are wide variations in the parameters for success by individual decision makers and disagreement about how to make the decision.

VALUE OF A MODEL

The value of having a model stems from the paucity of not having any model. A model is an identifiable system of thinking where not having a model is an unidentifiable frenzy of straw grasping.

Without a model, there is no guiding plan for discovery about decisions and performance. With the model, there is a strategy for discovery. That means the crucial elements of who, what, when and where of decisions and performance are subject to being pieced together within a broad framework instead of a more haphazard piece by piece basis in which the horizontal and vertical dimensions are not known. Even when completed, the model may not be correct but it is easier to reframe the issue than it is to restart piecing together the individual pieces.

At its core, there is the decision and there is the effect of the decision.

It is the words of the decision and the flurry of action that follows. Most of the time, it is easy to distinguish between the two but modern organizations are doing both at the same time so for the outside observer, the separation is not as evident. That is why we have to rely on better-informed participants in the decision–performance bridge to reveal what is happening inside the organization. That is a basis of our research. Because we have kept these participants confidential as well as the names of their organizations unrevealed (unless they are described in public case studies), we are reasonably assured of participant candor about good decisions, bad decisions and their consequences.

In organizations, there is more formality in tying decisions to performance more so than in our daily personal lives. Decisions are recorded in the organization and communicated to those responsible for executing the decision. In our personal lives, the registry of the decisions is in our heads. We are our own implementers as well. That is not what occurs in sizable business organizations. The recording of organizational decisions happens in the strategic plan, contracts with customers and suppliers, project charters, policies and directives are among the forms. The recording of decisions helps identify responsibilities and rate performance of individuals who are charged with making decisions work.

CHAPTER OUTCOMES

In this chapter, the effort is on building an approach to understanding decisions and the results of decisions in the dimension of performance. Decisions may or may not have performance results. In theoretical physics, a theoretical model may be constructed which explains a phenomenon but there are no real-world consequences. Einstein notably participated in thought experiments with other physicists. He and they did so because true experimentation was not possible yet the results of the thought-based experiments could be speculated on. Making decisions plays a part in thought experiments of science but not in businesses because it is a continuous set of decisions that have to touch base with the real world – in choices consumers make and where investors decide to invest. Performance and the measurement is in constant demand.

In our case, we want the model to as closely represent reality as possible. We don't want a thought experiment. We want a thought with an actual result. That is the added value of a business experiment that forms the crux of our model-building effort. It is a science-like approach but not a pure science approach. Organizational study searches for a reasonable explanation of how things work not an exact one. That is our approach. Start with the science but adjust to the social science. If the model reasonably replicates what happens in the arena of practice, then headway has been made. The model can be tested by others. It can be used in for-profit and not-for-profit organizations. That is an aim: models that produce real and measurable outcomes.

The process for model-building in this circumstance is:

1. Build the model. That is the focus of this chapter.
2. Apply the model. To the degree possible, fill in the model with results from the survey and interviews. That will happen in Chapters 5–7.
3. Analyze the results. At this stage, form conclusions about how the collected data conforms to the model or doesn't conform to the model. This will occur in Chapter 8.
4. Confirm, reset or abandon the model based on the analysis. This is the subject of Chapters 8 and 9.

All of these steps are a part of this book in forthcoming chapters and explicated in Chapters 5–9 in detail. At various points throughout the remaining chapters, the model will be referred to and used to pull together the purpose of this research to disaggregate and then link decisions and performance.

PERFORMANCE AND DECISION CONSIDERATIONS IN MODELING

Performance, as we have said, is the resultant of decisions. Ideally, we want the linkage to be direct between decision and performance but it must be acknowledged that reality may not fit the mold that has been created by modeling. An overall conclusion will be reached on this matter.

Decisions themselves can be elusive in revealing themselves. This is especially true of human resource management decisions. An executive who has been subject to a CEO's decision may have their departure couched in the proverbial term of "seeking opportunities elsewhere" while, in fact, nothing of the sort occurred. A particularly bad decision which has not been widely publicized within and outside the organization may be snuffed by the CEO before severe damage can occur. Behind the faint grimace of the CEO is the realization that their poor decision making has been buried. For our purposes, only strategic decisions which are widely known within the organization are under scrutiny.

Put another way, we very often see an organization's performance but we may not see the decision behind the performance. Executives may be hedging their performance bets by relying on emotions, even hidden emotions to affect decisions. The problem with this is that organizations want to ostensibly portray themselves as rational driven entities to their investors. You never read a CEO annual report letter saying they didn't like the CFO and pushed them outside the business. The real reason is obscured in language of reason. "To further gain market share, our financial operations and department have been reorganized to conform to our mission" might be an example from a CEO letter. Both a reason and an action are substituted for an emotional and personal decision in letters such as this.

A business decision that involves unvarnished deception is another that is not subject of our research but it is also a decision that happens to have severe consequences. These hidden decisions may occur as part of corruption in decision making or because the risks are too high if things go wrong. Tyco's CEO Dennis Kozlowski failed to tell his board of his decision to move money into different accounts to make Tyco stock look more attractive. Ken Lay, the Enron CEO made the decision to facilitate the setting up of off shore accounts to make Enron look more profitable.

Deceptive and concealed decisions very often involve different groups. For Enron, the deceptive decision by Ken Lay was to enrich a small subgroup of executives with the shell game of moving money from one off shore company to another. That was done with the cooperation of their accounting firm, Arthur Anderson. Only a few at Enron knew what was being done and benefited from it. Enron investors and employees were denied information about the scheme to show continued profits so the decision was technically connected to performance but, because the implementation phase did not include the organization as a whole, it cannot be considered a legitimate example of decision and performance linkage. The decision implementation phase will be part of our model as described shortly.

With these cautions and clarifications in mind, the task is now to construct our initial model of decisions and performance. That follows.

BOX 4.1 A MODEL OF DECISIONS AND PERFORMANCE

As a means of understanding the natures of decisions and performance, a useful step is to create a model of what and how decisions and performance are comprised and how the two interact.

A model is a representation of reality. It is what is projected to be the way something works. It is not absolute in that it can be modified if new realities intrude on its structure. Astronomers talk about the standard model of the universe which explains how the universe is structured and how it evolves.

Theory is an organized group of ideas that is supposed to be a valid reflection of what is. Theory depends on and originates from facts but theory itself is not fact in permanence. Yet we use theory to understand various aspects of our world. For the scientist, theory is only as good as it explains things as they now stand.

A model is a representation of our understanding of how the world works. Perhaps the most common examples are plastic models found in hobby stores. An airplane or car model glued together from plastic pieces is a depiction of an actual model but in smaller scale and in three dimensions. We think of models as having proportionality to what they represent but strict proportionality is not always the way to go. The forces acting on an airplane do not scale up in linear proportion. Drag is a squared force as velocity increases. This shows aerodynamic distortion of simple scaling up on a linear basis.

Our use of a model is more abstract, more like a theory than a model. Our model is more a set of interrelated ideas than a physical mock-up. Our realm is more a thought model à la the approach of science.

For our purposes, we are introducing a model that will be tested through observation. Our model will be described and the interviews and case studies we do will then be applied to the model to determine how appropriate it actually is. The revised process model will be presented to a group of respondents and they will be asked to judge it.

Those business executives and owners interviewed were asked which factors contributed substantially to the success of the decision. A listing of factors was provided that fall off the list originated from the literature cited in our research. Thus, all the literature which hypothesized or established a possible reason for a successful decision was the basis for inclusion. These factors were put in short form and the surveyed or interviewed participant simply checked off any and all of the factors they believed contributed to success. The source articles were mainly from the *Journal of Strategic Management* though other leading academic research journals were used as sources for factors. The journal articles have been cited in other chapters of this book.

The factors were (along with an explanatory note if the respondent needed clarification in parentheses):

1. Impact of the firm's prior performance on firm reputation (extent that the firm's reputation among customers explained performance).
2. Commitment to ethics (degree that perceptible ethical behaviors of the company explained performance).
3. Innovation (the degree the firm demonstrated innovation capabilities as a performance factor).
4. Team effectiveness (the degree that teams in the firm contributed to performance).
5. Resource sharing across diverse business units and/or product lines (extent that sharing of business unit resources instead of not sharing resources meant to performance results).
6. Employee satisfaction (if positive or negative employee satisfaction affected performance).
7. Human resource management (did policies and procedures of employee management affect performance?).
8. Popular management techniques (e.g. TQM, Sigma 6) (did popularly used tools of motivation, compensation and rewards affect performance?).

9. Competition between firms (does the number and strength of competitors affect performance of the firm in question?).
10. Data-driven decision making (the extent that data-based decision making affects performance as opposed to hunch or intuitive decision making).
11. Decision speed (i.e. fast versus slow strategic decision making).
12. Corporate governance (the impact of formal governance practices on the firm).
13. Board of directors (the influence of the board of directors on performance).
14. CEO pay (does the amount of money the CEO gets paid affect performance?).
15. CEO attributes (experience, tenure of the CEO and performance effects).
16. CEO autonomy/independence (does the extent of CEO freedom to make decisions have performance implications?).
17. Middle management (influence of middle management on performance). For very small businesses, some of the factors such as middle management, corporate governance, CEO autonomy/independence did not apply and these responses were left unchecked. Companies with over twenty employees tended to respond to these questions more than the very small firms.

These were the factors included in the survey and executive interviews. From the world of practice, other factors such as when the business was launched, how it was funded and what business model was used are no doubt important but our focus was on the research findings as sources for success because published research tends to be more rigorous than popular accounts of success contained in general media. The 17 factors used here came from empirical studies in academic journals as described earlier. Though the listing does not include factors one might consider such as the historic period of when the decision was made and the size and position of the organization within the industry life cycle, the factors that are present have been subject to empirical work. Thus, they come with a platform of evidence-based verification.

Mathematic notation is used to initially present the model. It is used to reduce the model to the simplest form without using words. The aim is to have basic but essential representations of causal relationships.

In its most basic form, the model is notated as $P = f(D)$ where P is performance, D is a strategic decision and f is a function of. A function is a "formula, rule, or procedure for taking a set of numbers and assigning to each number in the set precisely one value" (Gootman, 1997, p. 3). Calling the relationship a function means we can use numerical data in a generalized expression of a relationship between decisions and performance. We can't say that performance is directly a result of a strategic decision but it is related to a decision or, in mathematical parlance, a function of the decision. How much of a function the decision plays in the performance is the subject of study.

The very bare bones model can immediately be amended by adding factors which may uncontrollably intervene is a direct relationship between decision and performance. Chief among these factors are environmental factors which are very usefully captured in a commonly used technique of strategic management and that is the PEST framework where P = political-legal, E = economic factors, S = social and cultural and T = technological factors. These are "big tent" (used even though with the dissolution of the circus, big tents are becoming an artifact of the past) factors because they cover a large number of subfactors which are important in themselves. As an example, S includes demographic trends which is certainly a determinant of organizational success in terms of number and location of customers or patrons.

Some versions of PEST add an N for Natural factors. These could be weather and climate events, natural resource availability including water and other related happenings. We will add the N to the PEST making it PESTN as a more complete optic for evaluating outside influences on performance.

The commonality among the PESTN factors is that they are largely though not totally out of the control of executives making strategic decisions. The PESTN factors modify how the decision can result in performance that can occur.

The resulting revision to the model is:

$P1 = f\ D\ +/-\ PESTN$ where P1 is actual performance which is a function of the decision (D) as modified by PESTN factors. This can be read as: The actual performance is a function of decision plus or minus the influence of PESTN.

The new model introduces the idea of actual decision results versus intended results. The intended results are the modifications on performance caused by PESTN factors. The outside forces can have a great effect or a small effect but it is virtually certain they will have no effect.

Effects of PESTN may encompass all five components or only a single one. An example of a single dominant factor is technology on software applications businesses. Companies in this field are extremely dependent on advances in computing power to bring new applications into existence. These businesses are far less dependent on any of the other PESTN factors. On the other hand, consumer goods businesses are very dependent on all PESTN elements. Political-legal factors affect product safety regulations. Economic factors affect disposable and discretionary income available to consumers, Socio-cultural aspects affect the number, wants and needs of customers, technology affects the production of goods and services and the natural element affects basic sources of supply from minerals to water.

There are also interactive effects of the external factors on performance. Government regulation, taking the form of increased testing of new drug formulations, can have the effect of increasing the price of drugs therefore reducing consumer ability to pay for the drugs. New efficiencies in producing drugs if they win regulatory approval can alternately reduce the consumer cost in acquiring more efficiently produced drugs.

PESTN forces can enhance and reduce organizational performance and, as such, is an essential consideration in any assessment of strategic decision making. PESTN factors affect all the players in the organizational game. Any set of players encounter different levels of influence for each of the factors but all industry players are affected to some degree by PESTN.

HOW PESTN FACTORS WILL BE EVALUATED

The PESTN factors will be evaluated for their impact on performance by a subgroup of survey and interview participants. These respondents will respond to a question about the degree to which the PESTN factors modified the performance results and if that influence was positive, negative or neutral. Also, which of the factors had the greatest effect on performance will be explored with the respondents.

THE PROCESS MODEL

The preceding discussion of the connection between decisions and performance dealt with notations. Here, we will focus on the process for a more complete perspective on the subject. The notation offers a view of the relationship among the independent and dependent variables while the process model incorporates the element of time in the overall model by showing the sequence of events in the course of moving from decisions to performance results. The process itself that comprises the model is shown in Box 4.1. Each stage is enumerated and described briefly after the figure.

The way this process model will be assessed is by a select group of survey and interview participants who will be shown Box 4.1 and asked how applicable it is for their decision-making and performance evaluation practices. Your authors will derive conclusions and present findings in the following chapters.

Having developed both a symbolic depiction of the decision and performance along with a flow chart of the process, we will turn to some of the assumptions behind the models themselves.

ASSUMPTIONS OF PERFORMANCE PROCESS MODEL

The first assumption of the model is that the sequence of actions is that decision always precedes performance. This carries from our basic decision/cause, performance/effect model and further that the decision and the performance are not simultaneous. The demise of Radio Shack shows the fatal damage that can happen if too many decisions especially reversing ones can confuse employees about the standard decision and performance sequence. In essence, Radio Shack hopped around with its strategic decisions, moving from electronic parts, to CB radios, to services to computers to cell phones without coordination or phase in and out strategies. Where the company was on decision sequences was lost on employees and certainly lost on customers.

The second assumption is that there is freedom by agents of the organizations to make decisions. The agents are not totally independent and have obligations to boards of directors but the boards are not the primary controllers of strategic decisions. A related assumption is that once the decisions are made the agents of the organization are not free to control results since external PESTN factors come into play. We are assuming that our participants were or were connected with active agent CEOs.

The third assumption is that there is uncertainty over the outcomes of the decision. The assumption is that there is some level of risk to accompany some level of reward. This is a tenet of strategic management. If there was no uncertainty, then human decision making would be obviated by computer-based decision systems.

The fourth assumption is that the results of the decision are measurable. The measurement can be qualitative or quantitative but it must be tangible. In our case, much of the measurement will be categorical in nature and involve nominal data. A related assumption is that the measurement must be honestly done. Measurement of performance will be accepted when provided by the organization under study because it is confirming information of previously reported judgments of positive and negative performance experiences. The organizations themselves have volunteered this information as a core element of this study.

The fifth assumption is that the decision is strategic in nature. This is clarified for survey and interview respondents at the outset of the information gathering process from them. A strategy decision was provided to all survey and interview participants or it was extracted from the case studies reviewed or written by the authors.

The sixth assumption is that in the course of implementing the decision there is sufficient time to produce results. In other words, instantly reversed decisions are not subject to our analysis. An instantly reversed decision would take the form of a CEO who suspends the decision within days of its implementation. This assumption is needed because there is time required for potential external influences to impact the performance. As a guideline, we consider a year to be sufficient time for full implementation.

The seventh assumption is that the decision is a true decision with a choice between two or more courses of action which are distinctive enough in expected results and require substantial organizational resources to accomplish.

The eighth assumption is that the decision involved some level of analysis or consideration before implementation. This eliminates the "playing a hunch" type of decision making. Said another way, we are exploring decisions which have been subject to some form of discussion among members of the organization before they are enacted. This is a stricture of rational decision making. This assumption will be checked as a preface to the surveys and interviews but in prior research done by the authors in strategic management, there have been no instances of hunch playing by organizational leaders.

These eight assumptions, and the implicit requirements of respondents constrain some potential conclusions but also enable management of the study.

OBSERVATIONS ON THE PROCESS MODEL

As designed, the process model as presented has the capacity to take in both large and small businesses. In many cases, the difference between small and large businesses is a matter of scale. Both large businesses and small businesses are aimed at increasing shareholder wealth. They both have forms of governance and both require human labor to operate.

Also, as presented, it also can be used for profit-driven and not-for-profit organizations. Both for profit and not-for-profit make decisions to secure their futures. They both require human labor and they both have accountabilities.

By incorporating both internal and external influences on prospective influences, the model is a widespan one.

The process model shows a system which includes feedback which again has a place for continuous adjustment. It is based on our initial observations about organizational decision making. That suggests organizations are not like cargo ships in World War II. They do not abruptly run zig-zag courses to avoid torpedoes. For large organizations, this would be hard to do given the slow process of implementation of strategy decisions and for smaller organizations, a zig-zag course would reveal a lack of a "stick to the knitting" decision pattern. Smaller organizations need to be wily and flexible but not to the point they radically change strategy. Instead, the model poses that more gradual changes are made in strategy for the most part for organizations of both size categories.

EXCLUSIONS OF THE PROCESS MODEL

What the process model does not incorporate is what we call existential structural emergencies. While almost all organizations experience emergencies such as deaths of key executives and evaporation of customer bases or catastrophic product failure, these can be insured for or planned around. An existential structural emergency is something like having the entire organization fail in many dimensions at one time as the French enterprise building the Panama Canal. The bankruptcy of the French investors paved the way for the pathway between two continents by the United States. This demonstrates that ultimately, there may be success after failure. In the Panama Canal instance, the success resulted from a new means of technology – that of large industrial shovels and intensive use of dynamite instead of hand picks and strong backs.

WHO ARE SOURCES FOR MODEL INFORMATION?

The accuracy of the model depends on the quality of information provided to the authors. For the small businesses included, the information sources were either the owner/operators or those closely connected with the core operations and strategies of the organizations. For larger organizations, these individuals were CEOs, vice presidents, directors and managers who described themselves as having a say in the formulation of strategic decisions.

Providers of information were candid about offering information about good and bad decisions. All provided information about good decisions and the results and only a very few (four) were not able to describe a bad decision that was made. This originated from their brief tenure with the organizations they were reporting on. The fact that both good and bad decisions were readily described shows that organizations do not uniformly make good or bad decisions but a combination of both. More on this is reported in Chapter 6. A bouncing effect between a good decision and a bad decision that was detected among participants highly suggests that decision science is not a science in organizational life because there are no laws of nature on what causes good and bad decision making.

In the following chapter, Chapter 5, we are dedicated to describing how the research was conducted. The number and characteristics of respondents will be described. Immediately thereafter, the results of the survey and interviews will be presented in Chapter 6.

REFERENCE

Gootman, E. Calculus (1997) *Hauppauge*, New York: Baron's Educational Series.

5. First round findings

Up to this point, we have presented information on the aim of the book, discussed decisions and performance and have offered a model of assessing the performance outcomes of managerial decisions. Now, we delve into the original research done in our study. This chapter is devoted to describing how the research was conducted. The research methodology is presented together with the rationale for the methods used. The chapter will introduce the methods of research in a basic fashion that will be understandable to business practitioners and business students alike.

As far as we know, this is the first broad-based look at actual performance associated with decisions of managers and executives. Prior decision research has been constrained to setting up decision choices and having individuals make choices among several options. This is very much a laboratory setting for management specimens. It does not replicate the actuality of making management decisions based on partial information, fast-changing information or even bad information. This is the world of management practice though. As such, our intent was to bridge some of the differences between the academic and practical perspectives on decision making. For business managers, there has been a long-standing desire for research that is applicable in the daily world of business. For researchers, there is a need for an organized and coherent approach to uncovering commonalities and relationships among the disparate ways of decision making in businesses. Melding these perspectives has the chance of reducing some of the unknown aspects about decisions and their results. There is a mysterious component to this in the minds of the many in businesses who do not know how strategic decisions are made let alone how the consequences are produced.

ISSUES OF SOURCES OF DECISION MAKING DATA

All said, the sources of business decision making appear to come from a very narrow vessel. What we have are hundreds of thousands of decision making techniques coming from hundreds of thousands of businesses. How businesses make decisions depends considerably on the organization.

It is a very individualized process as a whole. That process we have found varies by size of organization and differences in the psychology of chief executives. It is demarked by industry and competitive intensity as well. Our observation is that not one single model of business decision making applies to the majority of American businesses. With such variance, it was important to select businesses in the study that were different from one another, and that was done.

There was much more uniformity on the performance resultant. By and large and as reported, revenues dominated the performance measures. The plus side of this was that most performance was measured by a unit of comparability with other firms – the dollar. The negative side was that revenue gains cannot be easily linked back to specific decisions. There are many factors that affect revenues – numbers and level of competition, cost controls, system efficiencies, the tax treatment of corporate income and the skills and talents of employees. Any linkage between decision and result was done by way of the judgment of the respondent or the judgment of the authors reviewing case information.

Both authors conducted the survey/interviews and both authors did the case studies. Periodically during the data gathering the authors met to compare their findings. This facilitated more uniform reporting of data along with consistent responses.

SOURCES OF DECISION MAKING AND PERFORMANCE

There were two main sources for the research data, as noted earlier. They were different sources though the content of the case study and interview/survey was very similar. Of the two methods, one was interviews with the owners, key executives or informed managers of companies selected for inclusion by the authors. This was a convenience sample of firms that the authors knew by virtue of knowing key decision makers in the organizations. The firms were also selected because they had successful performance results or unsuccessful results. To encourage their candid appraisal of decision making, they were assured of confidentially by the authors. This decision did lead to these individuals being forthright. They stated clearly that they were responsible for results. There was no experimentation involved in our effort. Actual decisions and actual results were reported. This was needed to get to primary source data.

The second source of data was from corporate histories and financial reports of larger companies. Almost all these companies had more than 1,000 employees. Their corporate histories were quite detailed and came from their corporate websites which were supplemented by business media accounts of their activities. The financial information came from SEC 10K filings and other SEC reports including quarterly reports. While interviews with individuals did not happen, the publicly reported history information and financial data gave us a picture of major decisions and performance. The performance information was not solely financial. Some firms reported market share information instead of or as a supplement to financial information. Not all the companies studied used financial information as a determinant of success, though most did.

Three years of performance information was sought for the interviews and the corporate histories and financial report information. Three years of performance information for the years after the strategic decision was made were asked for. Almost invariably, performance trend information was offered. This was turned into categorical data for the analysis that will be explained shortly.

Both successful and unsuccessful decisions were tracked this way. For the larger firms, the strategic decisions the company made were obtained from the corporate histories. We cannot claim that a specific decision led to certain performance results but there were associations between the decision and performance trends.

The period of time that the interviews and the corporate histories were conducted was between January, 2017 and August, 2017. There was a greater span in the time when the firms made the decision and the performance happened. This spanned 1980 through 2016. The successful and unsuccessful decisions did not always happen coincidentally. It may have been that a successful decision was followed by an unsuccessful decision or vice-versa. To have required a certain pattern of success and non-success would have constrained the free sequence of results.

The qualifications of the respondents were established because the respondents:

a) Were personally known by the authors to have substantial responsibility within their business organizations, or
b) Were not known personally by the authors yet they held positions within their organizations normally associated with strategic decision making, for example CEO, Chief Operations Officer, Chief Marketing Officer, owner or vice president or director.

Initial discussions of prospective interviewees established that the individuals understood what strategic decisions were and that had sufficient tenure with the organization to comment on the three year results of the decision.

We let the participants of the interview determine what constituted a successful or interchangeably a good business decision. For the case studies, we determined and differentiated the successful business decisions as opposed to unsuccessful decisions. The basis for differentiating between the good and bad decisions in the cases was the degree which the decision met articulated expectations. This decision categorization was found in annual reports, SEC filings, media releases by the firm and media stories by national business press.

For both the interviews and case studies, the stipulation of what performance measures were used was not forced on the respondent but left open. That was articulated in person by the interviewee and inferred by the authors for the case studies based on public records of the companies.

For the interviews which were all done solely by the authors, the interview sessions ran about an hour each. Notes were taken during the interviews by the authors. After each interview was conducted, the notes were reviewed. Key points were underscored and gaps in the requested information were noted for interviewee call backs.

The interviews occurred at prearranged times selected by the participant. The nature of the interview was described in advance to the respondent. An interview guide was used for the interviews. The interview guide asked for the product and/or services provided by the company. The responses were open ended. A description of a successful strategic business decision was asked for along with an unsuccessful decision. For both decisions, the responder was asked why the decision was successful or unsuccessful in the short term (meaning a year or less). The long-term consequences (over three years) were solicited. Additional information requested for both successful and unsuccessful decisions were the estimated effect of the decision on revenue for each of the three years. What had also been collected was overall revenues for the company so that reported revenue impacts could be gauged from the decision. A following question had to do with the top three performance measures. Respondents were asked to provide these as they determined overall success or failure of the decision.

The next question asked respondents to select from a list of 17 possible explanations of business decision success which applied to their organization. The possible explanations originated from empirical research articles from scholarly publications as discussed in Chapter 3. The intent was to establish if any of these factors was evident in the respondent reported decisions. The respondent simply said yes or no if that particular factor was consequential in the decision. The percentages for each factor were tabulated and reported from those who replied to the question.

A very open question was asked at the end of the interviews. That question inquired about what the single most important factor was that would lead to better strategic decisions for most businesses. This allowed

Table 5.1   Interviews and case studies decision results

Decisions	Personal Interviews	Case Studies
Decision Considered a Success	56	32
Decision Considered a Failure	25	50
Total	81	82

the respondent to reflect on their own responses and also step aside and offer their views for others to consider in improving decision making. A broad range of replies were provided and they were arranged by category to facilitate analysis. As a generalized note, respondents were very eager to share their thoughts about what businesses could do to improve strategic decisions. This question was at the end of the interview. It was not answered in the case studies because the case studies were not based on responses of individuals but reported data instead.

There was some limited follow-up with respondents to explore respondent questions that arose during the interviews. A few respondents wanted to elaborate on points not directly part of the interview but were nonetheless worth exploring. These comments are incorporated in Chapter 9 on recommendations.

All the data from the surveys and case studies was entered into an Excel spreadsheet. Descriptive statistics were obtained and reported in this chapter. The descriptive statistics include percentages of categorical responses, means and standard deviation. The principal analytical tool for this portion of the analysis was Excel. The findings are presented in Tables 5.1–5.5.

SUMMARY INFORMATION ON INTERVIEWS AND CASES

Let us begin by summarizing our decisions. There are 127 firms and a total of 163 unique decisions in our sample, as some reported both successes and failures. We collected information on 81 unique decisions from 57 personal interviews using the criteria described above. These interviews contained a total of 56 successes and 25 failures. The remaining data came from case studies for 70 different firms. These case studies included 82 decisions, 32 of which were successes and 50 of which were failures.

Responses in personal interviews tended to be skewed heavily towards successful decisions, with business leaders in our personal interviews reporting about twice as many successful decisions as unsuccessful decisions. In contrast, our business case studies tend to be skewed towards

Table 5.2   Long-term effects of decisions

	Strong Success	Moderate Success	No Change	Moderate Decline	Strong Failure	Totals
			Long-term Effects, Full Sample of 163 Decisions			
Successes	13	43	9	14	2	81
	(8%)	(26.4%)	(5.5%)	(8.6%)	(1.2%)	(49.7%)
Failures	10	15	8	30	19	82
	(6.1%)	(9.2%)	(4.9%)	(18.4%)	(11.7%)	(50.3%)
Totals	23	58	17	44	21	163
	(14.1%)	(35.6%)	(10.4%)	(27%)	(12.9%)	(100%)

unsuccessful decisions, as we collected roughly twice as many examples of unsuccessful decisions as successful decisions. This highlights one of the benefits of our mixed sample. By combining our sample in this way we have an even mix of successful and unsuccessful decisions.

When asked for more detail on the outcome, interviewees tended to report general information on trends rather than respond with detailed financial data. We converted this trend data to a five-point Likert scale. Values of our decision outcome range from a one through to five, with one being a strong increase in performance over a three-year period, two being a moderate increase, three being no significant change, four being a gradual decrease in performance, and five being a strong decrease up to and including bankruptcy. With written case studies, determinations were generally made by the author of the study using terms such as "strong growth," etc. In these latter cases we were able to classify the results on our scale. This method has the advantage over our first model of looking at actual performance, rather than a simple success or failure determination. This method also has an advantage in that it also allows us to use our full sample of data in our analysis.

Tables 5.2, 5.3, and 5.4 present the results from these five-point scales for the full sample, interviews, and case studies, respectively. The

Table 5.3   Personal Interviews

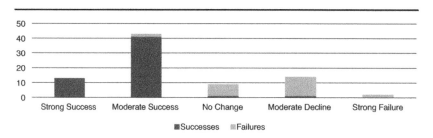

Initial Success/Failure vs Long-term Effects, 81 Personal Interviews

	Strong Success	Moderate Success	No Change	Moderate Decline	Strong Failure	Totals
Successes	13	41	1	1	0	56
	(16%)	(50.6%)	(1.2%)	(1.2%)	(0%)	(69.1%)
Failures	0	2	8	13	2	25
	(0%)	(2.5%)	(9.9%)	(16%)	(2.5%)	(30.9%)
Totals	13	43	9	14	2	81
	(16%)	(53.1%)	(11.1%)	(17.3%)	(2.5%)	(100%)

Table 5.4   Case studies

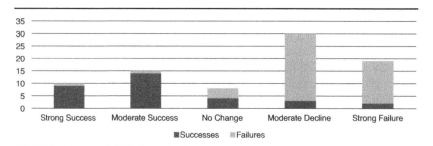

Initial Success/Failure vs Long-term Effects, 82 Case Studies

	Strong Success	Moderate Success	No Change	Moderate Decline	Strong Failure	Totals
Successes	9	14	4	3	2	32
	(11%)	(17.1%)	(4.9%)	(3.7%)	(2.4%)	(39%)
Failures	1	1	4	27	17	50
	(1.2%)	(1.2%)	(4.9%)	(32.9%)	(20.7%)	(61%)
Totals	10	15	8	30	19	163
	(12.2%)	(18.3%)	(9.8%)	(36.6%)	(23.2%)	(100%)

respective right- and left-skewed nature of the personal interviews and case studies can be seen in Table 5.2. We would expect to see a clear relationship between the simple success/failure determination and long-term trend outcomes as measured by values on our Likert scale. If we compare the success/failure results from personal interviews and case studies to the Likert scale values, we see the expected relationship between the two in the tables below:

By focusing on the personal interviews and case studies specifically, we can more clearly see the skewed relationships in Tables 5.3 and 5.4. Again, the majority of personal interviews generated examples of successes and the majority of case studies led to examples of failures.

We collected average sales revenue data from 60 observations. While seven of these observations were given to us in interviews, the majority of these figures were taken from publicly available data for publicly traded firms in our case studies. In the interviews, the most commonly reported figure is sales revenue, and this is what we generally focus on as well for the larger firms. Firms range in size from small franchises with $30,000 in annual sales to large corporations with tens of billions in annual revenue. In each of these cases, we collected the three-year trend for revenue during the three years associated with the decision. With the smaller businesses that generally face greater risk and wider swings in performance, successful decisions were mostly associated with relatively small increases in sales, though these increases were large as a percentage of total sales revenue. The smallest in our sample is a $5,000 increase in annual sales due to the implementation of a new marketing tactic, though this represents a 17 percent increase in the firm's sales. In contrast, successful decisions made by larger firms lead in many cases to seemingly insignificant outcomes when viewed as a percentage of annual revenue. In one case an increase in revenue of $1 billion led to an increase in sales revenue of less than 3 percent. The largest of these led to an increase of slightly more than $100 billion in annual revenue, representing an increase in this particular corporation's annual revenues of almost 200 percent.

The mean value for these figures is $28.5 billion. This seems like a high number but there are two reasons for this. First, we must remember that accurate sales data is coming mostly from larger firms, as actual sales figures for our smaller firms are more likely to be incomplete or missing. Second, the standard deviation is $60.4 billion. This is because there are five very large firms, such as auto makers, in our data with unusually large values for sales revenue. If we remove these from our sample and include only firms with less than $100 billion in average revenue our mean value falls to $12.7 billion with a standard deviation of $17.5 billion.

The size of a firm's revenue is related to the success or failure of a decision in our data. If we calculate Pearson correlation coefficients between a firm's size and success, we find a correlation coefficient of −0.26, which suggests that revenue has a somewhat weak correlation with the likelihood a decision is successful. This should not be surprising if we consider the fact that we have more complete financial data from the larger firms in our case studies. Because we also have more data on failed decisions from these firms, it should make sense that we observe a relationship in our data. We believe the observed relationship is due to our sample and therefore is not meaningful as we do not believe it would extend to the general population. This inverse correlation does not hold when we compare revenue to our Likert scale scores.

FINDINGS IN DETAIL

We now turn to specific factors that influence success or failure. Chapter 3 outlined 26 unique factors that theoretically can impact the likelihood of success or failure. Of these 26, we collected data on these 17 factors:

1. Firm's Prior Performance
2. Commitment to Ethics
3. Innovation
4. Team Effectiveness
5. Resource Sharing Across Diverse Business Units
6. Employee Satisfaction
7. Human Resources Management
8. Specific Management Techniques
9. Competition
10. Data-Driven Decisions
11. Decision Speed
12. Corporate Governance
13. Board of Directors
14. CEO Pay
15. CEO Attributes
16. CEO Autonomy
17. Middle Management.

We chose this subset of 17 due to the extensive empirical research conducted on each of these specific factors. We will discuss each of these separately and comment on meta-analyses that review this empirical literature.

The first of these factors is the impact of a firm's prior performance. Did a firm's prior reputation impact the ultimate success or failure of this decision? Ali et al. (2015) review 101 studies in the empirical literature. They find that a firm's prior reputation is more important in the United States than it is in the United Kingdom or in other countries, possibly due to greater media exposure. However, they also point out that a firm's "reputation" is difficult to define and measure. Going even further, they state that:

> [I]t is difficult, if not impossible, for any single, primary study to . . . provide a synthesized assessment regarding the relationship between corporate reputation and its antecedents and consequences with the specific aim of clarifying and possibly resolving some of the inconsistencies in previous research. (Ali et al., 2015, p. 1106)

This statement echoes the general feeling we get from the majority of these meta-analyses and highlights the difficulties inherent in this line of academic literature.

The brand loyalty that emerges from a firm's prior successes should not be underestimated. Gillette relied on consumer trust when they introduced the disposable razor (as opposed to razors with disposable blades). A startup firm may not have been able to introduce this product successfully. On the other hand, as we see in the introduction to the following chapter, brand loyalty was a major factor that was not adequately considered in Coca-Cola's introduction of New Coke. At any rate, most of the studies do find a positive relationship between prior performance and business outcomes. Therefore, we expect to see the same positive relationship with this factor.

Our second factor is commitment to ethics. Orlitzky, Schmidt, and Rynes (2003) find a complex but positive relationship between corporate social/environmental performance and corporate financial performance. The general consensus is that ethically questionable decisions may sometimes have a positive impact in the short term, but they ultimately tend to have a negative long-term impact. Margolis and Walsh (2001) suggest that the relationship between ethics and business outcomes is frequently oversimplified. In such cases it is normal for researchers to be expected to find a very small relationship if one at all. We cautiously expect to find a positive relationship because our measure is a simple yes/no question. Lululemon Athletica, a yoga wear retailer, successfully uses ethical business and production practices as its core marketing strategy. In contrast, ethics were discarded when Bernie Madoff decided to grow his company by creating a pyramid scheme. This was successful in the short term, but ultimately led to bankruptcy.

Our third factor is the effect of innovation. Rosenbusch, Brinckmann, and Bausch (2011) find that while the relationship between innovation and business performance is theoretically justified, it is difficult to see in small- and medium-sized enterprises because innovation is "context dependent." Again, this is not surprising given the findings of Ali et al. (2015) above. Despite its humble beginnings in an entrepreneur's garage, Amazon.com grew to become one of the largest retail firms in the country due to its ability to navigate technological changes. Similarly, Apple rose to prominence due to Steve Jobs' masterful focus on innovation. As firms can be highly successful primarily due to their successful innovation, some firms can fail because of their inability to innovate. For example, Sears Roebuck and Co. built up a phenomenal amount of infrastructure in their more than 100 years as a leader in mail order catalog sales. The ability to leverage this existing infrastructure should have given them an advantage over Amazon, yet Amazon grew to be the leader in online retail sales. It seems obvious that Sears management was reluctant to take risks. Sony's failed experiment with Betamax and later success with the compact disc shows that constant innovation with both positive and negative results is sometimes a part of a successful enterprise.[1] Because we see so many examples of both success and failure related to innovation, we remain agnostic on the relationship between innovation and business outcomes.

Our fourth factor is team effectiveness. The automobile industry provides examples of both success and failure. Toyota's strong focus on teamwork led to a competitive advantage in manufacturing early on. General Motors' widely publicized quality control issues in the 1980s stemmed partly from a weak focus on team building and poor morale. By some accounts, their Fremont plant was the "worst of the worst" (Shook, 2010, p. 63). In a joint venture, Toyota and GM operated what would eventually be known as the "NUMMI" plant. Toyota helped GM create an efficient workforce while GM helped Toyota navigate the U.S. regulatory environment. Mathieu et al. (2008) review the empirical literature and generally find positive relationships between team effectiveness and outcomes. They also note the difficulty with which team effectiveness can be measured, showing that this is little different than the other factors. We expect a positive relationship between team effectiveness and successful decisions.

The fifth factor is resource sharing across diverse business units. From soft drinks to automobiles, furniture to entertainment, it is easy to think of countless examples of multinational firms successfully marketing different products globally. However, there are just as many examples of firms attempting so with less than successful outcomes. Many of these involve marketing efforts that get lost in translation when international boundaries are crossed. A popular urban legend involving the NUMMI plant described above serves to illustrate this phenomenon. The first vehicle to emerge from the NUMMI plant was the Chevy Nova. As the story goes, "nova" is translated as "no go" in Spanish, and led to poor sales in Mexico. While this particular case is likely an urban legend, Scandinavian firm

Electrolux did try to market vacuum cleaners in the United States using the slogan "Nothing sucks like an Electrolux" and Kentucky Fried Chicken did find out the hard way that "finger lickin' good" didn't translate into Chinese the way it was intended. In these examples, resources were not shared effectively. Crook et al. (2008) conduct a meta-analysis of 125 studies and find a correlation between the shared use of "strategic resources" and business performance of 0.22. Liang, You, and Liu (2010) review 42 studies and find "strong evidence" that shared IT resources contribute positively to financial performance and efficiency due to their ability to strengthen an organization. We expect to see a positive relationship between shared resources and successful decisions.

The sixth factor is employee satisfaction. Was employee satisfaction a factor that contributed to the success of the decision? Was low employee morale a reason for the failure of this decision, as we see with GM pre and post NUMMI? In a popular meta-analysis of prior empirical studies, Harter, Schmidt, and Hayes (2002) document a clear positive relationship between employee satisfaction and business outcomes. Therefore, we expect to see a positive relationship as well.

The seventh factor is human resource management. In a review of the empirical literature, Subramony (2009) finds a positive relationship between HRM bundles (i.e. combinations of best practices) and business outcomes. SAS Institute is a pioneer in this factor and has a long history of providing generous benefits such as onsite daycare for its employees in order to reduce turnover. On the other hand, Amazon has recently experienced very high turnover in distribution and call centers nationwide. Both of these firms are successful leaders in their industries. We expect to see human resource management have a positive relationship with success in our data. Like the effect of ethics, however, we suspect that firms can be successful in the short run with mediocre human resource practices. Therefore, we also expect this relationship to be weak.

The eighth factor is specific management techniques such as Six Sigma, Lean, and Total Quality Management programs. Though originating at Motorola, Six Sigma was popularized through its use at General Electric in the 1990s in order to reduce variance in the production process. Lean originated with Toyota as a systematic method to reduce waste. While such programs provide clear benefits to automakers, they may create unnecessary bureaucratic red tape in small organizations. Nair (2006) finds that the impact of specific quality management practices is not always direct and that success is moderated by combinations of other factors. As with many of these factors, they theoretically matter but the direct effect is hard to measure. We cautiously expect to see a positive relationship with success in our data.

Our ninth factor is the influence of competition. Amazon's intense focus on increasing market share before profits is an example of a major strategic success. Motorola's status as an industry leader led to organizational inertia and a failure to compete effectively. Capon, Farley, and Hoenig (1990) review an astounding 320 studies and find that competition as measured by the Lerner Index of market share and/or its growth over time are both positively related to financial performance. They note that at the time of their study more work needed to be done on the possible synergistic relationships between factors. The level of competition in an industry should increase risk for all firms in that industry, and for this reason we expect a negative relationship with success.

The tenth factor is the influence of data-driven decisions. Bughin (2017) conducts a recent meta-analysis and finds that successful firms are ones that dedicate resources to data analytics. Toyota's Just In Time inventory system is an example of a successful use of data analytics. Their use of data to forecast demand for inputs and parts used in their manufacturing processes has become the model for others to follow. It should be rare for the use of data to lead to poor outcomes, but it can happen. In an extreme example, Nobel laureates Myron Scholes and Robert Merton's Long Term Capital Management (LTCM) used historical data to trade stock options with an apparent low probability of losing money, but because of high leverage they were unable to weather large losses from events that occurred with a higher than expected probability. The catastrophic failure of this firm led to a bailout organized by the Federal Reserve in order to avoid a domino effect. We believe that such cases where data contributes negatively to a firm's success are rare. Therefore, we "bet" there is a positive relationship between data usage and success and we believe we are not making the same mistake as LTCM when doing so. At any rate, the consequences are relatively benign if we're wrong.

Our eleventh factor is the speed at which decisions are made. While we discuss this in more detail in the next chapter, Coca-Cola was able to quickly reverse course when the New Coke marketing campaign failed, and the speed at which they were able to reverse course led to success. In contrast, Target's inability to quickly adapt to changing market conditions has led to a loss in market share. The "Great Recession of 2008" led customers to place a greater emphasis on value and price. Target's upscale business model has proven ill-suited to compete in the post-recession market. Baum and Wally (2003, p. 1107) collect data from 318 CEOs and find that "fast strategic decision-making predicts subsequent firm growth and profit." We expect to find the same relationship.

Corporate governance is our twelfth factor. Did successful management of competing interests between shareholders, management, and/or clients contribute to the success of the decision? In 2013, Dell went private in a bid to change corporate governance. CEO Michael Dell claimed this enabled the firm to focus more strongly on customers rather than shareholders. In a case that provides an example of the polar opposite approach, MF Global improperly balanced the interest of clients and stakeholders when it used customer funds to cover trading losses, eventually leading to bankruptcy. In our sample, respondents were asked if corporate governance contributed to the outcome following the decision. Daily, Dalton, and Cannella (2003) conduct a meta-analysis of the empirical literature and also find little conclusive results. For these reasons we do not speculate here about the hypothesized direction of the effect.

Influence from the board of directors is our thirteenth factor. The board's continued support of Tim Cook as Apple's CEO has led to continued success in an example of positive input from the board of directors. On the other end of the spectrum, Volkswagen's purposeful installation of devices designed to defeat emissions testing equipment has led to criminal investigations of multiple members of the board of directors. Dalton et al. (1998) find little in the way of clear relationships in a comprehensive meta-analysis of 85 studies. Similar to the last factor, we have no clear expectations for our data.

Our fourteenth, fifteenth, and sixteenth factors all involve the impact of the CEO on business outcomes. Tosi et al. (2000) conduct a meta-analysis of studies that examine the impact of CEO pay. While they find a positive effect, they also find that this effect is small and only accounts for around 5 percent of the variation in firm performance. There are notable instances of CEO pay having a negative effect on performance. For example, American Airlines' decision to cut employee pay while keeping CEO pay high had a predictably negative effect on employee morale. Given the relatively small empirical findings in the literature, we expect to find little here.

CEO attributes, such as tenure and prior experience, may impact outcomes as well. In a survey of 121 CEOs not unlike ours, Peterson et al. (2009) find that CEO optimism is positively related to success. In a survey of 770 employees associated with 128 CEOs, Agle et al. (2006) find a positive relationship with CEO charisma. Amazon's Jeff Bezos and Apple's Steve Jobs are examples of CEOs who displayed a high degree of perseverance in challenging environments over a long tenure before their firms finally took off. Martin Shkreli's lack of experience may have led to his focus on profits at all costs. His decision to raise the price of Daraprim from $13.50 to $750 per pill led to a large amount of negative publicity for Turing Pharmaceuticals and a high degree of scrutiny from regulators. We expect to see positive CEO attributes have a positive relationship with success in our data.

The final CEO-related factor is autonomy. Quigley and Hambrick (2012) study 181 firms and find that in cases where former CEOs remain as board members after their tenure, a theoretical negative effect on autonomy for the new CEO should exist. They also find a negative link

Table 5.5   Performance factors: summary

Factor	Number of Interviews Citing this Factor (out of 81 total)	Case Studies Citing this Factor (out of 82 total)	Significant Difference Between Proportions? (Pearson's χ^2)
Firm's Prior Performance	42 (51.9%)	48 (58.5%)	0.74
Commitment to Ethics	30 (37%)	25 (30.5%)	0.78
Innovation	19 (23.5%)	39 (47.6%)	10.33*
Team Effectiveness	36 (44.4%)	31 (37.8%)	0.74
Resource Sharing Across Diverse Business Units	30 (37%)	28 (34.1%)	0.15
Employee Satisfaction	36 (44.4%)	17 (20.7%)	10.44*
Human Resources Management	30 (37%)	14 (17.1%)	8.24*
Specific Management Techniques	22 (27.2%)	13 (15.9%)	3.08 (10%)
Competition	28 (34.6%)	45 (54.9%)	6.80*
Data-Driven Decisions	22 (27.2%)	30 (36.6%)	1.67
Decision Speed	19 (23.5%)	28 (34.1%)	2.27
Corporate Governance	8 (9.9%)	26 (31.7%)	11.76*
Board of Directors	4 (4.9%)	32 (39%)	27.51*
CEO Pay	14 (17.3%)	35 (42.7%)	12.50*
CEO Attributes	31 (38.3%)	49 (59.8%)	7.53*
CEO Autonomy	20 (24.7%)	43 (52.4%)	13.23*
Middle Management	28 (34.6%)	24 (29.3%)	0.53

with outcomes in cases where the former CEO remains "on board." The same two above examples can be used here as well. Steve Jobs was given considerable freedom during his tenure, with the board uncritically signing off on risky decisions he made. While the same was apparently true with Martin Shkreli, the ultimate outcome was quite different.[2] We feel that Jobs' autonomy was a critical factor in Apple's success, but this was likely a unique case and it isn't clear what relationship we should expect to see in our data.

The seventeenth and final factor is the effect of middle management. Because middle management handles the day-to-day tactical operations of the firm, they can make or break the strategic decisions made by upper management. Walt Disney's decision to empower low-level employees with authority traditionally reserved for middle management has led to an enhanced level of customer satisfaction. In contrast, a widely reported confrontational management culture at Nokia may have led to an unwillingness to take risks and bureaucratic inertia. This caused a failure to effectively respond to competition and the sales of their mobile devices division to Microsoft. With examples of successes and failures, we will not predict any relationship with our data.

Table 5.5 lists each of these 17 factors and the number of interviews and case studies that cite each of the factors. Because the publicly traded firms in our case studies are generally larger than those in our interviews and more likely to provide an example of a failed decision, we produce cross tabulations of our data and compare the two groups. In the next chapter we will be examining the impact of each of these factors on the probability of success.

Tests of differences between two proportions were conducted for each variable. Innovation is significantly more likely to be chosen as a factor with case studies than with interviews. Perhaps smaller firms are less likely to be innovative, or less likely to remain in business if they do innovate. It is also possible that small firms that do innovate successfully, such as Amazon and Facebook, do not remain small for long. A similar story could be told about competition, which is also more likely to be chosen in case studies. Larger firms may be more likely to face fierce competition.

In addition to the two factors above, all of the factors associated with corporate leadership (i.e. corporate governance, board of directors, CEO pay, CEO attributes, and CEO autonomy) are more likely to be chosen as factors in case studies. This should not be unexpected; as smaller firms are more likely to have relatively simple leadership structures. With the smaller firms in our interviews, if such factors exist at all, their function is reduced compared to that of a large corporation.

Employee satisfaction and human resources management are the only two factors that were more likely to be cited as factors in interviews. It may be the case that CEOs of smaller firms are closer to their employees than CEOs of large firms. These two factors were the only factors that had findings that we did not expect to see. It is unclear why we see such a large difference between larger and smaller companies concerning employee satisfaction and human resources management. These two factors are likely related to one another, and it is surprising that smaller firms tend to focus more on employee relations.

SINGLE MOST IMPORTANT FACTOR

In addition to the 17 factors highlighted above, business leaders were given an open ended opportunity to list the single most important factor that contributed to business success. Most of our interview respondents declined, claiming that success was due to a combination of factors that couldn't be distilled down to one. However, 26 respondents did list a single factor. We list these below:

Executive dedication (x2)
CEO competence and employee satisfaction
Awareness of and response to customer and employee concerns
Market research / marketing (x4)
Workplace culture / employee quality (x3)
Focus on core business strategy
Firm's prior performance / brand trust (x2)
Middle management (x3)
Providing a high value to customers (x7)
Communication
Data-driven decisions.

Interestingly, a strong focus on customer relations was the most common factor cited, with a total of seven responses. While we are not surprised by this, a strong customer focus is something that is almost impossible to measure beyond these anecdotal responses. Our second most common factor cited was employee quality, with five responses listing employees alone or in combination with another factor. Marketing was the third factor cited with four responses, followed by the effect of middle management with three. With middle management, we were given anecdotal stories of managers failing to meet organizational goals due to shirking. In each of these three cases, owners/CEOs felt this could have been avoided with better oversight. We feel that a case could easily be made for including these three observations as examples of poor employee quality.

CONCLUSION

In this chapter we introduce the structure of our dataset and provide summary statistics. We also briefly review the associated empirical literature in order to justify why we chose the variables we did but also so we can get an idea of what to expect as far as relationships between variables in our data. Though both personal interviews and case studies appear in our data, we find that there are some key differences between interviews and case studies and we discuss them above. Of particular importance is the fact that case studies tend to represent larger firms, and are also more likely to provide examples of unsuccessful decisions in our data. In the next chapter we examine successful and unsuccessful decisions in detail. Because larger firms are also more likely to experience issues with corporate governance, the board of directors, and CEOs, we might expect to see a negative relationship with success and these factors in simple hypothesis tests. This provides motivation for the use of the regression model introduced in the next chapter, which will control for this possibility and allow us to gain a clearer picture of the underlying relationships.

NOTES

1. The Beta and VHS were two competing cassette tape video formats from the 1980s. Though almost identical in design and function, VHS caught on as the standard format and Beta was relegated to the dustbin of history. Sony immediately continued its innovation, however, with the development of the compact disc.
2. Shkreli was eventually replaced by the board, apparently not due to his controversial decisions as the CEO of Turing, but rather due to a federal indictment on securities fraud.

REFERENCES

Agle, B.R., Nagarajan, N.J., Sonnenfeld, J.A., and Srinivasan, D. (2006) Does CEO Charisma Matter? An Empirical Analysis of the Relationships Among Organizational Performance, Environmental Uncertainty, and Top Management Team Perceptions of CEO Charisma, *Academy of Management Journal*, 49(1), 161–174.

Ali, R., Lynch, R., Melewar, T.C., and Jin, Z. (2015) The Moderating Influences on the Relationship of Corporate Reputation With its Antecedents and Consequences: A Meta-Analytic Review, *Journal of Business Research*, 68(5), 1105–1117.

Baum, Robert J. and Wally, S. (2003) Strategic Decision Speed and Firm Performance, *Strategic Management Journal*, 24, 1107–1129.

Bughin, J. (2017) Ten Big Lessons Learned from Big Data Analytics, *Applied Marketing Analytics*, 2(4), 286–295.

Capon, N., Farley, J.U., and Hoenig, S. (1990) Determinants of Financial Performance: A Meta-analysis, *Management Science*, 36(10), 1143–1159.

Crook, T.R., Ketchen, D.J., Combs, J.G., and Todd, S.Y. (2008) Strategic Resources and Performance: A Meta-analysis, *Strategic Management Journal*, 29(11), 1141–1154.

Dalton, D.R., Daily, C.M., Ellstrand, A.E., and Johnson, J.L. (1998) Meta-analytic Reviews of Board Composition, Leadership Structure, and Financial Performance, *Strategic Management Journal*, 19(3), 269–290.

Daily, C.M., Dalton, D.R., and Cannella, A.A. (2003). Corporate Governance: Decades of Dialogue and Data, *Academy of Management Review*, 28(3), 371–382.

Harter, J.K., Schmidt, F.L., and Hayes, T.L. (2002) Business-unit-level Relationship between Employee Satisfaction, Employee Engagement, and Business Outcomes: A Meta-Analysis, *Journal of Applied Psychology*, 87(2), 268–279.

Liang, T.P., You, J.J., and Liu, C.C. (2010) A Resource-based Perspective on Information Technology and Firm Performance: A Meta-analysis, *Industrial Management & Data Systems*, 110(8), 1138–1158.

Margolis, J.D., and Walsh, J.P. (2001) *People and Profits? The Search for a Link between a Company's Social and Financial Performance*, Mahwah, NJ: Lawrence Erlbaum.

Mathieu, J., Maynard, M.T., Rapp, T., and Gilson, L. (2008) Team effectiveness 1997–2007: A Review of Recent Advancements and a Glimpse into the Future, *Journal of Management*, 34(3), 410–476.

Nair, A. (2006) Meta-analysis of the Relationship between Quality Management Practices and Firm Performance: Implications for Quality Management Theory Development, *Journal of Operations Management*, 24(6), 948–975.

Orlitzky, M., Schmidt, F.L., and Rynes, S.L. (2003) Corporate Social and Financial Performance: A Meta-analysis, *Organization Studies*, 24: 403–441.

Peterson, S.J., Walumbwa, F.O., Byron, K., and Myrowitz, J. (2009) CEO Positive Psychological Traits, Transformational Leadership, and Firm Performance in High-technology Start-up and Established Firms, *Journal of Management*, 35(2), 348–368.

Quigley, T.J., and Hambrick, D.C. (2012) When the Former CEO Stays On As Board Chair: Effects on Successor Discretion, Strategic Change, and Performance, *Strategic Management Journal*, 33(7), 834–859.

Rosenbusch, N., Brinckmann, J., and Bausch, A. (2011) Is Innovation Always Beneficial? A Meta-analysis of the Relationship between Innovation and Performance in SMEs, *Journal of Business Venturing*, 26(4), 441–457.

Shook, J. (2010) How to Change a Culture: Lessons from NUMMI, *MIT Sloan Management Review*, 51(2), 63.

Subramony, M. (2009) A Meta-analytic Investigation of the Relationship between HRM Bundles and Firm Performance, *Human Resource Management*, 48(5), 745–768.

Tosi, H.L., Werner, S., Katz, J.P., and Gomez-Mejia, L.R. (2000) How Much Does Performance Matter? A Meta-analysis of CEO Pay Studies, *Journal of Management*, 26(2), 301–339.

6. Detailed findings and analysis

Our goal is to document the characteristics of decisions that business leaders themselves feel are important. In doing so we collected a total of information on 88 decisions that were considered successes and 75 decisions that were considered failures as described in Chapter 5. This data comes from both personal interviews with owners and/or managers of a broad selection of small businesses as well as popular case studies that include public information from large corporations.

In the last chapter we examined the differences between our interviews and our case studies. In this chapter we will begin by examining the differences between successful and unsuccessful decisions. We will focus specifically on the characteristics associated with successful and unsuccessful decisions, while the next chapter focuses on the impact of these decisions over time. Before we jump right into the analysis, let us provide a little background to explain why we feel our approach is warranted.

In Chapter 4, we saw that individual performance results might not follow decisions clearly or may do so in unpredictable ways. One of history's most notable examples can be used to illustrate this point. In the late 1970s and early 1980s, Pepsi conducted a marketing campaign known as the "Pepsi Challenge." In shopping malls throughout the country, individuals were asked to participate in a free blind taste test between Pepsi and Coke. Tasters were then asked to sip two small samples of soda, then pick their favorite before being shown which was Pepsi and which was Coke. In the majority of cases tasters chose Pepsi. Pepsi heavily publicized these results and Coke began to lose market share. In response, in 1985 Coca-Cola's marketing team chose an unprecedented reformulation of Coca-Cola that fared better on these blind taste tests. The introduction of "New Coke" (and the subsequent discontinuation of the original formulation) led to a strong backlash from consumers, further declining sales, and even a formal declaration of "Cola War victory" from rival Pepsi. In response to the backlash, Coca-Cola admitted their mistake, made a quick reversal later that year, and reintroduced the original "Classic" formula.

By all accounts, the introduction of New Coke frequently ranks at the top of lists of "bad business decisions." However, its ultimate effect on shareholder value is unclear. Paradoxically, the ultimate effect on shareholder value may actually have been positive. To understand why this was the case we will dig a little deeper into the taste tests. To begin with, the initial taste test results were real and have consistently been replicated in numerous independent academic studies (McClure et al., 2004; Koenigs and Tranel, 2007). However, it is important to understand that the Pepsi Challenge was conducted only with blind sip tests, testers were not allowed more than a small sample, and could not switch back and forth. In such cases, we consistently see that the sweeter of two samples is more likely to be chosen. While Pepsi's current 41 grams of sugar per 12oz serving compared to Coke's 39 grams of sugar per 12oz serving doesn't seem like a large difference, Pepsi is anecdotally known to be sweeter than original Coke. This is also the reason why the New Coke formulation was even sweeter, so it would emerge at the top of these blind sip tests. However, the independent tests also show that individuals also tend to prefer the original classic Coke formulation in tests other than blind one sip tests. That is, individuals tend to prefer Coca-Cola when asked to perform these blind tests more than once or asked to test a larger sample (i.e. more than a small sip). Paradoxically, the sweetness that leads Pepsi to victory in blind sip tests quickly becomes overpowering relative to Coke for the majority of cola drinkers. Further, we also know that that the majority of individuals consistently prefer Coke from the outset in non-blind tests, perhaps for cultural reasons that are difficult to measure. Another explanation is that tasters expect a certain familiar flavor from the Coke they grew up with, and the reformulation was somewhat offensive to them. One would have the seemingly insurmountable task of finding tasters who have never tasted Coke in order to eliminate this possibility.

At any rate, with the reversal and the return of the original classic Coca-Cola, the company went on to more than regain the lost market share. Customers may have been convinced by the Pepsi Challenge that they preferred the taste of Pepsi, but the New Coke fiasco somehow convinced them otherwise. Regardless of the mechanisms at play, the introduction of New Coke is one of the most famous examples of a "bad" business decision, but by most accounts led to a positive outcome for the company.

In contrast, not all "successful" business decisions (or at least decisions that in retrospect seem to be correct by anyone's account) will necessarily lead to a favorable business outcome. For example, Eastman Kodak invented the first digital camera in the 1970s. By all accounts, this was a successful business decision. They went on to introduce the "DC" line in the mid-1990s, which was the first digital cameras marketed to the public. Digital photography would eventually bring the downfall of traditional film cameras. Kodak's unwillingness to capitalize on this would eventually mean that Kodak as a firm would follow film cameras into obscurity. It would be inappropriate to classify Kodak's early research into digital technology as a mistake. Kodak's fear that digital technology would cannibalize sales of film cameras was legitimate, but their myopic marketing focus on film cameras could not stop the proliferation of digital cameras. Their lukewarm approach to digital led to a loss of sales and eventual bankruptcy, though arguably none of this would have happened had they not pioneered digital technology to begin with. If we separate the earlier decision to conduct research in digital technology from their latter anemic marketing decisions, it might be reasonable to classify the former as a success and the latter as a failure, though both were linked and both necessarily contributed to the poor performance of the firm.

These two examples illustrate two reasons why our approach differs sharply from that of previous works that focus on specific outcomes to determine "success" or "failure." First, outcomes may be driven sometimes by "luck" or at least factors that are difficult to predict in advance. Coca-Cola sales revenue consistently continued to rise throughout the 1980s and stock doubled in value from 1985 to 1990. Their strong positive performance throughout the latter half of the 1980s and beyond may be a poor indication of the quality of the decision to introduce New Coke. Second, it can be difficult to define a clear-cut "decision," and in doing so we may be forced to oversimplify complex issues or introduce our own personal biases as researchers. It would be misleading to classify Coca-Cola's marketing efforts in 1980s as a single well-defined decision that resulted in "success" or "failure." It would also be misleading for us to do the same for Kodak's foray into digital photography, and may also be inappropriate to suggest that Kodak's invention of the technology itself was a mistake.

For these reasons, we do not focus as strongly on objective criteria to measure the actual outcomes, such as stock prices, return on equity, or market share. Rather, we allow business leaders themselves to use whatever criteria they feel is important to gauge the degree of "success" or "failure" of a particular decision. This approach differs from that of previous works such as Carroll and Mui (2008) in that we do not produce a list of objective criteria such as bankruptcies, write offs, or discontinued operations, that we use in order to classify a decision as a success or failure. Rather, we use subjective criteria such as the opinion or the business owner or manager as criteria for inclusion. We also remain agnostic about what constitutes a business decision, and similarly allow business leaders to define a "decision" as best they see fit.

What characteristics of decisions are more likely to lead to "success" or "failure?" We begin by classifying these decisions according to their relationships to the 17 criteria discussed in Chapter 5. We conduct tests of

Table 6.1   Impact of a firm's prior performance

Pearson's ρ = -0.06 Pearson's χ^2 = 0.67	Not a Factor	Is Considered a Factor	Totals
Successful Decision	42 (48%)	46 (52%)	88
Unsuccessful Decision	31 (41%)	44 (59%)	75
Totals	73	90	163

Table 6.2   Impact of a commitment to ethics

Pearson's Rho =−0.03 Pearson's χ^2 = 0.17	Not a Factor	Is Considered a Factor	Totals
Successful Decision	59 (67%)	29 (33%)	88
Unsuccessful Decision	48 (64%)	27 (36%)	75
Totals	107	56	163

differences between two proportions in order to see which of the criteria are likely to impact success or failure.

The first factor we consider is the impact of a firm's prior performance. As discussed in the previous chapter, we expect to see a positive relationship with prior performance and successful decisions. However, as Table 6.1 shows, this basic relationship does not clearly emerge in our data. Prior performance is actually cited as a factor in slightly more unsuccessful decisions (59 percent) than successful decisions (48 percent). While a good reputation is beneficial for firms and a bad reputation is costly for firms, our results suggest the effect of a bad reputation is stronger, but the difference between these two proportions is not statistically significant.

Our second factor is commitment to ethics (Table 6.2). Commitment to ethics is cited in roughly one-third of both successful and unsuccessful decisions. While a clear relationship between success and ethics does not immediately emerge from the cross-tabulations below, we were prepared to see little if any relationship given the findings from previous empirical literature. Ethically questionable decisions are difficult to clearly measure and have negative long-run consequences. As our data on this factor results from a single question with a simple yes/no format, and our outcomes are

Table 6.3   Impact of innovation

Pearson's $\rho = -0.01$ Pearson's $\chi^2 = 0.01$	Not a Factor	Is Considered a Factor	Totals
Successful Decision	57 (65%)	31 (35%)	88
Unsuccessful Decision	48 (64%)	27 (36%)	75
Totals	105	58	163

Table 6.4   Impact of team effectiveness

Pearson's $\rho = 0.22^*$ Pearson's $\chi^2 = 7.95^*$	Not a Factor	Is Considered a Factor	Totals
Successful Decision	43 (49%)	45 (51%)	88
Unsuccessful Decision	53 (71%)	22 (29%)	75
Totals	96	67	163

examined for only the three years following a decision, we are not surprised with the weak results for this factor.

Innovation is our third factor (Table 6.3). We had no clear expectations with this variable, and similar to the previous case, we found no relationship between outcomes and innovation being cited as a factor. Innovation was cited as a factor in 65 percent of successes and the ratio was identical for unsuccessful decisions. Our only explanation is that innovation is as likely to lead to success as failure. However, we still believe that firms must innovate to stay alive in competitive industries.

Team effectiveness (Table 6.4) is our fourth factor and is also one in which we clearly expected to find a positive relationship. We find a relatively strong relationship, with a statistically significant Pearson correlation coefficient of 0.22 and a statistically significant difference between the two proportions. With successful decisions, team effectiveness was cited as being a factor in roughly half of our cases. However, with unsuccessful decisions, team effectiveness was cited in only 29 percent of the cases. Effective teams clearly contribute more to success than they lead to failure in our data and we are not surprised by this finding.

Our fifth factor is resource sharing across diverse business units (Table 6.5). We expected to see a positive relationship between shared resources

Table 6.5   Impact of shared resources

Pearson's rho = −0.08 Pearson's χ^2 = 1.11	Not a Factor	Is Considered a Factor	Totals
Successful Decision	62 (70%)	26 (30%)	88
Unsuccessful Decision	47 (63%)	28 (37%)	75
Totals	109	54	163

Table 6.6   Impact of employee satisfaction

Pearson's ρ = 0.22* Pearson's χ^2 = 7.92*	Not a Factor	Is Considered a Factor	Totals
Successful Decision	51 (58%)	37 (42%)	88
Unsuccessful Decision	59 (78%)	16 (22%)	75
Totals	110	53	163

and successful decisions. However, we do not find this relationship in our sample, though only about a third of our responses reported this factor (or lack of it) as contributing to success or failure. In fact, there was a slightly larger proportion of citations with unsuccessful outcomes. While this is the exact opposite of what we predicted, this difference is not statistically significant.

Our sixth factor is employee satisfaction (Table 6.6). Here we expected to see a positive relationship with success. As we expected, employee satisfaction is cited as a reason for success in 42 percent of our successful decisions. In contrast, it is cited as a factor in only 22 percent of the unsuccessful decisions. The difference between these two proportions is statistically significant. Business leaders are more likely to attribute success to employee satisfaction than to blame low morale for failure.

Our seventh factor is human resource management (Table 6.7). We do find the difference we expected, with human resource management being cited as a factor in 30 percent of successes and only 19 percent of unsuccessful decisions. This difference is small, however, and only marginally significant at the 10 percent level of confidence.

Our eighth factor is the usage of specific management practices such as Six Sigma or Lean (Table 6.8). We cautiously expected to see a positive

Table 6.7   Impact of human resource management

Pearson's ρ = 0.13 Pearson's χ^2 = 2.59 (p = 0.108)	Not a Factor	Is Considered a Factor	Totals
Successful Decision	62 (70%)	26 (30%)	88
Unsuccessful Decision	61 (81%)	14 (19%)	75
Totals	123	40	163

Table 6.8   Impact of specific management practices

Pearson's ρ = −0.12 Pearson's χ^2 = 2.22 (p = 0.138)	Not a Factor	Is Considered a Factor	Totals
Successful Decision	73 (83%)	15 (17%)	88
Unsuccessful Decision	55 (73%)	20 (27%)	75
Totals	128	35	163

Table 6.9   Impact of competition

Pearson's ρ = −0.03 Pearson's χ^2 = 0.20	Not a Factor	Is Considered a Factor	Totals
Successful Decision	50 (57%)	38 (43%)	88
Unsuccessful Decision	40 (53%)	35 (47%)	75
Totals	90	73	163

relationship. In our data, specific practices are cited in a slightly larger proportion of unsuccessful decisions than successful decisions, though this difference is not statistically significant at any standard level of confidence. We are not surprised by this result.

Our ninth factor is the effect of competition (Table 6.9). Because an increase in the level of competition should increase the level of risk a firm faces, we expected to see an inverse relationship with the likelihood of a successful outcome. We do find a very slight relationship, with successful

Table 6.10   Impact of data-driven decisions

Pearson's ρ = 0.05 Pearson's χ² = 0.42	Not a Factor	Is Considered a Factor	Totals
Successful Decision	58 (66%)	30 (34%)	88
Unsuccessful Decision	53 (71%)	22 (29%)	75
Totals	111	52	163

Table 6.11   Impact of decision speed

Pearson's ρ = −0.15* Pearson's χ² = 3.46* (p = 0.063)	Not a Factor	Is Considered a Factor	Totals
Successful Decision	69 (78%)	19 (22%)	88
Unsuccessful Decision	49 (65%)	26 (35%)	75
Totals	118	45	163

decisions citing competition 43 percent of the time compared to unsuccessful decisions at 47 percent of the time. However, this difference is not statistically significant and should be interpreted cautiously. We are somewhat surprised by this weak result.

Our tenth factor is the impact of data usage to drive decision making (Table 6.10). We predicted a positive relationship between data usage and success. We do find that successful decisions are more likely to cite data at a rate of 34 percent to 29 percent, however as with the last factor this finding is not statistically significant.

Our eleventh factor is decision speed (Table 6.11). We expected to find that decision speed is positively related to success. However, we see the opposite, finding that decision speed is more likely to be cited as a factor in unsuccessful decisions than successful decisions. Unsuccessful decisions were more than twice as likely to have cited decision speed. While initially surprising, it is important to note that this difference is only statistically significant at the 10 percent level and not at the 5 percent level, with a p-value of 0.06. Some of our business leaders cited decision speed in unsuccessful decisions, as the failure to act quickly led to an unsuccessful outcome. Therefore, this finding does not contradict our initial hypothesis.

Table 6.12   Impact of corporate governance

Pearson's ρ = −0.16* Pearson's χ^2 = 4.29* (p = 0.038)	Not a Factor	Is Considered a Factor	Totals
Successful Decision	75 (85%)	13 (15%)	88
Unsuccessful Decision	49 (65%)	26 (35%)	75
Totals	124	39	163

Table 6.13   Impact of board of directors

Pearson's ρ = −0.22* Pearson's χ^2 = 7.93* (p = 0.005)	Not a Factor	Is Considered a Factor	Totals
Successful Decision	76 (86%)	12 (14%)	88
Unsuccessful Decision	51 (68%)	24 (32%)	75
Totals	127	36	163

Corporate governance is our twelfth factor (Table 6.12). Given our review of the literature, we were agnostic about the effect of corporate governance. However, we find that corporate governance is over twice as likely to be cited in unsuccessful decisions as successful decisions. While this appears to be a large significant finding, we must be cautious. This finding could be driven by the fact that our larger firms were more likely to cite corporate governance than small firms without corporate governance issues. These large firms were also more likely to provide examples of unsuccessful decisions. Our larger regression model below will be used to disentangle the effects of these two factors.

Though we had no clear expectations with our thirteenth factor that examines the impact of the board of directors (Table 6.13), we do we find a large statistically significant difference. We feel this is very similar to the effect of the previous factor, in the proportion of successful and unsuccessful decisions that cited the board of directors as a factor is roughly identical to the proportions that cited corporate governance.

Our fourteenth factor is the impact of CEO pay (Table 6.14). We expected to see a positive relationship between CEO pay and successful

Table 6.14   Impact of CEO pay

Pearson's $\rho = -0.10$ Pearson's $\chi^2 = 1.47$ ($p = 0.22$)	Not a Factor	Is Considered a Factor	Totals
Successful Decision	58 (66%)	30 (34%)	88
Unsuccessful Decision	56 (75%)	19 (25%)	75
Totals	114	49	163

Table 6.15   Impact of CEO attributes

Pearson's $\rho = -0.00$ Pearson's $\chi^2 = 0.00$ ($p = 0.95$)	Not a Factor	Is Considered a Factor	Totals
Successful Decision	45 (51%)	43 (49%)	88
Unsuccessful Decision	38 (51%)	37 (49%)	75
Totals	83	80	163

outcomes, and we do in fact find this relationship. However, this relationship is not statistically significant. As with decision speed, it could be the case that some of our respondents cited low CEO pay as a reason for unsuccessful decisions. It could also be the case that inappropriately high CEO pay itself contributed to the "unsuccessful" determination.

Our fifteenth factor is CEO attributes (Table 6.15). We expected to see a positive relationship with success. However, we find no relationship at all. In fact our responses were split evenly down the middle. The proportion of successful responses choosing CEO attributes as a factor is exactly identical to the proportion of unsuccessful responses. Good CEOs can lead to success and bad CEOs can lead to failure.

Our sixteenth and final CEO factor is autonomy (Table 6.16). Though we were not sure what to expect with this factor, we find it slightly more likely to be cited in unsuccessful decisions than successful decisions. This difference is marginally statistically significant only at the 10 percent level. It could be the case that larger firms are more likely to cite CEO autonomy as a factor simply because CEOs generally have more freedom at small firms. Because in our data larger firms are more likely to provide examples

Table 6.16   Impact of CEO autonomy

Impact of CEO Autonomy			
Pearson's $\rho = -0.13$ Pearson's $\chi^2 = 2.62$ ($p = 0.11$)	Not a Factor	Is Considered a Factor	Totals
Successful Decision	59 (67%)	29 (34%)	88
Unsuccessful Decision	41 (55%)	34 (45%)	75
Totals	100	63	163

Table 6.17   Impact of middle management

Impact of Middle Management			
Pearson's $\rho = 0.08$ Pearson's $\chi^2 = 0.97$ ($p = 0.32$)	Not a Factor	Is Considered a Factor	Totals
Successful Decision	57 (65%)	31 (35%)	88
Unsuccessful Decision	54 (72%)	21 (28%)	75
Totals	111	52	163

of unsuccessful decisions, we could be capturing this result. It is peculiar, however, that this would be the case with the autonomy variable and not the CEO pay or CEO attributes variables. As with our decision speed variable, our regression model will be able to solve this mystery.

Our seventeenth and final factor is the impact of middle management (Table 6.17). We had no expectations about this variable and find a weak positive correlation with success, but one that is not statistically significant. As input from middle management can "make or break" a decision, we are just as likely to see citations in examples of successes as failures.

LOGIT MODEL

If we combine the results from Chapter 5 with the results from the previous section, both decision speed and CEO autonomy raise an interesting question. Is it the factor itself that matters, or is it simply the fact that a factor is correlated with the size of the firm, and the size of the firm is what really matters for success or failure? In this section we answer these questions and generate a more comprehensive predictive model. We will first analyze these decisions using a regression model to predict which of the above characteristics are most likely to contribute either positively or negatively to business success and/or failure. We will then use this model to generate predictions about how the probability of success will change when factors themselves change.

We begin by estimating the following model:

Decision Outcome (Success or Failure) = β_0 + β_1 firm's prior performance + β_2 commitment to ethics + β_3 innovation + β_4 team effectiveness + β_5 resource sharing across diverse business lines + β_6 employee satisfaction + β_7 human resources management + β_8 specific management techniques + β_9 competition + β_{10} data driven decisions + β_{11} decision speed + β_{12} corporate governance + β_{13} board of directors + β_{14} CEO pay + β_{15} CEO attributes + β_{16} CEO autonomy + β_{17} management teams + β_{17} interview + ε

We have a total of 163 observations and our dependent variable is also coded as a dummy variable, as each decision resulted in either a success or a failure. In addition, each of the explanatory variables is also coded as a dummy variable. A one indicates a particular characteristic may have contributed to the success (or failure) of the decision. We also include a dummy variable for interviews. As we found in the previous chapter, interviews are more likely to experience success in our data than case studies. It is also the case that interviews were more likely to be conducted with small firms. By using interviews as a control variable we can ensure we're isolating the effect of each factor, and not indirectly capturing the effect of small versus large firms.

This data structure also allows us to estimate the model using a logit procedure. A logit model is a natural choice when dealing with a dependent variable that takes on only two values: 0 and 1. The logit is especially useful when the goal is to predict the probability of a certain outcome with respect to certain factors. With this model we can provide more accurate predictions than a simple ordinary least squares regression because it constrains the impact of each explanatory variable to between 0 and 1. This impact, which we refer to as a "marginal effect" should be interpreted as the change in probability of a successful outcome given that we include that particular criteria while holding everything else constant. In a sense, if we hold everything else constant with a given firm, then "switch on" the criteria, the probability of success will change. In other words, how much more likely are we to see a successful outcome? The marginal effect tells us exactly how much this probability will change.

While the logit model allows us to estimate the likelihood of changes in each factor to influence the outcome of the decision, it also allows us to generate odds ratios and estimate a propensity score. The odds ratio allows us to interpret our results in a different way and present our information from a slightly different perspective. From the data that we have, we can estimate the likelihood of a success for a firm that meets the particular criteria (as well as whatever other criteria they meet), relative to firms that do not meet that criteria. This should not be confused with the marginal effect approach described above. If we compare firms that meet a given criterion to firms that do not in our data, what is the ratio of success to failure? Finally, the propensity score predicts the probability that a given factor is present given a decision is deemed to be a success, and this should not be confused with the odds ratio above.

Table 6.18 presents the results from our model. Again, our coefficient estimates can be interpreted in slightly different ways. Coefficients are converted into both marginal effects as well as odds ratios and propensity scores in the table.

DISCUSSION OF RESULTS, LOGIT MODEL

Factor 1: Firm's Prior Performance

Beginning with our first criterion, where the firm's prior performance impacted the decision in some way, our marginal effect estimate is a −0.0978, or a −9.78 percent. This should be interpreted to mean that if a typical firm theoretically changes this one characteristic (i.e. changes a firm where prior performance does not exist or at least has no impact to a firm where prior performance matters), then the chance of a decision to lead to a favorable outcome will drop by an estimated 9.78 percent. Using the odds ratio we see that firms for which previous reputation impacted the decision are 67 percent as likely to experience a successful outcome as those for which previous performance did not impact the decision.

Both the marginal impact and the odds ratio clearly suggest that decisions impacted by the firm's prior performance are less likely to be successful. However, the magnitude of the effect is relatively small and the direction of the effect may even be unclear, as the underlying statistic used to generate these measures is not statistically significant. If we rely on estimates for this category at all, we must be cautious when doing so.

Our propensity score estimate suggests that if we take a random

Table 6.18   Simple logit model, success versus failure

Criteria	Coefficient	p-value (level of significance)	Marginal Effect	Odds Ratio	Propensity Score
Firm's Prior Performance	−0.396653 (0.4561197)	38%	−0.0978	0.672567	0.5227
Commitment to Ethics	−0.0779243 (0.4385629)	86%	−0.01933	0.925034	0.3295
Innovation	0.1560498 (0.4224457)	71%	0.038572	1.168884	0.3522
Team Effectiveness	1.052653* (0.4961712)	3%	0.252607	2.865242	0.5114
Resource Sharing Across Diverse Business Units	−0.9735772* (0.5232307)	5%	−0.23867	0.377729	0.2955
Employee Satisfaction	0.8654515 (0.5648927)	11%	0.207361	2.376079	0.4204
HR Management	−0.4422596 (0.6665796)	51%	−0.10997	0.642583	0.2955
Management Techniques	−0.4297353 (0.5278389)	41%	−0.10692	0.650681	0.1705
Competition	0.2939211 (0.4942355)	55%	0.072613	1.341678	0.4318
Data-driven Decisions	0.9714746* (0.4672221)	3%	0.23099	2.641837	0.3409
Decision Speed	−0.3242347 (0.497512)	52%	−0.08062	0.723081	0.2159
Corporate Governance	−0.5113655 (0.53028)	33%	−0.12711	0.599676	0.1477
Board of Directors	−0.9246505* (0.5356645)	7%	−0.22685	0.39667	0.1364
CEO Pay	0.6456459 (0.519747)	20%	0.156221	1.907219	0.3409
CEO Attributes	0.3368401 (0.5218442)	52%	0.083269	1.400515	0.4886
CEO Autonomy	−1.306207* (0.5786318)	2%	−0.31532	0.270845	0.3295
Middle Management	0.1661662 (0.5123757)	75%	0.041037	1.180769	0.3523
Constant	0.2368817 (0.3262315)	47%	–	1.267291	–

successful firm, we estimate a 52 percent probability (close to 50/50) that this firm would consider prior performance to be a factor. The propensity score should not be confused with the marginal effect, as it is a different statistic. Some factors that might have a large positive effect (i.e. a large marginal effect) could rarely show up in our data (and thus would have a low propensity score). In this case, our propensity score estimate suggests close to a 50/50 chance that prior performance matters, given a successful outcome. This weak result should not be particularly surprising given that these estimates are not statistically significant.

Factor 2: Commitment to Ethics

Similar to the previous criteria, commitment to ethics has a surprisingly small estimated impact on the likelihood of success for a given decision. Our estimates suggest that when ethical questions are raised the ultimate outcome may actually be negative. The marginal effect is slightly negative and the odds ratio and propensity score both suggest that successful firms are less likely to list this as a factor. However, the standard error of our estimate was large and not statistically significant. In fact, the size of the coefficient relative to its standard error (i.e. t-stat) was the smallest in our model. It is surprising that we do not have more evidence to conclude the ultimate effect of ethical decisions on decision outcomes, and this warrants further discussion. There are at least three reasons for why we feel we do not have strong results with this category.

First, it could be that ethical decision makers can sometimes pass on questionable business deals as they place more weight in the long-term viability of the firm. In these cases, we would be unlikely to see the decision in our data. A successful decision to not undertake an activity would appear to be no decision at all. Second, it could also be that decisions that are not necessarily ethically questionable (from the position of business leaders) may be perceived as ethically questionable by the public, and may indeed have negative consequences. For example, Ford Motor Company's historical conflicts with Union labor raised ethical questions during the Great Depression. In a famous 1937 example known as the Battle of the Overpass, union organizers were demanding higher hourly pay for fewer work hours.[1] Ford security was caught on camera beating the organizers during an event that came to be known as the Battle of the Overpass. Though the organizer's demands may have been unrealistic at the height of the Great Depression and a few Ford security officers may have acted in a way that did not accurately represent the wishes of Ford's management, this led to immediate negative consequences for Ford. In short, Ford paid the price as if they made an ethically questionable decision, when it is not clear that one was actually made.

Third, decisions that are obviously unethical may not immediately lead to failure. For example, Bernie Madoff's decision to construct a Ponzi scheme to defraud investors appeared to lead to initial success. Only when the decision became publicly known did the firm fail. A myopic focus on immediate profits may lead to decisions that are successful at first. Our data focuses on the three years following the decision, and therefore may be revealing some of this effect as well. In addition, we may also be capturing the opposite effect, with ethical decisions appearing to be unsuccessful in the short term. For example, Nike's use of low wage child labor in third world countries was a controversial practice throughout the 1990s. In 1998, Nike CEO Phil Knight pledged to end this practice, though the firm did not begin to experience strong positive growth until years later. Whatever the explanation, there is substantial variation in outcome with this variable and our results are not statistically significant.

Factor 3: Innovation

Innovation is the first on our list to have an estimated positive effect on decision outcomes. But similar to the previous two criteria our results are not statistically significant and the effect does not seem large. However, this is less surprising than the finding for ethics. Innovation in a given industry may positively or negatively affect firms. Successful innovation (e.g. Apple) generates failure in the same industry for firms that fail to innovate (e.g. Nokia and Motorola). Firms attempting to innovate are also engaging in risky behavior. As in the case of Eastman Kodak, innovative firms may be so risk-averse that they do not market their products effectively, which can also lead to failure. Firms operating in highly technical industries with a large degree of innovation will either succeed or fail. In these industries we do not see much of a middle ground and there are just as many winners as losers.

Factor 4: Teamwork

Teamwork is the first factor on our list to have a large clear statistically significant impact on decision outcomes. Specifically, in cases where decisions were impacted by a firm culture that promotes teamwork, decisions were over 25 percent more likely to lead to success. In our data such firms were a whopping 2.86 times more likely to report a successful outcome than those for which teams were not a consideration. However, the propensity score suggests a successful firm only lists this as a factor 51 percent of the time.

It is clear that not all successful firms cite teamwork as a factor. However, it is also clear that when present, the impact of teamwork is positive. The example of the Toyota/GM joint venture at the NUMMI plant provided in the previous chapter illustrates the importance of focusing on teamwork. It should be no surprise to anyone that organizations with strong cohesive teams are more likely to produce successful outcomes, regardless of the context, and more attention should be given to this factor.

Factor 5: Resource Sharing Across Diverse Business Units

When resources are shared across different business units, we have an increased likelihood of unsuccessful outcomes. When this is a factor, firms are an estimated 24 percent more likely to face an unsuccessful decision. The odds ratio suggests such firms in our data are 2.65 times as likely to face an unfavorable outcome as those who do not share resources across different units.[2] The propensity score suggests that successful firms list resource sharing as a factor approximately 30 percent of the time. Shared resources may become stretched. We can think of two reasons for why this may be the case. First, during the great recession, firms focused on cost-cutting strategies to remain viable. This led to a case where employees and managers had to "wear many hats," and perform multiple diverse job functions in order for the firm to stay afloat. In such an environment, workers became stressed and were less productive than they otherwise could have been.

Second, over-diversification may lead to a case where firms lack a clear focus on their core competency. The existence itself of diverse business units can be a sign of trouble. A famous example of this is Henry Ford's attempt to diversify into upstream and downstream production processes. Ford attempted to produce the entire supply chain for the Model T in-house, going so far as to purchase rubber plantations in Brazil and attempt to produce raw rubber used as an input. Ford management attempted to export American culture and management techniques to an unfamiliar agricultural production process on a different continent. Fordlandia was a major failure as Ford's management was unable to function effectively in this environment. Further, Ford marketed wood scraps left over from wooden car body production by turning them into charcoal and selling. While the Kingsford charcoal that emerged from this side project was more successful, it was eventually spun off as its own firm. Ford's core competency was at the time and is today automobile mass production. A foray into anything else would be an excessively risky business decision.

Factor 6: Employee Satisfaction

In cases where employee morale was a factor, decisions are approximately 21 percent more likely to lead to success. In our data, these firms were 2.37 times as likely to be successful than firms not concerned over employee morale. We know from previous studies that high employee morale leads to a greater chance of success, so the result is not surprising. What is surprising is that our propensity score estimate suggests that a successful firm will list employee satisfaction as a factor only 42 percent of the time. However, these results are only marginally statistically significant at the 10 percent level of significance. In a substantial number of cases decisions are made to improve employee morale specifically because of management's understanding that this will lead to improved performance. Google's generous employee benefits are an obvious example of this. However, there are some examples of failed decisions that in retrospect may have been associated with low employee morale. Nokia's corporate culture that focused on existing products and discouraged innovation also unintentionally contributed to low employee morale. The existence of these two types of observations mixed in our data may have led to results that were weakly statistically significant. We explore this factor in more detail in our second model later in this chapter, finding stronger results.

Factor 7: Human Resources Management

Do human resource issues contribute positively or negatively to decision success? Our model was unable to definitively answer that question though our propensity score predicts a successful firm will cite human resources 30 percent of the time. This category is very similar to the effect of innovation; as positive human resource practices are just as likely to lead to success as the lack of human resources will cause problems.

Factor 8: Specific Management Techniques

Though we cautiously expected a positive finding, we find no statistically significant impact on successful outcomes for specific management techniques such as TQM, Six Sigma, and Lean. Our propensity score predicts that successful firms will cite management techniques 17 percent of the time. We found examples of both successful implementation as well as failures in the literature. From our data it seems that this factor as well as the previous factor of human resource management might not be all that impactful. Strong effective management is strong effective management, regardless of particular techniques and/or practices.

Factor 9: Competition

The relationship between the existence of competition and business success is unclear, as successful firms have navigated competitive industries and unsuccessful firms have been driven out by competition. We find no statistically significant impact of competition on success or failure. Recent technological advances that have emerged following the rise of the internet in the 1990s provide countless examples of both. Facebook emerged as a highly successful firm in a highly competitive environment. Myspace was the nearest competitor that was unable to successfully compete. The winner-take-all nature of this market was the crucial factor in the respective success and failure of both firms. A successful firm is predicted to cite competition as a factor 43 percent of the time. These results should not be surprising and should not suggest that competition in itself is not a decisive factor.

Factor 10: Data-driven Decisions

We find that decisions made after using data as an input were more likely to be successful than those that did not. Using data relative to not using data will increase the probability of success by 23 percent, and we expect to see 2.64 times as many successful data-driven firms as successful firms that do not use data. However, our propensity score suggests that successful firms that use data are still a minority, as they will only cite data an estimated 34 percent of the time. Again, the marginal effect should not be confused with the propensity score. The marginal effect predicts the impact of data and the propensity score predicts the likelihood that a successful firm is using data. In today's world, firms that do not rely on information technology are at a large competitive advantage, yet our data suggests most firms are still not using data as much as they should be. These results seem conclusive enough for us to make an obvious suggestion – more firms should be moving in this direction.

Factor 11: Decision Speed

As with a number of these measures, the ability to make quick decisions doesn't appear to have a strong influence, and we find no statistically significant impact. In our sample we have examples of firms that were successful because of their ability to quickly change directions and win business. Coca-Cola's reintroduction of Coke Classic is the textbook example. We also have examples of firms that were unable to do so. Motorola's anemic response to Apple's introduction of the iPhone led to their downfall. Our propensity score prediction suggests that successful firms are likely to cite decision speed as a factor only in a minority (22 percent) of cases.

Factor 12: Corporate Governance

Though also a statistically insignificant factor, corporate governance was an issue with more unsuccessful decisions than successful decisions. Also, successful firms cite corporate governance as a factor an estimated 15 percent of the time. Part of these results can be explained by likely multicollinearity with influence from the board of directors. In other words, firms that cite one in our data are likely to cite the other, since these two factors have a high degree of correlation. Because of this, our regression model produces large standard errors for both and has difficulty isolating the effect of one factor over the other. As an alternative explanation, this outcome likely mirrors the outcome from commitment to ethics in that we have examples of both positive and negative outcomes in our sample. By offering sales commissions to loan originators for bad loans that would later be sold to other firms, Countrywide mortgage did not appropriately weigh the interest of all stakeholders and ultimately failed as a result, later being purchased by Bank of America at a fire sale price. On the opposite end of the spectrum, Dell computers' privatization was an act taken specifically to remove shareholders from the equation. According to Michael Dell, it was an act taken specifically to improve corporate governance and by all accounts was successful.

Factor 13: Board of Directors

Given the findings from corporate governance, we might expect a statistically insignificant effect with board of directors as well. However, a clear negative effect was found in cases where the board of directors was involved in the decision-making process. Specifically, such firms were 23 percent less likely to experience a successful outcome and experienced failure at 2.5 times the rate as firms that made decisions without input from the board of directors. Firms that are successful will cite the board of directors as an influence an estimated 14 percent of the time. Two reasons explain this. First, board members may not have timely access to the same information as decision makers, but may still micromanage and push for the status quo in cases where this may cause issues. Second, the board of directors may be involved because of known issues in the organization that may themselves lead to failure. In these latter cases we should expect to see other factors emerge as well. We will explore this possibility in the next chapter.

Factor 14: CEO Pay

As we predicted, little relationship between success and CEO pay was found. CEO pay is estimated to be a factor in roughly one third of success-ful decisions, but there is no statistically significant difference with unsuc-cessful decisions. From the existing empirical literature, the impact of CEO compensation is small and more likely to affect long-term effectiveness of an organization.

Factor 15: CEO Attributes

We expected to find a positive relationship between CEO attributes and outcomes. However, the positive relationship we found was not statistically significant. Our model predicts roughly 50 percent of successful decisions can at least partly be attributed to CEO attributes. This is surprising given the strong findings from the empirical literature. We feel that a partial explanation comes from cases where failed decisions can be attributed to CEO characteristics. Bernie Madoff's Ponzi scheme and Martin Shkreli's drug price hike are two popular examples of these cases.

Factor 16: CEO Autonomy

While we were unsure what to expect with CEO autonomy, we did find it to be a statistically significant predictor of success. CEO autonomy was cited as a factor in more failures than successes, and led to a 32 percent drop in chance of success. Firms that reported this as a factor were 3.7 times as likely to experience failure than those who did not. Successful firms are predicted to cite CEO autonomy as a factor only 33 percent of the time. If we compare this with the results above from influence from the board of directors, we can infer that restrictions on CEO autonomy were the main driver of these results. It also raises an interesting question about the effect of multiple factors working together. We will explore this possibility in the following chapter. For now, it doesn't appear from our data that restrictions on CEO autonomy are productive, however we must remember that the majority of our data was reported by CEOs themselves.

Factor 17: Middle Management

We expected to find little impact one way or another from middle manage-ment, and we did in fact find no statistically significant impact. Our model predicts successful decisions will cite middle management approximately one third of the time, but this is not found to be different from unsuccessful decisions.

In summary, our logit model finds that of the 17 factors we analyzed, teamwork, the use of hard data, influence from the board of directors, and the amount of freedom given to the CEO all matter. While this first level analysis provides fewer conclusive results than we would have liked, it does raise some very interesting questions. Specifically, are there combinations of factors that matter? Is there a magic formula for success? Is there a poisonous combination that leads to failure? To explore these and other ideas, we will turn to a more detailed model in Chapter 7. Before we do so, let us first analyze our decisions using the five-point Likert scale outcomes.

LOGIT MODEL, LIKERT SCALE

Because the first model produced fewer conclusive results than we would have liked, we turn now to a more sophisticated model that examines the actual outcome after the decision, rather than the simple subjective determination of success or failure. We will use the values from our Likert scale as the dependent variable in our second model, which is described in the following section below.

In our previous section, our main focus was on the subjective valuation of "success" as evaluated by the business leaders in question. In effect, success was a simple yes/no question in the previous model. In this section we will focus on the firm's performance in the three years following the decision in order to gain a clearer picture of exactly "how" successful each decision was over time.

We have a total of 163 decisions, 88 of which were deemed successful and 75 of which were unsuccessful. The impacts of these decisions were compared to the performance of the firm over the next three years. As explained in Chapter 5, each firm's performance was rated on a five-point Likert scale. To recap, a score of one represents a strong increase in performance over a three-year period, two represents a moderate increase, three represents no significant change, four represents a gradual decrease in performance, and five represents a strong decrease up to and including bankruptcy. Strong growth was experienced by 23 of our firms and moderate growth was experienced by 58 firms. Over the three years following the decision, only 17 of our firms remained stable, with no significant change. We attribute this to sample selection, as decisions with neutral outcomes such as these were unlikely to be reported as an example of a successful or unsuccessful decision. There were 44 firms that experienced a moderate decline in performance, and 21 firms that experienced a strong decline and/or bankruptcy. Our data is bimodal, with a large group of firms that experienced growth and a large group that experienced a decline. Again, this should not be surprising given the nature of our survey.

A small majority (81 versus 63) of these were associated with positive performance over the three years following the decision. However, positive performance would later turn negative with 12 of these. This could be due to a short-term focus as explained in the Kodak example. These could also be caused by an event not necessarily related to the successful decision or due to factors beyond the firm's control.

If we compare the Likert scores to the financial size of the firms in our sample, there is no clear relationship. That is, we have no evidence to conclude that smaller firms are more or less likely to make decisions that are ultimately judged to be more or less successful than larger firms. Large businesses do not appear to have a strong advantage over smaller firms, or at least small business leaders are no less optimistic than large business leaders are. This finding alleviates some of the concern we have about sample selection bias and suggests that responses from our interviews provide a good representative sample of firms throughout the business spectrum.

ORDERED LOGIT MODEL

In this section we will introduce an ordered logit model. Our five-point scale provides slightly more detailed information than the simple yes/no success/failure outcome variable analyzed above. However, the simple logit model we estimated above is only appropriate for binary dependent variables that take on values of 0 or 1. The ordered logit model is an extension that can be used to analyze dependent variables that take on additional integer values. Instead of predicting the probability of a movement from failure to success, we're now essentially predicting the probability of different outcomes on our Likert scale. We can use this to see how the probability of all five particular scores on our scale change when we change one of our 17 impact factors. The only additional assumption that we must add to generate this model is that distance from 1 to 2 is the same as the distance from 2 to 3 and the same as 3 to 4 and so on. In other words, the change from a neutral outcome to a moderate growth in sales (i.e. a movement from a 3 to a 2) would be the same size change as a change from a strong failure to a moderate decline (a movement from a 5 to a 4). The ordered logit model we will estimate is described below:

Decision Outcome (1–5) = β_0 + β_1 firm's prior performance + β_2 commitment to ethics + β_3 innovation + β_4 team effectiveness + β_5 resource sharing across diverse business lines + β_6 employee satisfaction + β_7 human resources management + β_8 specific management techniques + β_9 competition + β_{10} data driven decisions + β_{11} decision speed + β_{12} corporate governance + β_{13} board of directors + β_{14} CEO pay + β_{15} CEO attributes + β_{16} CEO autonomy + β_{17} management teams + β_{18} interview + ε

This model is similar to the simple logit model in the previous section above in that each of the same 17 criteria will be used as explanatory variables as well as an interview variable to control for the difference in size between small and large firms. However, this model is slightly different in that the interpretation is more complicated. Specifically, each factor no longer impacts a simple "success" or "failure," but now will impact the probability of different values on the Likert scale. It will also allow the effect of each criteria to change over the range of values, and allows us to evaluate the effect of multiple criteria together. Initial coefficient estimates are listed in Table 6.19, and will be interpreted below.

With the logit analysis in the previous section, there were five factors that produced a statistically significant effect. These were team effectiveness, resource sharing, data-driven decisions, board of directors, and CEO autonomy. In this section, there are also five factors including team effectiveness, employee satisfaction, data-driven decisions, board of directors, and CEO autonomy. The effect of employee satisfaction was marginally significant in the first model, and resource sharing was less so in the second model. Rather than go through the entire list of 17 factors in our interpretation, we will focus only on those six factors that produced a statistically significant effect in either of our models for comparison purposes.

Factor 1: Team Effectiveness

In order to interpret the results of our ordered logit model, we predict the likelihood of each of the outcomes on our Likert scale, holding each of the criteria at their average value in our data and holding the team effectiveness variable at zero. We then change the team effectiveness variable to a one, then observe how our predictions change. We use the delta method to produce a confidence interval for the change (Table 6.20).

From Table 6.20, interpretation is straightforward. When present, team effectiveness increases the probability of a moderate success by 11 percent, decreases the probability of a moderate decline by about 12 percent, and decreases the probability of a strong failure by over 6 percent. There is no clear effect on neutral outcomes, as we should expect to see more neutral

Table 6.19   Ordered logit model, Likert scale

Criteria	Coefficient	z-score (coefficient / standard error)	p-value (level of significance)
Firm's Prior Performance	−0.0708069 (0.3648845)	−0.10	85%
Commitment to Ethics	0.170448 (0.3535454)	0.48	63%
Innovation	−0.5203491 (0.3520275)	−1.48	14%
Team Effectiveness	−0.7943513* (0.3886365)	−2.04	4%
Resource Sharing Across Diverse Business Units	0.5535747 (0.405221)	1.37	17%
Employee Satisfaction	−1.064594* (0.4544747)	−2.34	2%
HR Management	0.2229259 (0.5314415)	0.42	68%
Management Techniques	0.2691648 (0.4232612)	0.64	53%
Competition	−0.1615159 (0.3808251)	−0.42	67%
Data-driven Decisions	−0.600142* (0.3570925)	−1.68	9%
Decision Speed	0.4157026 (0.4029916)	1.03	30%
Corporate Governance	−0.1094492 (0.4138595)	−0.26	79%
Board of Directors	1.174114* (0.4263721)	2.75	1%
CEO Pay	−0.1306583 (0.3865044)	−0.34	74%
CEO Attributes	−0.4072029 (0.4139209)	−0.98	33%
CEO Autonomy	1.138319* (0.4486447)	2.54	1%
Middle Management	0.376134 (0.3866639)	0.97	33%

outcomes from firms in decline, and less neutral outcomes from successful firms. Both of these effects cancel each other out. It may seem peculiar at first that we do not see a statistically significant increase in the probability of a strong success, however the effects are not as strong in cases in the tails of the distribution. The increase in the probability of a strong success

Table 6.20   Predictions after ordered logit, team effectiveness

Outcome Probabilities	Team Effectiveness not a factor	Team Effectiveness is a factor	Change in probability	95% Confidence Interval	
				Upper Bound	Lower Bound
1 = Strong Success	0.0831	0.167	0.0840	−0.0044	0.1723
2 = Moderate Success	0.337	0.4488	0.1118*	0.0080	0.2156
3 = Neutral	0.1279	0.1127	−0.0153	−0.0388	0.0082
4 = Moderate Decline	0.3282	0.2115	−0.1167*	−0.2277	−0.0058
5 = Strong Failure	0.1237	0.06	−0.0637*	−0.1262	−0.0013

Table 6.21   Predictions after ordered logit, resource sharing across diverse business units

Outcome Probabilities	Resource Sharing not a factor	Resource Sharing is a factor	Change in probability	95% Confidence Interval	
				Upper Bound	Lower Bound
1 = Strong Success	0.0798	0.1311	−0.0513	−0.1217	0.0191
2 = Moderate Success	0.3297	0.4157	−0.0860	−0.2132	0.0413
3 = Neutral	0.1277	0.122	0.0057	−0.0057	0.0171
4 = Moderate Decline	0.3343	0.2531	0.0812	−0.0335	0.1959
5 = Strong Failure	0.1285	0.0781	0.0504	−0.0296	0.1304

is barely not statistically significant at the 5 percent level (but is at the 10 percent level). On the other side of the coin, the decrease in the probability of a strong failure is barely statistically significant at the 5 percent level.

Factor 5: Resource Sharing

The second criteria is resource sharing across diverse business units. While the effect was not statistically significant in this second ordered logit model, the effect of this factor on "success" or "failure" was statistically significant in the first model (Table 6.21). We include it here for comparison purposes only.

The estimated effect in general is that when resources are shared across business units, the probability of success falls and the probability of failure increases. While the effects are weak, they may be meaningful when interpreted in light of the results from our first model.

Table 6.22   Predictions after ordered logit, employee satisfaction

Outcome Probabilities	Employee Satisfaction not a factor	Employee Satisfaction is a factor	Change in probability	95% Confidence Interval	
				Upper Bound	Lower Bound
1 = Strong Success	0.2049	0.0816	0.1233	0.0012	0.2454
2 = Moderate Success	0.4683	0.3337	0.1346	0.0363	0.2328
3 = Neutral	0.102	0.1279	−0.0259	−0.0598	0.0081
4 = Moderate Decline	0.1775	0.331	−0.1534	−0.2769	−0.0300
5 = Strong Failure	0.0473	0.1258	−0.0785	−0.1435	−0.0136

Factor 6: Employee Satisfaction

Though the effect of employee satisfaction is not statistically significant in the first model, it certainly is in this second model (Table 6.22).

Here, we can see that employee satisfaction, when present, increases the probability of a strong success by 12 percent and decreases the probability of a moderate success by 13 percent. It also decreases the probability of a moderate decline by 15 percent and decreases the probability of a strong failure by 8 percent. These results themselves should not be surprising. However, it is surprising that they did not emerge as strongly in our initial model. The difference simply means there is a stronger correlation between actual outcomes and employee satisfaction than there is between subjective "success" or "failure" determinations and employee satisfaction. Perhaps business leaders underestimate the importance of this factor, and this in itself is an important finding.

Factor 10: Data-driven Decisions

When data is used to inform a decision, our first model estimated a 23 percent increase in the probability of success (Table 6.23). While not statistically significant at the 5 percent level, results from our second model agree. We find that when data is used to make a decision, the probability of a strong success will increase by roughly 7 percent, the probability of a moderate success will increase by 8 percent, the probability of a moderate decline will fall by 9 percent, and the probability of a strong failure will fall by 5 percent. The fact that these results are not statistically significant at the 5 percent level (but are at the 10 percent level) suggests that perhaps data-driven decisions are not as important as business leaders perceive. It could be the case that data is being given more credit for influencing the outcome of a decision than it should be.

Table 6.23   Predictions after ordered logit, data-driven decisions

Outcome Probabilities	Data-driven Decisions not a factor	Data-driven Decisions is a factor	Change in probability	90% Confidence Interval	
				Upper Bound	Lower Bound
1 = Strong Success	0.159	0.094	0.0650	−0.0056	0.1356
2 = Moderate Success	0.4428	0.3594	0.0835	0.0064	0.1605
3 = Neutral	0.1149	0.1279	−0.013	−0.032	0.0059
4 = Moderate Decline	0.2199	0.309	−0.089	−0.1757	−0.0023
5 = Strong Failure	0.0634	0.1098	−0.0464	−0.0905	−0.0023

Table 6.24   Predictions after ordered logit, influence from board of directors

Outcome Probabilities	Influence from Board of Directors not a factor	Influence from Board of Directors is a factor	Change in probability	95% Confidence Interval	
				Upper Bound	Lower Bound
1 = Strong Success	0.0479	0.14	−0.0921	−0.1518	−0.0324
2 = Moderate Success	0.239	0.4255	−0.1865	−0.3212	−0.0519
3 = Neutral	0.1155	0.1199	−0.0044	−0.032	0.0232
4 = Moderate Decline	0.3949	0.2418	0.1532	0.056	0.2503
5 = Strong Failure	0.2027	0.0728	0.1298	0.0101	0.2496

Factor 13: Board of Directors

Our first model suggests that influence from the board of directors has a negative effect on the success of a decision either due to micromanagement or some other problem that causes the board of directors to become involved. This second model generally agrees with those findings (Table 6.24).

Influence from the board of directors will decrease the probability of a strong success by an estimated 9 percent and decrease the probability of a moderate success by 19 percent. It will also increase the probability of a moderate decline by 15 percent and increase the probability of a strong failure by 13 percent.

Factor 16: CEO Autonomy

As with our first model, the effect of CEO autonomy is identical to that of influence from the board of directors (Table 6.25).

Table 6.25   Predictions after ordered logit, CEO autonomy

Outcome Probabilities	CEO Autonomy not a factor	CEO Autonomy is a factor	Change in probability	95% Confidence Interval	
				Upper Bound	Lower Bound
1 = Strong Success	0.0588	0.1632	−0.1044	−0.1856	−0.0232
2 = Moderate Success	0.2743	0.4461	−0.1717	−0.3063	−0.0372
3 = Neutral	0.1223	0.1137	0.0085	−0.0123	0.0294
4 = Moderate Decline	0.3747	0.2155	0.1592	0.0419	0.2766
5 = Strong Failure	0.1699	0.0615	0.1084	0.0084	0.2083

Table 6.26   Predictions after ordered logit, joint impact of board of directors and CEO autonomy

Outcome Probabilities	Neither Influence from Board NOR CEO Autonomy are factors	Both Influence from Board AND CEO Autonomy are factors	Change in probability	95% Confidence Interval	
				Upper Bound	Lower Bound
1 = Strong Success	0.0244	0.2018	−0.1774	−0.2777	−0.0770
2 = Moderate Success	0.1423	0.4672	−0.3249	−0.4757	−0.1741
3 = Neutral	0.0842	0.1029	−0.0187	−0.0602	0.0228
4 = Moderate Decline	0.4109	0.1800	0.2309	0.1348	0.3270
5 = Strong Failure	0.3382	0.0482	0.2900	0.0682	0.5119

When CEO autonomy is an issue, the probability of a strong success falls by an estimated 10 percent and the probability of a moderate success falls by 17 percent. It will also increase the probability of a moderate decline by 16 percent and increase the probability of a strong failure by 11 percent.

One of the benefits of the ordered logit procedure is that it allows us to examine the impact of multiple factors at once. If influence from the board of directors is related to CEO autonomy, then we can examine their joint impact. Table 6.26 reports the results of this joint analysis.

When taken together, if both of these factors are an issue, the probability of a strong success falls by 18 percent, the probability of a moderate success falls by 32 percent, the probability of a moderate decline rises by 23 percent, and the probability of a strong failure rises by 29 percent. These large effects reflect the negative impact of a power struggle between the CEO and the board. These large effects also point out how strongly these factors can be when they work together.

CONCLUSION

In conclusion, we find six of our 17 factors that independently produce statistically significant effects on decision outcomes. These are summarized in Table 6.27.

Table 6.27   Summary of findings, Chapter 6

Factor	Impact on "Success" or "Failure," Logit Model	Impact on 5-point Likert Scale, Ordered Logit Model
Team Effectiveness	Positive effect on success, cited by successful firms roughly half the time	Positive effect on moderate success Negative effect on moderate decline and strong failure
Resource Sharing Across Diverse Business Units	Negative effect on success, cited by successful firms an estimated 30% of the time	Apparent negative effect on success and positive effect on failure, but not statistically effect
Employee Satisfaction	Positive effect on success, not statistically significant, only cited by successful firms approximately 42% of the time	Positive effect on probability of success Negative effect on probability of failure
Data-driven Decisions	Large positive effect on success, only cited by successful firms an estimated 34% of the time	Statistically significant positive effect on moderate success only at the 10% level Statistically significant negative effect on the probability of failure only at the 10% level
Influence from the Board of Directors	Large negative effect on success, only cited by successful firms an estimated 14% of the time	Negative effect on probability of success Positive effect on probability of failure
CEO Autonomy	Large negative effect on success, only cited by successful firms an estimated 33% of the time	Negative effect on probability of success Positive effect on probability of failure
Board of Directors + CEO Autonomy, Joint Impact	N/A	Large negative effect on probability of success. Large positive effect on probability of failure

Team effectiveness contributes positively to subjective measures of success. Unsurprisingly it also has a positive relationship with successful outcomes for the three years following the decision. Resource sharing has the opposite effect, as it contributes negatively to subjective measures of success and is negatively related to successful outcomes. This makes sense as resources can become stretched and organizations can lose focus.

Employee satisfaction, while not a statistically significant factor that determines the success or failure of a particular decision, is certainly a statistically significant factor that determines actual outcomes after the decision. We suspect that business leaders, while aware of the effect of worker morale, may still underestimate its importance over the long term. The propensity score of 42 percent provide evidence consistent with our suspicion.

Data-driven decisions are found in the first model to have a large statistically significant effect on success. We would suggest that more firms should increase their reliance on data. However, in our second model which examines the actual outcomes in the three years following the decision the effect is still positive but statistically significant only at the 10 percent level. Perhaps business leaders overestimate their usage of data attribute success to their reliance on data when such factors are overstated.

Influence from the board of directors and CEO autonomy were two factors that individually had large negative effects on success in both models and tended to show up only in a minority of successful cases. They were also found to have an even larger joint effect, suggesting that when these two factors coexist they act as symptoms of a larger underlying problem.

While the relationship between the board of directors and CEO autonomy is an obvious example of certain factors working together, it is not clear which other combinations of factors will matter. We will focus specifically on these joint effects in the next chapter.

NOTES

1. The United Auto Workers were demanding $6 for a 6-hour workday. According to the Bureau of Labor statistics, the average worker in the motor vehicle manufacturing industry in 1937 was being paid roughly $6 for an 8-hour workday. The purchasing power of a dollar in 1937 is roughly equivalent to slightly more than $17 in 2017.
2. The odds ratio suggests firms that share resources are successful at a rate of 0.377 to 1 compared to firms that do not share resources. $1/0.377 = 2.65$.

REFERENCES

Carroll, Paul B. and Mui, Chunka (2008) *Billion-Dollar Lessons: What You Can Learn from the Most Inexcusable Business Failures of the Last 25 Years.* London: Penguin.

Koenigs, Michael and Tranel, Daniel (2007) Prefrontal Cortex Damage Abolishes Brand-Cued Changes in Cola Preference, *Social Cognitive and Affective Neuroscience*, 3(1), 1–6.

McClure, Samuel M. et al. (2004) Neural Correlates of Behavioral Preference for Culturally Familiar Drinks, *Neuron*, 44(2), 379–387.

7. Underlying performance factors

The 17 criteria we analyzed in the previous chapter do not affect an organization in a vacuum. Rather, these factors will work together and sometimes in opposition to ensure the success or failure of any business decision. The focus of this chapter is on these joint impacts. Is there a magic formula for success? Are there certain poisonous combinations that ensure failure? In this chapter we will use exploratory factor analysis to answer these questions.

We assume that there is some unobservable set of "success" criteria. Each of the 17 factors described in the previous chapter likely matter in some way only because of their relationship to unobservable underlying characteristics. For example, in the last chapter we hypothesized that influence from the board of directors and CEO autonomy are two variables that are related to some unobservable level of intra organizational conflict. In other words, when conflict within an organization reaches a certain level, we see interference from the board of directors and we also see issues with CEO autonomy. While we do not have a measure of "organizational conflict" in our data, these two factors may be related to it. Our focus in this chapter is to look for these unobserved factors in our data. Once found, we will revisit a version of the analysis in the previous chapter using the factors we discover.

We begin by looking at simple Pearson correlation coefficients for our 17 explanatory variables (Table 7.2). Correlation coefficients and p-values are provided in the table on the following page using the abbreviations detailed in Table 7.1.

For the purposes of this analysis, we will define a moderate correlation as one greater than 0.30 (Cohen, 1988). We expect variables that are correlated here to emerge in our more detailed analysis below as parts of the unobservable factors we are searching for. We will begin with our first variable and move across the columns from left to right.

Firm's prior performance has moderate statistically significant correlations with commitment to ethics, competition, CEO attributes, and CEO autonomy. It seems reasonable to think that ethical CEOs tend to stay around for a while, and these correlations may be capturing this relationship.

Table 7.1   Table of abbreviations for impact factors

Abbreviation	Description
FPP	Firm's Prior Performance
CTE	Commitment to Ethics
I	Innovation
TE	Team Effectiveness
RS	Resource Sharing across diverse business units
ES	Employee Satisfaction
HRM	Human Resource Management
MT	Management Techniques
C	Competition
DDD	Data-Driven Decisions
DS	Decision Speed
CG	Corporate Governance
BOD	Board of Directors
CP	CEO Pay
CAT	CEO Attributes
CAU	CEO Autonomy
MM	Middle Management

In addition to being correlated with prior performance, commitment to ethics is marginally correlated with employee satisfaction. This makes sense as ethical firms are thought to treat their employees well.

Innovation is correlated with resource sharing across diverse business units and marginally correlated with competition and decision speed. This suggests there may be a link between innovation and risk-taking with multiple new products being quickly introduced in a competitive market.

Team effectiveness has stronger correlations with resource sharing, employee satisfaction, human resource management, as well as middle management. These correlations make sense, and may reflect the general effectiveness of labor in the organization. When all of these work well, we should expect to see a fairly well-oiled "human machine."

In addition to being correlated with team effectiveness, resource sharing has a strong correlation with middle management. If resources are being shared well (or poorly) across diverse business units, then it seems likely the case that middle management is either working well (or poorly) across these units.

Employee satisfaction is highly correlated with human resources management and moderately correlated with middle management. We also see that human resources management itself is moderately correlated with

Table 7.2   Pearson correlation coefficients

	FPP	CTE	I	TE	RS	ES	HRM	MT	C	DDD	DS	CG	BOD	CP	CAT	CAU
CTE	0.366 (0)	1														
I	0.077 (0.331)	0.029 (0.714)	1													
TE	0.176 (0.025)	0.078 (0.321)	0.108 (0.169)	1												
RS	0.136 (0.084)	0.067 (0.394)	0.294 (0)	0.366 (0)	1											
ES	0.204 (0.009)	0.270 (0.001)	0.031 (0.692)	0.485 (0)	0.151 (0.054)	1										
HRM	0.112 (0.154)	0.068 (0.390)	0.023 (0.772)	0.538 (0)	0.356 (0)	0.609 (0)	1									
MT	0.050 (0.524)	0.125 (0.112)	0.017 (0.829)	0.140 (0.075)	0.235 (0.003)	0.052 (0.513)	0.223 (0.004)	1								
C	0.389 (0)	0.206 (0.008)	0.258 (0.001)	0.251 (0.001)	0.284 (0)	0.086 (0.275)	0.289 (0)	0.220 (0.005)	1							
DDD	0.193 (0.014)	0.004 (0.962)	0.206 (0.008)	0.017 (0.832)	0.161 (0.040)	0.031 (0.697)	-0.023 (0.768)	0.059 (0.456)	0.231 (0.003)	1						
DS	0.225 (0.004)	0.189 (0.016)	0.286 (0)	-0.042 (0.597)	0.265 (0.001)	-0.048 (0.545)	-0.097 (0.218)	0.346 (0.001)	0.272 (0.001)	0.225 (0.004)	1					
CG	0.128 (0.103)	0.074 (0.350)	0.155 (0.049)	-0.061 (0.442)	0.056 (0.480)	-0.002 (0.982)	-0.047 (0.550)	-0.011 (0.889)	0.084 (0.285)	0.167 (0.033)	0.088 (0.263)	1				
BOD	0.182 (0.020)	0.051 (0.519)	0.222 (0.004)	-0.054 (0.493)	0.097 (0.220)	-0.117 (0.137)	-0.097 (0.216)	0.010 (0.902)	0.145 (0.065)	0.143 (0.068)	0.201 (0.010)	0.455 (0)	1			
CP	0.214 (0.006)	0.033 (0.677)	0.072 (0.363)	0.187 (0.017)	-0.035 (0.657)	0.088 (0.266)	0.124 (0.116)	-0.180 (0.022)	0.271 (0.001)	0.183 (0.020)	-0.016 (0.841)	0.059 (0.458)	0.135 (0.086)	1		
CAT	0.366 (0)	0.194 (0.013)	0.065 (0.410)	0.202 (0.010)	0.091 (0.247)	0.236 (0.003)	0.210 (0.007)	0.025 (0.756)	0.276 (0)	0.144 (0.066)	0.107 (0.172)	0.070 (0.376)	0.187 (0.017)	0.427 (0)	1	
CAU	0.310 (0)	0.142 (0.070)	0.042 (0.598)	0.028 (0.720)	-0.050 (0.526)	0.014 (0.861)	-0.043 (0.588)	0.045 (0.567)	0.349 (0)	0.322 (0)	0.102 (0.197)	0.151 (0.055)	0.155 (0.049)	0.4698 (0)	0.582 (0)	1
MM	0.034 (0.666)	0.087 (0.270)	0.069 (0.384)	0.391 (0)	0.441 (0)	0.312 (0)	0.374 (0)	0.251 (0.001)	0.231 (0.003)	0.096 (0.221)	0.107 (0.173)	0.070 (0.376)	-0.079 (0.317)	-0.047 (0.553)	0.144 (0.066)	-0.084 (0.288)

middle management. Taken together these variables may be capturing the general effectiveness of the management team.

Management techniques are only correlated with decision speed. Perhaps this reflects a firm's level of organization as firms that have an existing framework such as Six Sigma, TQM or Lean in place may also have other mechanisms that enhance (or slow) the speed at which decisions are made.

Competition and data-driven decisions are correlated with CEO autonomy, though it is a little more difficult to speculate on the reasons for this. It is obvious why corporate governance is correlated with influence from the board of directors, and why CEO pay, attributes, and autonomy are all correlated with one another. However, it is not obvious why board of directors is so weakly correlated with CEO autonomy, given the results we found in the previous chapter. We expected to see a strong correlation between these two, given that their joint effect is so powerful. But perhaps this speaks to the limitations of the analysis performed in the last chapter, and perhaps relationship between these two variables is more complicated that it seems.

We now turn to our exploratory factor analysis. In this section, we will "collapse" our 17 variables that are correlated with one another into synthetic variables that are not correlated with one another and capture more clearly key relationships and underlying principles. The unobservable (latent) variables we find from this exploratory factor analysis should somewhat mirror what we find in the correlations above.

We compute unique vectors (i.e. combinations) of our 17 variables that explain as much of the variance in our data as possible. After finding the vector that explains the most variation, we find a second, completely uncorrelated vector that explains as much of the remaining variance as possible, and so on. Though we could technically compute as many of these as we have explanatory variables (i.e. 17), at some point the additional variation we would be able to explain would be small and would not be theoretically justifiable. We assume that these vectors represent independent latent factors (i.e. principal components). The Kaiser (1960) criterion suggests we discard any component with eigenvalues less than 1. Cattell's "scree" test suggests we examine the "scree plot" of eigenvalues and discard additional factors after we visually determine a "leveling off" in the plot. These values are presented in Figure 7.1. The Kaiser criterion suggests we should produce 5 principal components. Cattell's scree method suggests we choose 4, 6, or 8, as we see a leveling off after all of these in Figure 7.1. While we experimented with different numbers of factors, we will choose six principal components as these are more theoretically justifiable with our data.[1]

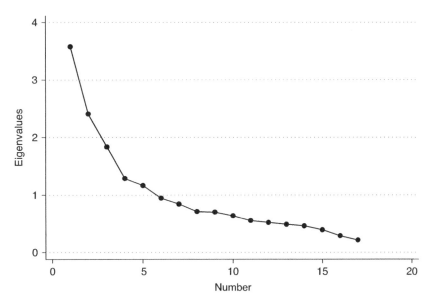

Figure 7.1   Scree plot of eigenvalues after factor

Table 7.3 presents each of the six principal components, the variance in our 17 variables that is explained by the component, and the variables in each component for which at least a moderate correlation exists.[2] For example, our first component explains about 16 percent of the variation in our 17 variables. This first component is correlated primarily with five key variables. The first of these, team effectiveness, has a correlation coefficient with the first principal component of 0.7741, and so on. For team effectiveness in particular, our six components explain all but 36 percent of its variation. We discuss each of these principal components below.

Principal Component 1: Labor Effectiveness

As we see above, team effectiveness, resource sharing, employee satisfaction, human resource management, and middle management are all correlated with each other to a high degree, relative to other factors. These five variables form the bulk of our first principal component, which explains 16 percent of the variation in all of our independent variables. The high degree of correlation combined with the straightforward theoretical interpretation of this "human machine" variable gives us a high degree of confidence in this measure.

Table 7.3 Principal components

	Principal Components						Unique Variance
	1	2	3	4	5	6	
Proportion of Variance Explained	0.1571	0.1401	0.0957	0.0935	0.087	0.0860	--
Cumulative Variance Explained	0.1571	0.2972	0.393	0.4865	0.5735	0.6596	--
FPP		0.3816				0.6385	0.3962
CTE						0.8521	0.2542
I			0.8425				0.2598
TE	0.7741						0.3571
RS	0.4608		0.5175	0.3506			0.3824
ES	0.7474					0.3293	0.3132
HRM	0.8396						0.2784
MT				0.8544			0.2464
C		0.4545	0.3975				0.4635
DDD		0.4225	0.3782				0.5993
DS			0.4747	0.546			0.3428
CG					0.8864		0.2108
BOD					0.7733		0.3224
CP		0.736					0.342
CAT		0.7211					0.3683
CAU		0.8574					0.2278
MM	0.6127			0.4174			0.4225

Principal Component 2: CEO Tenure

The second principal component is very highly correlated with CEO pay, CEO attributes, and CEO autonomy. It is correlated to a lesser extent with a firm's prior performance, intra industry competition, and data-driven decisions. Though this is similar to a relationship we found in the simple correlations above, it is interesting that we do not find the same relationship between a firm's CEO and ethical decision making. At any rate, over 14 percent of our data can be explained by forces surrounding a firm's CEO.

Principal Component 3: Marketing/R&D

Our third principal component explains a further 10 percent in the variation of our 17 variables. This component is highly correlated with innovation. It is moderately correlated with resource sharing across diverse business units, competition, data-driven decisions, and decision speed. These variables are all linked to a firm's marketing, research and development. Firms must evolve in fast-paced industries, and must quickly change directions when needed to market new products.

Principal Component 4: Operations Management

Our fourth principal component explains 9 percent of the variation in our 17 variables. It is highly correlated with specific management techniques, and moderately correlated with resource sharing across diverse business units, decision speed, and middle management. This component captures the efficiency at which the organization operates on a daily basis.

Principal Component 5: Corporate Governance and Board of Directors

Our fifth principal component explains an additional 9 percent of the variation in our variables. It is highly correlated only with corporate governance and influence from the board of directors. It is interesting that these two variables so strongly produce a separate component themselves.

Principal Component 6: Ethical Reputation

Our sixth and final component also explains an additional 9 percent of the variation in our explanatory variables. While highly correlated with commitment to ethics, this component is also correlated with a firm's prior performance and employee satisfaction. It makes sense that these three variables are combined here, as ethical decisions (and the lack thereof) tend to follow firms over time and can "snowball" as future decisions are viewed as (un)ethical by those biased by a firm's previous actions. In many cases, including for example American Airlines' pay cuts, such decisions directly affect employees themselves.

In effect, we can collapse our 17 explanatory variables into these six uncorrelated principal components. These should be thought of as underlying factors that "matter" in some way for successful decisions. Together, these six components explain 66 percent of the variation in our 17 explanatory variables. For each of the 163 observations in our data, we estimate principal component scores for each of these factors. We will then use these scores to conduct an analysis similar to that in the previous chapter.

PRINCIPAL COMPONENTS LOGIT MODEL AND DATA

In this section we estimate a model similar to that in the previous chapter. However, rather than using each of the 17 dummy variables as explanatory variables, we will now use the six principal component scores.

Specifically, our model is:

Decision Outcome (Success or Failure) = β_0 + β_1 Labor Effectiveness + β_2 CEO Tenure + β_3 Marketing/R&D + β_4 Operations Management + β_5 Corporate Governance / Board of Directors + β_6 Ethical Reputation + β_7 Interview + ε

Our explanatory variables are all standardized with mean zero and standard deviation equal to one. Scores represent the value of each firm's principal components in standard deviations. Values for these scores are shown in Figures 7.2 through 7.7. As can be seen in these histograms, these variables are all right-skewed, indicating relatively low principal component scores for most observations, and high scores for relatively few observations. This is particularly the case for the fifth and sixth components, though these are also the least important two of our components.

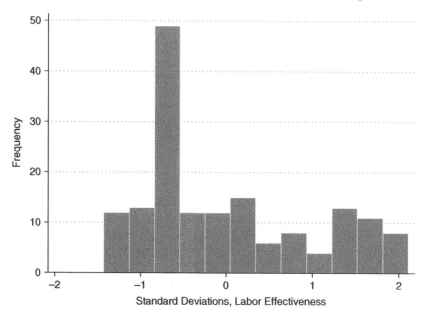

Figure 7.2   Labor effectiveness

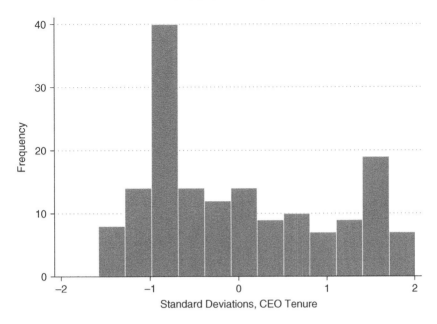

Figure 7.3   CEO tenure

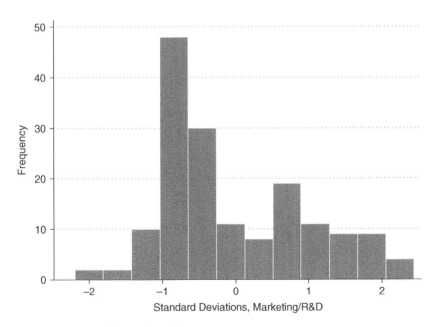

Figure 7.4   Marketing / R&D

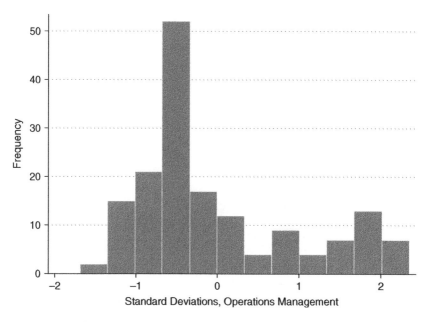

Figure 7.5   Operations management

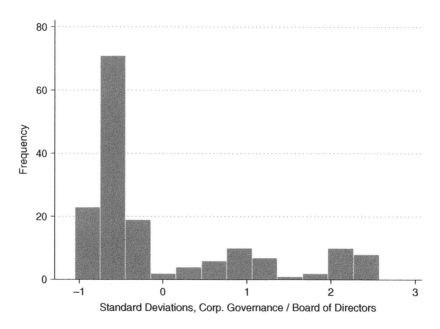

Figure 7.6   Corporate governance / board of directors

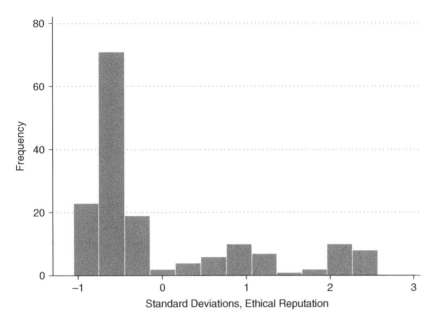

Figure 7.7   Ethical reputation

Results for our logit model including marginal effects are presented in Table 7.4.

Labor effectiveness has a strong positive effect on the probability of success. A one standard deviation increase in this principal component score increases the probability of a successful decision by approximately 12 percent. Keep in mind that a one standard deviation increase in this component is equivalent to a one standard deviation increase in the weighted factors of team effectiveness, resource sharing, employee satisfaction, human resource management, and middle management being reported as related to a given decision. For example, in this particular case a one standard deviation increase would be roughly equivalent to moving from a situation where only three of these factors were considered impactful to a situation where all five mattered. The firms that jointly list all five of these factors are more likely than others to experience success. If we must pick only one result to present from our findings it can be summed up by simply stating that labor relations matter. The night and day difference in performance between GMs Fremont plant and the later NUMMI joint venture is explained by this one factor, and may be the best case study to illustrate our most powerful finding. That this factor itself is important should not be surprising, but the fact that it is so much

Table 7.4   Logit model, success versus failure as predicted by principal components

Criteria	Coefficient	p-value (level of significance)	Marginal Effect
Labor Effectiveness	0.4933488* (0.1776276)	0.005	0.1225301
CEO Tenure	−0.0120958 (0.1714524)	0.944	−0.0030042
Marketing/R&D	−0.0071008 (0.1662268)	0.966	−0.0017636
Operations Management	−0.4126800* (0.1740209)	0.018	−0.1024949
Corporate Governance Board of Directors	−0.4688523* (0.1750604)	0.007	−0.116446
Ethical Reputation	−0.1291623 (0.1681313)	0.442	−0.0320793

more important than all other factors is our main contribution from this chapter.

The second principal component is the one reflecting CEO tenure. It is not found to be a statistically significant predictor of decision success. This is a surprising result because in our first model in the previous chapter CEO autonomy was a strong predictor of success, and CEO autonomy is very highly correlated with this component with a coefficient of 0.86. It must be the case that the unique CEO characteristics which explain decision success are those that are unique and not part of this principal component. In other words, about 23 percent of the variation in CEO autonomy is not explained by our 6 principal components. This unexplained variation must be what is driving success. Anecdotally we can use CEO autonomy to explain why this may be the case. For example, Steve Jobs brought something to Apple's table that contributed to success. His independence was a key factor in Apple's continued success over the years. However, this unique independence was not directly related to his salary or his attributes. Our second principal component will only measure characteristics that are related to all three. While CEO attributes themselves are strong predictors of success, we must conclude that our second principal component is not a reliable predictor of success. Firms that jointly list CEO autonomy together with CEO attributes, CEO pay, data-driven decisions, competition, and firm's prior performance, are no more or less likely to experience success.

Our third principal component measures the effectiveness of marketing, research and development, broadly speaking. While innovation is the major factor in this principal component, innovation itself is not a statistically significant predictor of decision success. Unsurprisingly, neither is this third principal component. Firms that jointly list the factors in this component (i.e. innovation, resource sharing, decision speed, data-driven decisions, and competition) are not more or less likely than other firms to experience success.

Our fourth principal component captures the effect of operations management practices. The major factor in this component is management techniques, such as Six Sigma, TQM, and Lean. Other factors in this component are resource sharing across diverse business units, decision speed, and middle management. Firms that jointly list these four factors are less likely to experience success. Specifically, a one standard deviation increase in this principal component score will reduce the probability of success by an estimated 41 percent. In our data, a one standard deviation increase is roughly equivalent to a change that includes particular management techniques as a factor. From the histogram above, we see that these factors are less likely to be listed as factors that impact the success of decisions. When they are listed in our data, we suspect that this is because there are specific issues that hinder the firm's operation. Operations management is a critical function that runs in the background and is only noticed by top leadership when problems arise. This is an important set of factors that should not be neglected.

Our fifth principal component captures the joint effect of corporate governance and the board of directors. When listed, these two factors negatively impact the success of a decision. A one standard deviation increase in these two factors will decrease the likelihood of a successful outcome by approximately 47 percent. A one standard deviation increase in our data would be equivalent to less than the change from neither of these variables being listed to just one of them being listed as a factor. As the histogram of this component and Table 7.5 show, most of the firms in our data do not list these factors as a contributor to success or failure, but when listed they are more likely to explain failure. This is similar to the individual effect of the board of directors found in our first model. The

Table 7.5 Relationship between corporate governance and board of directors

	Corporate Governance		Board of Directors	
	Is a factor	Not a factor	Is a factor	Not a factor
Failure	21	54	24	51
Success	13	75	12	76

implication of this is straightforward. When listed, these factors are likely to be a sign of trouble within the organization.

Our sixth and final principal component is ethical reputation, comprised mainly of commitment to ethics, firm's prior performance, and employee satisfaction. As with the previous principal component, firms are less likely to list these factors. Unlike in the previous case, when these variables are jointly listed they are just as likely to be cited in successes as failures. Our results are not statistically significant and we should be cautious when interpreting the effect of this principal component. We believe ethical reputation is important and these weak results can be explained by the two competing reasons for why business leaders list these factors.

PRINCIPAL COMPONENTS ORDERED LOGIT MODEL

Following the format of the previous chapter, we now turn to our final model, which is an ordered logit model. Rather than examining the impact of the 17 impact factors themselves, it examines the impact of our six principal component scores on our Likert scale measure of decision outcomes. Formally stated, the model we estimate is:

Decision Outcome (1-5) = β_0 + β_1 Labor Effectiveness + β_2 CEO Tenure + β_3 Marketing/R&D + β_4 Operations Management + β_5 Corporate Governance / Board of Directors + β_6 Ethical Reputation + β_7 Interview + ε

Logit coefficients, z-scores, and p-values are provided in Table 7.6.

In order to interpret these coefficients, we will use them to generate predicted probabilities of specific outcomes. The interpretation of this model will differ slightly from that of the previous chapter in that we will be predicting the effect of one standard deviation changes in principal component scores rather than discrete changes in our factors themselves. We focus on our first principal component, labor effectiveness, in Table 7.7.

As we move from one standard deviation below the mean value of this principal component to one standard deviation above the mean value, we see a positive impact on the probability of strong success. We also see that the effect increases in size, from a 4.6 percent increase to a 6.8 percent increase, as the value of labor effectiveness increases. Put differently, increases to labor effectiveness have a bigger impact on success for firms above the mean value of labor effectiveness.

Increases in labor effectiveness increase the probability of moderate

Table 7.6   Results, ordered logit with principal components

Principal Component	Coefficient	z-score (coefficient / standard error)	p-value (level of significance)
Labor Effectiveness	−0.5179186 (0.1486732)	−3.48	0
CEO Tenure	0.0841936 (0.1467565)	0.57	0.576
Marketing/R&D	−0.0715883 (0.1394762)	−0.51	0.608
Operations Management	0.4105197 (0.1460205)	2.81	0.005
Corporate Governance Board of Directors	0.3590642 (0.1391346)	2.58	0.01
Ethical Reputation	−0.0063614 (0.1431901)	−0.04	0.965

Table 7.7   Predictions after ordered logit, principal component 1 – labor effectiveness

Outcome	Labor Effectiveness, Mean Value − 1 s.d.	Labor Effectiveness, Mean Value (change from previous)	Labor Effectiveness, Mean Value + 1 s.d. (change from previous)
1 = Strong Success	0.0782	0.1246 (0.0464)	0.1928 (0.0682)
2 = Moderate Success	0.2908	0.3707 (0.0799)	0.4294 (0.0587)
3 = Neutral	0.1180	0.1191 (0.0011)	0.1056 (−0.0135)
4 = Moderate Decline	0.3469	0.2795 (−0.0674)	0.2061 (−0.0734)
5 = Strong Failure	0.1661	0.1061 (−0.0600)	0.0660 (−0.0401)

success as we move from one standard deviation below the mean to one standard deviation above. However, the size of the estimated effect falls slightly as the level of labor effectiveness rises.

As should be expected, changes to labor effectiveness have no clear effect on neutral outcomes. This is because increases to labor effectiveness

Table 7.8   Predictions after ordered logit, principal component 2 – CEO tenure

Outcome	CEO Tenure, Mean Value − 1 s.d.	CEO Tenure, Mean Value (change from previous)	CEO Tenure, Mean Value + 1 s.d. (change from previous)
1 = Strong Success	0.1341	0.1246 (−0.0095)	0.1157 (−0.0089)
2 = Moderate Success	0.3823	0.3707 (−0.0116)	0.3586 (−0.0121)
3 = Neutral	0.1178	0.1191 (0.0013)	0.1200 (0.0009)
4 = Moderate Decline	0.2675	0.2795 (0.012)	0.2914 (0.0119)
5 = Strong Failure	0.0983	0.1061 (0.0078)	0.1143 (0.0082)

are reducing the probability of failures (and therefore creating neutral outcomes) as much as they are increasing the probability of successes (and therefore reducing the number of neutral outcomes).

One standard deviation increases in labor effectiveness reduce the probability of a moderate decline by approximately 7 percent, and reduce the probability of a strong failure by somewhere between 4 and 6 percent. These results should not be surprising and are somewhat comparable to the ordered logit results from team effectiveness in the previous chapter.

Predictions for the next principal component, CEO tenure, are presented in Table 7.8. We estimate a very small decrease in the probability of success and a very small increase in the probability of failure. However as with the binary logit model above, the effect of CEO tenure is not statistically significant and these estimates should be interpreted with caution if used at all.

Similarly, the effect of marketing / R&D is not statistically significant, for reasons also explained above (Table 7.9). Firms listing factors included in this principal component are not significantly more or less likely to experience success.

The effect of our fourth principal component, operations management, is statistically significant (Table 7.10). A one standard deviation increase in the impact of factors included in this principal component serve to reduce the probability of a strong success by between 4 percent and 5 percent and reduce the probability of moderate success by between 5 percent and 6 percent. As may be expected, the effect on probability of neutral

Table 7.9   Predictions after ordered logit, principal component 3 – marketing / R&D

Outcome	Labor Effectiveness, Mean Value − 1 s.d.	Labor Effectiveness, Mean Value	Labor Effectiveness, Mean Value + 1 s.d.
1 = Strong Success	0.1170	0.1246 (0.0076)	0.1326 (0.008)
2 = Moderate Success	0.3604	0.3707 (0.0103)	0.3806 (0.0099)
3 = Neutral	0.1199	0.1191 (−0.0008)	0.118 (−0.0011)
4 = Moderate Decline	0.2897	0.2795 (−0.0102)	0.2693 (−0.0102)
5 = Strong Failure	0.1130	0.1061 (−0.0069)	0.0995 (−0.0066)

Table 7.10   Predictions after ordered logit, principal component 4 – operations management

Outcome	Labor Effectiveness, Mean Value − 1 s.d.	Labor Effectiveness, Mean Value	Labor Effectiveness, Mean Value + 1 s.d.
1 = Strong Success	0.1767	0.1246 (−0.0521)	0.0863 (−0.0383)
2 = Moderate Success	0.4200	0.3707 (−0.0493)	0.3080 (−0.0627)
3 = Neutral	0.1094	0.1191 (0.0097)	0.1195 (0.0004)
4 = Moderate Decline	0.2210	0.2795 (0.0585)	0.3345 (0.055)
5 = Strong Failure	0.0730	0.1061 (0.0331)	0.1517 (0.0456)

outcomes is effectively zero, as just as many successful outcomes become neutral outcomes as neutral outcomes become failures. Factors included in operations management increase the probability of a moderate decline by roughly 5.5 percent, and increase the probability of a strong failure by somewhere between 3 percent and 5 percent.

The effect of our fifth principal component is almost identical to that

Table 7.11   Predictions after ordered logit, principal component 5 –
corporate governance / board of directors

Outcome	Labor Effectiveness, Mean Value − 1 s.d.	Labor Effectiveness, Mean Value	Labor Effectiveness, Mean Value + 1 s.d.
1 = Strong Success	0.1693	0.1246 (−0.0447)	0.0904 (−0.0342)
2 = Moderate Success	0.4149	0.3707 (−0.0442)	0.3162 (−0.0545)
3 = Neutral	0.1110	0.1191 (0.0081)	0.1200 (0.0009)
4 = Moderate Decline	0.2282	0.2795 (0.0513)	0.3281 (0.0486)
5 = Strong Failure	0.0765	0.1061 (0.0296)	0.1452 (0.0391)

of the fourth (Table 7.11). A one standard deviation increase in the inclusion of corporate governance and influence from the board of directors as factors influencing a decision's outcome will lead to a decrease in the probability of a strong success of roughly 4 percent and a decrease in the probability of a moderate success of between 4 percent and 5 percent. Neutral outcomes remain unaffected for the same reasons – successful outcomes become neutral and neutral outcomes become failures at similar rates. The probability of moderate decline increases by roughly 5 percent, and the probability of a strong failure increases by between 3 percent and 4 percent.

Our last principal component is ethical reputation (Table 7.12). As we explained above, while we believe these factors matter, ethical considerations are just as likely to have been reported as reasons for success as reasons for failure. There is no statistically significant impact of this component.

In conclusion, we find statistically significant impacts for changes in only three of our six principal components (Table 7.13). Increases in the factors included in the labor effectiveness principal component tend to increase the probability of success and decrease the probability of failure. Increases in factors related to operations management and corporate governance / board of directors tend to have the opposite effect.

Table 7.12   Predictions after ordered logit, principal component 6 – ethical reputation

Outcome	Labor Effectiveness, Mean Value − 1 s.d.	Labor Effectiveness, Mean Value	Labor Effectiveness, Mean Value + 1 s.d.
1 = Strong Success	0.1239	0.1246 (0.0007)	0.1253 (0.0007)
2 = Moderate Success	0.3698	0.3707 (0.0009)	0.3716 (0.0009)
3 = Neutral	0.1192	0.1191 (−0.0001)	0.119 (−0.0001)
4 = Moderate Decline	0.2805	0.2795 (−0.001)	0.2786 (−0.0009)
5 = Strong Failure	0.1067	0.1061 (−0.0006)	0.1055 (−0.0006)

Table 7.13   Summary of results, Chapter 7

Principal Component	Impact on "Success" or "Failure," Logit Model	Impact on 5-point Likert Scale, Ordered Logit Model
Labor Effectiveness	Positive effect on success	Positive effect on strong success and moderate success
		Negative effect on moderate decline and strong failure
CEO Tenure	No statistically significant impact	No statistically significant impact
Marketing/R&D	No statistically significant impact	No statistically significant impact
Operations Management	Negative effect on success	Negative effect on strong success and moderate success
		Positive effect on moderate decline and strong failure
Corporate Governance Board of Directors	Negative effect on success	Negative effect on strong success and moderate success
		Positive effect on moderate decline and strong failure
Ethical Reputation	No statistically significant impact	No statistically significant impact

NOTES

1. We initially conducted this analysis with five principal components. In doing so, the third factor in our current six-component analysis (marketing) was essentially combined with our current fourth factor (operations management). The other factors in our current six-component analysis were virtually unchanged from a five-component analysis. We feel that the two functions of marketing and operations management are both important and different enough that they should not be combined in this analysis.
2. We define a moderate correlation as one greater than 0.30 and a strong correlation as one greater than 0.50 (Cohen, 1988).

REFERENCES

Cohen, J. (1988) Set Correlation and Contingency Tables, *Applied Psychological Measurement*, 12(4), 425–434.

Kaiser, H.F. (1960) The Application of Electronic Computers to Factor Analysis, *Educational and Psychological Measurement*, 20(1), 141–151.

8.   Overall research conclusions

In Chapters 6 and 7, specific and focused findings were presented. In this chapter, we will step back to synthesize these discoveries into broader patterns of relationships between decisions and performance.

Our premise is that the decisions and performance results are lessons for decision makers.

The overwhelming choice of performance measurement was revenues. This was more so for smaller firms than for larger firms but it dominated both classifications. Smaller firms looked more at employee productivity and customer loyalty as indirect measures of success while the larger firms of our study used financial measures. Our belief is that the financial measures are more standardized and can be verified. They are a common language of all businesses and for established firms that may be looking for acquisitions, mergers and joint ventures, the financial measures can be used to compare relative corporate value for businesses in different industries.

The use of revenues helps make this study cohesive in its dependent variable in spite of the fact that example firms were large and small, had experiences over thirty year spans, had very successful and catastrophic results and came from many different industries. We can use revenue for all of these examples and revenues also provide a common language, in dollars, of decision impacts on performance.

Businesses are very complex and very socialized systems. Even if revenues dominate as measurement, only the very small businesses use revenue as a sole performance measure. Small businesses we interviewed utilize informal performance measures. They may not conduct formal employee satisfaction surveys as larger businesses do but they do check in with employees with open ended questions like "how is it going" which is an invitation to uncover what employees feel.

Chapter 3 discussed performance in detail mainly from the perspective of the literature on performance. We encountered an expansion of performance measure in the research that are used in the practice of management.

They are market standing for one. His is not strictly market share but a mixed measure of how much respect there is for a particular firm in comparison to others. Standing can be used relative to competitors and market potential in the future.

Innovation is another performance factor which is looked at somewhat differently by practitioners. We found it to be a matter of if a company is innovative in its bones rather than a producer of innovations. It is less tangible but nonetheless meaningful for real world managers. "Either you are an innovative company or not" is the way one CEO put it. Being innovative counts and is looked at positively in every company we looked at. Not having a reputation for innovation is seen as being a detriment in the evaluation of other companies by firm CEOs surveyed. Though innovation was not a finding of great importance in our database, as it was cited as being a factor in 65 percent of successes and an almost identical 64 percent of failures, it still had an impact on firm reputation.

From practical management, we also found that the firm's physical resources were judged to be important as performance measures. This was less the case from the empirical studies. "How big is their plant? How old is it and how automated is it?" were questions asked by a CEO about a competing firm.

Financial measurements were shared as performance factors for practical managers and researchers.

Manager development was a performance measure informally used by real-world executives and less by academic researchers. The issues of manager development in decision making will be explored later. For many executives who made poor decisions, manager development is a salvation for their careers.

Manager performance and development along with worker productivity versus competitor worker productivity are used as human resource performance measurement. These can be done on an individual or aggregated basis.

Finally, public responsibility is a measure that has grown on both sides as being important. Academic studies have continued to explore the dimensions of public responsibility in considering issues of sustainability and how to make decent profits decently, a phrase used by business professors in melding the profit goal of businesses with the social goal of doing so in publicly acceptable ways. A host of initiatives among companies in the areas of community support, social investing, environmental sensitivity and other actions mark corporate responses to public responsibility. Public responsibility was not mentioned often in our sample and it is more a factor for larger businesses.

RECONCILING SHORT-TERM AND LONG-TERM PERFORMANCE MEASURES

In the interviews with business leaders, what became apparent was that the leaders were concerned with who was setting the performance standards. It was not only the business leader, it was outside parties for publicly traded firms. The investment community is the origin of one performance measure that was troublesome for CEOs. As put by the former CEO of Century Insurance of Iowa, Irv Burling, "I have to keep chasing down solid quarterly reports which show financial strength for investors. It makes pursuing long-term goals difficult because the long-term stuff does not show immediate results." This concern was a commonly expressed CEO comment. Burling understood that his ability to attract investors requires continuous financial performance but focus on that reduces the possibility of internal investment on promising but latent long-term returns. An example is a high technology company that thrives on new inventions yet still has to keep investors happy for the short term. CEOs in this position attempt to reduce costs of promising innovation, form partnerships with other organizations to share costs and sell equity interests in the future innovation. Objectives of innovation do conflict with financial performance objectives.

Who sets performance objectives in our study is a subject of concern for business executives. While they believe they can establish objectives themselves without board of directors or investor interference, they know that performance measures come in from the outside and these measures can conflict with the measures they set themselves. It is apparent company leaders take a broader view of their organizations than investors who can pick and choose who they can invest in.

UNEXPECTED FINDINGS AND CONCLUSIONS

To a person, the survey information showed that participants were quite willing to elaborate on both good and bad decisions. They had thought about examples of each before the interviews. The result was good detail on either extreme. In a sense, the range of decisions has been articulated by the participants. What's more, they had diagnosed both the positive and negative decisions that were made. The decisions were consequential for their businesses and it was clear that "never again" was the outcome of the negative decision. That meant carefully reviewing contracts with suppliers, doing more due diligence in hiring to get effective employees and doing more thorough marketing research before putting products into the market.

For the positive decisions, there was far less determination of what would be done next. Several interviewees believed the conditions for the original positive decision would not occur again. Others exploited the decision by following up with indicated demand on the part of customers. These responders believed the positive decision could be followed up on one way or another.

There was one interesting instance reported when timing meant everything. A non-domestic beer manufacturer decided to enter the U.S. market. That decision failed. Yet the company made the same decision a few years later and the decision was a success. The successful decision was made when U.S. beer drinkers became open to craft beers and reformulations of domestic beers. The importer obtained a foothold in the American market. The conclusion in this case is that exactly the same decision can be made in different market conditions and it can be a success even though the first try was a failure. A recommendation is to diagnose why an initial decision failed. If the diagnosis is correct and the decision problems fixed, the subsequent decision may succeed.

The decision makers interviewed had much more apprehension about making strategic decisions than tactical decisions. They were concerned about the downside of a bad decision and their concern was understandable.

The developer of the IBM PC was resurrected from failure and led a team that created the PC while off site in Boca Raton. The word at IBM was that after his failure, he expected to be dismissed. Instead, he was given another chance. His supervisor reportedly told him after the failure that he had just learned a very valuable lesson. It cost IBM a lot but they retained the manager and he launched the very successful PC for IBM after the company lagged behind others in PC development.

All of those interviewed knew what strategic decisions were. The definition of strategic decisions was written before the survey was conducted. For the case studies, your authors knew what decisions were strategic in nature and could therefore screen out tactical decisions.

When strategic decisions produced disastrous consequences, the deciders departed the company.

A further observation is that those who made strategic decisions all used some type of formality in making the decision except in the cases of very small firms where the owner acted as chief strategic decision maker. In other words, larger firms used some form of consultation with others in the firm or outside the firm in the decision process. They also used the rational decision model described in Chapter 2 or a variant of it in deciding. The "having a hunch" basis for making a decision was not used by survey participants.

What were some of the methods used for strategic decision making.

Very large firms used established consulting agencies such as KPMG or the McKinsey Group. Aside from the survey results, some of these large firms used agencies as justifiers for decisions already made. The consulting group was present just to put its approval mark on a decision in the view of the executives who arranged the consultation. A prestige consulting firm can give the decision just enough support to win wide approval from managerial staff.

STRATEGIC ORIENTATION

Strategic orientation is the matter of how organizations look at strategy when thinking about and acting on decisions. Based on probe questions of survey respondents and review of corporate histories, we observed there were differences between smaller (under 100 employees) and larger businesses. Smaller business owners and executives did not advance the notion that they thought of strategic decisions in a separate way than larger businesses did. Smaller businesses do not have levels of decision making the way larger organizations do. With smaller organizations, there are not as many strategic decisions to be made. The decision to survive and do everything to make that happen is predominant. For larger organizations, there are many other decisions: What to do with established revenue streams? What dividends to pay? Acquisitions? Research and development initiatives that are self-funded?

Larger organization leaders were more familiar with strategy since they encountered the subject as business school students. They were also more familiar with the tools of strategic decision making. Thus, their orientation was more strategic in nature. They knew that strategic decisions were going to have to be made in many different areas.

A generalized observation is that smaller firms were more transaction-oriented and larger firms more transformation-oriented. That poses an irony in that larger organizations are more difficult to organizationally transform.

Smaller firm owners and leaders were much more sensitive to individual customers than were the larger organizations. We heard stories of staying late to be available for a single customer and making after hour deliveries to customers for the smaller firms. For the larger organizations, the concept of customer equality came into play. Though not openly articulated, those who owned larger firms did not want it known they would go out of their way for certain but not all of their customers.

The small organizations may have wanted to become larger but they did not plan for it. A few told us they were just fine with the size they had become and did not want the managerial complications of becoming major firms.

Our conclusion on this is that businesses should be aware of their own strategic orientation and make the decision about whether they want to stay small or not. If they do, it will require much forward thinking and planning. This is a decision for leaders themselves and for their employees. A decision to grow will only be successful if correct decisions are made.

The results of bad decisions were felt equally by whatever classification of size. The scope of the bad decision was different of course for larger organizations. Privately, smaller business owners wished they could take back the bad decisions while in larger organizations with more and flexible resources had fewer regrets on the part of their leaders. That may be because they survived in their organizations while the individuals with worse judgment left the firm. This result reflects our further observation that the larger companies have more resource resilience and belief that eventually there will be success than the smaller companies.

LEARNING ORIENTATION

Learning from decisions can happen in two ways. One is on an individual basis and the other is organizational learning as in Peter Senge's *Fifth Discipline* (1990). Individuals can learn formally by going to school or informally through experience. A commitment to learning, a shared vision and open-mindedness are examples of cultural learning. These characteristics are inculcated in the organization and become ways of doing business. A learning organization actively seeks information about how its environment changes and acts on it.

For smaller organizations, owners and executives who discussed this almost always had prior experience with the business they were in. It came from previously managing an advertising agency, a hair salon, realty operation or print shop among other categories. This self-learning experience was used to guide their owned operation. Thus, none of our sample had formal vocational school or college training in the business. For decision makers in larger organizations, their learning was home grown in the form of tenure in the same organization and, very importantly, some measure of success at it. There was more academic experience in the larger firms evidenced by having more business degrees and MBAs present than the smaller firms.

Smaller firm respondents described themselves as Jacks and Jills of all trades and they did so for the fundamental reason that they could not afford to hire expertise. So, we found in either size of organization a learning orientation. This is true because none of our small firm participants inherited the business. Entrepreneurial small firms in our study were naturally learning organizations. Their founders had invented something or managed to find a new way of providing a service. These founders knew much less about businesses because they were educated in the sciences. The survival of these new firms depended greatly on their learning business skills or hiring people who did.

Both the small firms and the larger firms had an immense variety of decisions to make though it numbered more for the larger firms. Small firms' decision spans included physical facilities to distribution and warrantees, following the complete value adding process in the value chain.

There was no particular patterning to decision making in either small or large firms. To say that another way, if a company made a bad decision in their marketing program, there was almost no occurrence of a good decision. Although fix decisions were made to solve very major problems in one functional area, the tendency was that another problem and decision happened in another functional area, say the production process. Sometimes, the decision maker was named as the source of a problem but this stimulated a search for another root cause in our study. Taking a cue from H. Edwards Deming (2000)who believed processes and not people were the sources of problems, we are inclined to look at the process that was used to make the decision and not the individual. It is easier to replace people than fix systematic problems. Replacement is an answer but the underlying ways the decision was made lurks.

Are bad decisions hidden? Business organizations may knowingly make bad decisions but they make them anyway. An example may be a Hobbesian choice between two bad decisions. One might be to fire employees and another might be to default on a loan payment.

There can also be the example of concealed bad decisions. These happen when a business owner decides to do something illegal as did Bernie Madoff.[1]

If the decision is concealed it is difficult to do a diagnosis of it unless a party outside the decision uncovers it. A concealed decision that is consequential also destroys confidence in decision makers as eventually happened with Enron.[2]

We encountered several concealed decisions which turned out to be fatal for the business in the research. They were restricted to larger firms and they became business infamy as a result. We did not discover concealed strategic decisions for small firms. In one case though, the owners of the company were hiding an impending investment by a large outside firm. They did not want to share that with employees because they were concerned employees would leave for other jobs. Concealment to put together a deal was another category of hidden decisions. In this instance too, it led to resentment and distrust.

It is possible we could have discovered more instances of hidden bad decisions but most of the small firms included in the study had owners we did not personally know well, so it is a matter of sheer speculation to guess how much concealment happened in small firms.

What were the types of decisions made in small companies compared to larger companies? Initial location, initial location, initial location, location supplier contracts, alliances with recommenders, hiring staff, ethical climate, buying right equipment, small customers, buy out father, reducing staff size. Of these, the initial location decision predominates.

The types of decisions that led to unsuccessful outcomes told a different story. Among the negative decisions were allowing an underperforming employee to return to work. Other decisions were to pay employees poorly, too rapid business expansion, losing a major client, hiring outside IT providers, incomplete business plan, getting investors in the business, adding food products to retail line, lost opportunity to take over a successful business, expensive loans for the business and other related human resource management issues. The category of issues that dominated in terms of frequency of mentions were human resources issues, IT issues and financing issues.

It was a different story for the larger firms. As suggested earlier, there was a greater variety of positive decisions that led to successful outcomes. The positive decisions were to streamline models of customer products (multiple times), entry into U.S. markets, file for bankruptcy, win new investors, offer new products (multiple times), efficient operations, selling products compatible with leading firms, investing in new capital equipment, introducing new products (multiple times), multi-state operations (multiple times), creating a new search engine, internal call center, safety focus, credit insurance product, relaxation of customer qualifications, obtaining loans, lean manufacturing, flexible and open store design, new product introductions, acceptance of buyout offer, acquisition of other firms, new CEO and building staff loyalty were decisions that were cited as being positive decisions. Among the decisions, operational efficiencies, new products, new markets, acquisitions and financing methods dominated the list of positive decisions.

On the negative side of decisions for larger businesses, examples cited were too ambitious growth plans, decision not to take American Express cards, pursuit of production using carcinogenic materials, signing sponsorship with discredited celebrities, stock buybacks, decision to accept erroneous market research. Failure to control fixed costs, neglect of core product line, failure to shift to digital product line, expansion of parks to Europe, franchisee-based expansion, human resource management decisions, entry to China market, exclusion of line employees in management decisions, poorly designed programs to increase product utilization, poor employee satisfaction, failure to replace poor performing CEO, retaining poor performing products, entry into Canadian market, inconsistent product strategies, CEO ethics, massive database construction, insensitivity to cash flow, failure to detect obsolete products are among the poor decisions made. The most frequently mentioned decision failures were CEO ethics and poor performance, too ambitious growth plans, human resource management practices, product line management and new market entry. There were decisions made related to all these issues.

For both larger and smaller firms, human resource management issues were a commonality for poor decisions that frequently were observed.

As a conclusion for practitioners, the suggestion is to classify occurrences of types of problems for larger and smaller business. After determining which classification your firm belongs in, calculate the frequency of decisions and concentrate on those decisions which appear to be the major sources of positive and negative consequences. As for which to concentrate first, select the decisions which produce the best or the poorest results and ask about the extent of damage that can occur. Compare that to the amount of good that can happen from pursuing a positive decision. If the value of the gains from the good decision are projected to be greater than losses from the bad decision, then the good decision should be followed up on. A cost–benefit analysis of each alternative should be done. Organizations have their own cultures, of course, and the resolution of this choice may be anchored more in culture than mathematics. Risk-averse cultures would be more inclined to take the fix of a bad decisions while opportunity-seeking firms might seize the chance for more gain from the positive decision.

The review of positive and negative examples for both small and larger companies has not uncovered any new dimensions of decision-making results. Some of the decisions may seem mundane, even trivial but they were important for the organization in question at the time.

A conclusion about decisions and performance from the study at hand demonstrates that decisions are not isolated and discrete events. They are a continuum of other decisions. The creation of a business alone is a consequence of hundreds of decisions on the part of the founder. It is at the point after the formation of the business that we have taken up the trail of events. The founder has given us their decision sequence to work with. What we have found originates after that point in time. We also do not know what happens with our organizations except in the very few cases of business dissolutions. As a result, we talk about the continuum but we have only explored three years of decisions and performance. This may seem a short period of time but the interviewed business leaders agreed this was sufficient time to experience the results of the decisions.

There was some follow-up with a few but not many of the interviewees. This was for clarification of their comments or to ask their interpretation of overall results. These helpful comments led to affirmation of our own conclusions.

There were two different attitudes about participating in the interviews which were shared equally. About half actively looked forward to our interpretations of their decisions and consequences while the other half were a bit more reluctant, at least at first about the interviews. However, we were able to have all speak openly about the subject once we proceeded with the questions.

As an overall observation on our part, we found that all interviewees believed that decisions were an integral part of management. None felt that strategic decisions should be made by any other means than people. Decisions made by decision support systems should be confined to tactical decisions. They all recognized that strategic decisions are made under conditions of uncertainty and for several commented word to the effect that this is why I get paid the big bucks.

Business organizations can be looked at as the consequences of many decisions but the subjects of the interviews also believed they could influence but not control performance outcomes. If asked the reasons for poor performance, none of the individuals blamed macroeconomic conditions or government for the results.

An observation on the larger businesses incorporated in the study is that most reported revenue growth for either successful or unsuccessful decisions. The immediate expectation would be that poor decisions would lead to fewer revenues. However, larger businesses are, in effect, money machines. They can raise revenues by cutting costs more so than small businesses. They have established reputations and can dip into their brand equity. They can buy out competitors. They can greatly influence pricing as oligopolies. They hold greater reserves and have tax treatments that give them advantages other than rich revenue streams. The revenue streams may also be protected by long-term contracts with customers, a circumstance that small companies which are struggling to build reputations cannot do.

Larger businesses do not turn on a dime, so to speak. They make far fewer decisions that change their strategic paths. Like so many aircraft carriers, they do not easily change course and tend to "stick to their knitting" in a compound metaphor that at least is colorful if not entirely profound.

Our remedy for the protected revenue stream for larger businesses was to purposely include businesses that did not have continuously positive revenue growth. Some ten firms that were researched were definite failures. Their revenue flows declined and the business unit failed. This enabled us to include more variance in the firms with respect to growth and declines in revenues.

The examination of revenues was important because most of the firms, large and small, considered it to be the most important measure of performance. Very large firms we looked at sometimes stated in their mission statements that service excellence, exceptional customer experience and other generalized measures were what the company strived to achieve but there was far less objective measurement of how these goals were achieved. Customer satisfaction was cited by a few firms but this was measured by rating scales of satisfaction instead of behavioral parameters such as: Would you recommend this company to others?

Our conclusion is that meaningful measures of customer views about a firm on a cumulative and not simply a transaction basis have not fully been implemented. As a result, financial measures of performance remain in place among most firms. Interestingly, very small firms here take the pulses of their customers in informal but informative ways. Owners of the very small (five or fewer employees) companies depend on individual customers and the owners want to know and ask about what their customers think about them. It is very often part of the socialization rituals of sales where business owners edge into discussions about how well they are doing in the eyes of customers. They can do it because they have fewer customers than the larger firms and they need to do it because every customer counts for the small firm.

As an overall conclusion on the interview-based portion of our business review, the decision makers believed they were making every effort to win and retain customers.

When decision makers referred to making decisions in their business practices, they used the terms, "decisions I have to make" or "there are some hard decisions I am facing." We took these comments to mean that they were not looking forward to making decisions. The consequences of the decisions could have been layoffs or reduction in research and development both unpleasant outcomes. It might have also been true that the consequences were not as dire but the basis for making the decision was not clear. "Well, I'll have to play my hunch on this one," is the revelatory pronouncement of this situation. Or it could also be that the decision is recorded and assignment of that decision is made to a key leader in the organization. The results of these strategic decisions are set in stone and the decision maker's lifetime decision hitting record is something permanent. While a major league baseball hitter like Mickey Mantle might say, "I struck out or flew out two-thirds of the times at bat but if I got a hit one third of the time, I was a star," if a business decision maker only got their company on base a third of the time, they would not be considered stars. They would be in the minor leagues of business if in that field at all.

But there were positives expressed when the decision making actually occurred. "I was relieved when it was finally over," they would say.

Some responders would share the emotions of decision making. "If it was a really big decision with a lot of unknowns and big resource commitments, I would stay up all night before the decision was finally made. That's how upset I was," said a state public service commissioner. "I knew that the parties to the commission decision would scrutinize my logic and at least one side would seriously disagree with me." Another state mediator said the difficult decisions required detailed explanation to the loser in the case. "You wrote it up and 90 percent of the verbiage had to do with why the loser was wrong. The winner didn't really care why they won. But the loser always wanted a good explanation from you."

While some of the decisions we heard about emerged from sources and reasons outside the organization, many others emerged from inside. These were what we call dispute resolutions and they covered about a quarter of overall decisions. Very typically, they came from disputes between different departments that could not be resolved by the departments themselves and instead were escalated up the organization. An example would be a dispute between a marketing department that wanted to introduce a new menu item for a restaurant chain while the production department wanted to push out more established menu items. Decisions in this context required a referee with sound attention to pertinent facts. "It's easy to make a mistake in your thinking as you make a decision about who should win," said one vice president charged with resolving the debate.

MODEL REVISION

The model for business performance has been revised in light of this research to propose that performance is a function of decisions as modified by the external PESTN factors and internal factors chiefly labor effectiveness. In short, $P = f (D +/- PESTN, LE \text{ (labor effectiveness)})$. This formulation is subject to further study.

NOTES

1. Madoff, founder of Bernard L. Madoff Investment Securities, LLC, built a classic Ponzi scheme and delivered unusually consistent high returns for early investors in order to

solicit funds from new investors. It was later discovered that funds were essentially being taken from new investors in order to hide losses.
2. In a popular example, senior management with the energy brokerage firm Enron had hidden billions in losses from shareholders for years, eventually resulting in the firm's bankruptcy by 2004.

REFERENCES

Deming, W.E. (2000) *The New Economics: For Industry, Government, Education* (2nd edn), Cambridge, MA: MIT Press.
Senge, P. (1990) *The Fifth Discipline*, New York: Currency Doubleday.

9. Recommendations for business

This chapter focuses on recommendations your authors have for businesses. The recommendations are based on the research findings about decisions and performance. The way this chapter is organized is by way of first, an explanation of why these recommendations are pertinent, second, a presentation of findings and implications for businesses and third, some overall conclusions about this exploration of the decision and performance connection.

As a preliminary notation, though the focus of this chapter is on businesses, readers will find the suggestions can be applied to non-business organizations and are thus not exclusively business recommendations. The reader is the best judge of recommendation applicability. If you are in a governmental agency, a not-for-profit body or a quasi-public organization, the choice is yours. If the benefits of good decision making are expressed in terms of customer satisfaction rather than revenue growth, you will find the recommendations very likely to be useful.

HOW THE RECOMMENDATIONS CAN HELP

The immediate way that the recommendations can help is by offering ideas on optimizing decisions that have, for comparable other firms, produced better decisions. Replication of a decision making practice that produces intended results rather than unintended consequences is a desired decision outcome. This is a way of saying the predictability quality is high.

Another way recommendations can help to form a decision is when the reader notes a very similar set of internal and environmental conditions encountered by a business. If the same decision is made, there is a high probability that very similar results will happen for the reader's business.

There were major differences found in decision making and performance between smaller and larger organizations. These differences affect the recommendations as explained in this chapter.

The first recommendation for businesses under 100 employees is that they should realize they are very different in decision making practices than larger organizations. Businesses with over 100 employees tended to have more organizational superstructures than smaller businesses. The superstructures, in the form of boards of directors, were involved in review and approval of strategic decisions. The larger firms were organized as corporations while the smaller organizations took the form of sole proprietorships and partnerships. Based on this, the recommendation is for smaller organizations to have sounding boards of individuals who can advise on strategic decisions. While sounding board functions happen with boards of directors for larger organizations, such is not the case with the small business. The sounding board advisers can be volunteers or they can be paid per diems or retainers for their service of providing advice to business owners and executives about decisions. The decisions commonly made which sounding boards can aid with include major investment decisions, relocations, product and service initiation and expansion as well as merger, acquisition and joint venture options.

A sounding board of five or so members works well because there can be little mainly decorative and passive participation by members. A critically important element of sounding boards is that they provide expertise, skills and attributes that the business personnel do not have. A business lawyer member can advise on legal requirements for business formations in another state. A CPA member can help with building accounting reporting systems.

The sounding board, or as it may be known, advisory committee, will not have the authority or responsibilities for decisions but the stake will most likely be an interest in having the small business be successful. Retired executives from the industry that includes the small business in question are helpful.

The members of the sounding board also need to be truly objective in how they look at potential strategic decisions. Family members may not be appropriate as they can pull in the wrong direction with emotional ties to the business decision maker.

Small businesses lack the resources that larger businesses have in terms of decision making resources. This means less access to management consulting firms, using decision making application software and databases and hiring research personnel to aid in decisions. Experienced advisers can provide a resource that does not cost the small firm and that uses their own honed decision making skills. The advisers can ask "what if" questions of the small firm owner that may not occur to the small business executive, such as: What are consequences of the decision which might be unwanted and what assumptions have been made about the decision which are not realistic? For the adviser, the point is not to get into a discussion of repeating an irrelevant war story from the past, but to pose critical questions about current decisions the company faces.

Recognizing the value of outside opinions on decision making, another recommendation is to team up with other small firms and share resources for making better decisions or optimizing performance of the decisions. Some management consulting firms specialize in small business consulting for doing market and marketing research. Several small firms that do not directly compete with one another can pool resources to hire a research firm to collect decision data from other similar businesses which the individual client firms share among themselves. What makes this work is frank discussion about issues that the cooperating businesses face such as government regulation, changing customer demand, community relations and supplier issues. These subjects can be discussed without giving up company secrets to competitors if the participants agree to discuss issues rather than instances and the specifics of a particular problem are not revealed.

For larger businesses, sounding boards are likely to be less usable, especially if there is not a tradition of listening to outsider advice. Board members may feel disengaged in providing advice as they believe the company can and will buy the advice from well-known and expensive consulting firms.

The nature of decisions was different between larger and smaller businesses. For smaller businesses, most of the bad decisions were in personnel matters, contracts with suppliers and financing, financing of the business. Recommendations for personnel issues such as giving fired workers a second chance would be to involve a neutral party for advice on whether or not to offer a second chance. For contracts, legal review of the supplier contract can avoid problems later. Financing was an area in which poor decisions were made and small businesses could have avoided cash flow problems by planning for decreased revenues and increased costs in their business plans for businesses we examined. Managing cash flow is a special problem with small companies.

Larger organizations quite naturally experienced more varied bad and good decisions. While personnel, supplier and financing decisions are again present, distribution becomes a source of problems as distribution systems become more complex with larger businesses. Distribution problem solutions are highly individualized to the firm but a strong recommendation for the larger company is to have a long-term distribution strategy. The distribution strategy addresses current distribution but also encounters future distribution issues when changes in distribution fundamentals become more difficult. Company owned versus independent agents, number and role of channel intermediaries and exclusive versus wide distribution are among the decisions of concern for the larger firm.

An area of bad decisions for larger businesses comes with corporate governance. This is far less a concern with smaller businesses which have far less formalization of accountability. For larger businesses, relations between the board of directors and the CEO were found to be the source of poor decisions and performance. There are instances we discovered where the CEO took bold moves for a vision they wanted for the company that the board did not want and other instances of passive CEOs who played largely caretaking roles. A recommendation depends on the circumstances but an effort to assure alignment of CEO and board agreement on long-term strategy and goals is certainly in order.

One large credit union president told us that there are decision making tensions between the credit union board of directors and the CEO. "You have to go into board members knowing your decisions will be backed," he said. "If you start losing, it's a steep slide downward."

The recommendation here is to consider that decisions by CEOs are made in a band of acceptance. Boards will accept decisions in the range of no strategic decisions by inert caretaker CEOs and wildly opposing (to the board) decisions by an imperial and combative CEO. This may seem a wide breach but running companies is not always a matter of meeting financial performance targets but fit with corporate board values. The values may be ethical in nature or more subjective like employee satisfaction.

The CEO should track his or her decision performance record with the board. By keeping track of a win/loss record of strategic decisions, the CEO's standing will be revealed. Perplexed CEOs who find themselves with losing records without knowing why might want to check on the nuances of decision making. Was a board member humiliated? Were discussions on decisions cut off prematurely by a CEO bent on ratification without dissent? It might be as simple as corporate manners that explain board alienation from CEOs. Boards of directors are people with egos and simple good manners. One CEO of a large financial company described how manners evaporated when he announced his retirement. His executive committee acted bored when he wanted to elaborate on an agenda item. "They just nodded and pressed on to the next item," he said still smarting from the slight years later.

If advice can be encapsulated in a word, that word is "systematic." That applies to companies of any size. Systematic means to not be fixed on hunches in making decisions. Instead, it means using established methods to gather and analyze information and arrive at logically driven decisions. The use of hunches in decision making and the tendency to not change a decision if contradictory information is revealed introduces considerable individual human bias into corporate decision making.

Business leaders who use hunches may be able to explain their reliance on hunches based upon their opinion that playing their hunches in past decision making accounted for their success in business. They might also be reluctant to explain how they arrived at decisions preferring instead to project it as a mystery as to how they make decisions, perhaps fearing that a simple method they use will be easily adopted by others and they will lose their "power" in decision making.

Objectively, there is no reason to believe that using hunch decision making causes better decisions to be made than decisions made which follow accepted organizational decision making practices. When considering individual decision making, there is agreement that diligent groups make better decisions in the long run. Janis and Mann (1977) are researchers who long ago classified individual problems as seeing the consequences of inaction will not be great, leaping to the first available solution without analysis, passing the decision to someone else and reacting in a panic mode unnecessarily. Very plainly, the solution may be worse than the problem in such circumstances. The straightforward recommendation here is to do some level of team analysis of the prospective decision. This is a barebones systematic response to strategic decision making.

RECOMMENDATIONS FOR DECISION MAKING TOOLS

A major recommendation for businesses both small and large is the use of tools for making strategic decisions. Tools used in business analysis can be used systematically in decision making. As a guideline in practice, using decision analysis tools helps in the following ways:

- Tools reduce the reliance on hunches, guesses and intuition in strategic making. The use of these very subjective methods causes poor decisions to be made.
- Tools provide a means to trace backwards on decisions and establish if or if not a particular tool is associated with a positive or negative decision outcome.
- Tools deal with more objective facts and measurement of outcomes and can accordingly offer a common language for analysis of decisions.
- Within business, there are commonly accepted business analysis tools. Different industry groups use similar measurement tools. This enables single businesses to compare their position in the industry.
- Tools that are used for decisions have been proven more so than non-established decision evaluation methods such as informal consensus of success or failure.

- Established decision tools have longer lifetimes than informal tools.
- Decision tools often build on one another to increase their robustness while the informal tools generate and are replaced as management fashion dictates.
- Tools can be taught and learned to preserve their longevity whereas individualized decision making tools may reside only in the mind of a key business decision maker.

This review offers rationale for subjecting decisions to a method for making them with emphasis on how this differs from the alternative of non-quantitative, intuitive-based decision making. Our interviews strongly endorsed the use of data-based decision making and this itself is a consequential finding.

DECISION MAKING TOOLS SPECIFIED

Financial Analysis Tools

For most businesses, financial analysis is at the heart of sound decision making. The common thread of these tools is the use of numbers. It is hard to argue with numbers if the assumptions behind them are correct and the calculation is accurate. These advantages are countered by the other side of numbers. They can be difficult to produce and induce criticism.

Presented in an ascending order of their comprehensiveness in this sequence are common tools used to analyze business strategic decisions:

a) Payback: This is a simple tool which reveals how long it will take for a decision to return the amount of money invested in the decision. As an example, if the decision to do something costs $100,000 and the businesses gains $1,000 a year as a result of the decision, the payback period is ten years.

b) Return on investment and other ratio tools: A very commonly used method which compares the returned revenues to the initial investment as a percentage. Return on decision investment is calculated as the annual return on the investment divided by the total investment amount. It is expressed as a percentage. Like payback, it is conceptually straightforward. Return on investment is a very common ratio tool for evaluating decision results but there are other ratios as well.

c) Decision trees: This tool takes an initial decision question and branches it out to defined choices and outcomes as a result of choices. The estimated probabilities of each outcome and the value of that outcome is calculated and a decision path optimizing value is selected by decision makers. The decision tree produces a series of decisions that will result in the most optimal result, typically in terms of dollars of gain. The key to having the decision tree work is accurate estimates of the possible gains or losses from each path as well as the probability of each outcome.

d) Cost–benefit and cost effectiveness techniques: These are time value of money techniques in which the stream of benefits over the years are compressed to a present day figure. It is based on the idea that a bird in the hand is worth two in the bush. A company can invest in alternatives other than internal options and receive income over a period of time. A decision that is made has to beat the results that would happen if the firm invested in outside choices such as equities available in the stock market. The cost–benefit or cost effectiveness analysis has to show a gain above other decisions to be justified. Cost–benefit and cost effectiveness analysis are done the same way but cost–benefit is used for yes or no decisions on major projects and cost effectiveness is used to compare several projects and to decide which one should be selected.

The way these tools work is that the expected benefits and costs are lined up on a timeline. The length of the timeline is set as the time over which the costs and benefits will occur. The costs are usually expressed in dollars and the benefits the same way. The costs and benefits are assigned to specific times on the timeline. The difference is found between the costs and benefits for each time point (usually a year) and the results are multiplied by the present value interest factor for that year. The present value interest factor is usually the firm's cost of capital. The time point differences as adjusted by the present value interest factors are then added up. If the sum is more than $1.00, the decision is worth making as an investment. It is worth making because the compressed value is more than what the company would gain from investing at its cost of capital.

When to Use and Not Use Specific Tools

Table 9.1 advises on the matter of when to use or not use a particular tool we have presented.

A Caution with Tools

The tools of making decisions are plentiful but too many tools can spoil the broth, so to speak. As reviewed, different tools produce different

Table 9.1   Choosing decision tools

	When to Use	When Not to Use
Payback	Short duration where time value of money not significant	When substantial benefits happen after payback period
Ratio	For basic, simple comparisons with other decisions	When scale of investment is important
Decision Tree	When optimal decision is based on many other decisions	When probabilities of decision outcomes and value of outcomes cannot be determined
Cost–Benefit/Cost Effectiveness	Major decisions with multiyear impacts and when other investment choices available when decision is scrutinized in financial terms	When data is not available. For very short-term projects

Source: From Bolland (2017).

measures and the decision maker will have to decide which tools work best based on the result they produce.

Using too many tools may produce contradictory results about the deci-sion results. Making one decision may produce a relatively high 15 percent rate of return but only $100 of revenue. The decision measurement should be done with reference to the firm's overall strategy and superfluous measures should be discarded.

Another caution is that newly introduced decision measurement tools should not be used until they have won acceptance by industry and financial analysts. This same caution applies to decision support software programs. In fact, measurement tools should not be used when they are incompletely understood by those who uses them and not understood by those who make business policy on the basis of them.

It is not only new tools of decision evaluation that should be avoided, it is that the tools that are in use are used with great frequency should be employed. These tools can be quickly revealed by trade journals, consult-ing agencies, 10K reports with the Securities and Exchange Commission, annual reports and informed reporters are some sources. Using standard industry measures allows comparisons of performance among the industry players.

Table 9.2   Tracking decisions

	Number of Decisions/ Year	Number of Successful Decisions	Percent of Successful Decisions	Comments
Executive / Key Administrative				
Production				
Legal				
Financial				
Marketing / Sales				
Administrative Support				

Another recommendation is to categorize business decisions by type of decision and then compile the results of the decisions. The categorization might be based on the functional areas of the business. Using this as an example and displaying it in the form of a table, the depiction would be as shown in Table 9.2.

The key piece of information from this table would be the percentage of successful decisions and what functional area the decisions came from. The functional area with the lowest percentage of successful decisions might be a candidate for improving decision making. The table only shows numbers of decisions though and the value of the decision could also be weighed by functional area or even each decision within the functional area. Executive decisions count more than administrative support decisions. This would be a consideration for the weighing of functional areas in the review of decisions.

The table will spotlight where decision making could improve. A follow-up step would be to look more closely at how decisions are made in the functional area using the standard rational decision making process of problem identification, analysis, development of alternative solutions, selection of a solution, implementation and evaluation. Each of these steps can be explored as root causes of decision making flaws. Was the implementation phase done correctly? Was the problem accurately specified? These are examples of further digging for an answer.

This tool is straightforward and leads to solutions but the difficulty may be in coming up with the data on decisions and recording them. It is essential to record the critical decisions which are strategic in nature and avoid minor decisions with few consequences.

Bain & Company (2016) has offered ways to make better decisions as a process. Decision effectiveness can be benchmarked by quality, speed, yield and effort. Decision criteria are needed to start the process. Next, it is necessary to focus on key decisions because it is not possible to consider the thousands or even millions of decisions that businesses face daily. Focus on strategic decisions is obvious but operational decisions that may not appear to be major but are still made frequently and can cumulatively affect the entire organization should be attended to. Estimating the value at stake and the degree of management attention required are two screens to determine criticality of the decision. The next step is to make the decisions work by making sure exactly what decision has been. This is coupled with who will be involved in each aspect of decision formulation and action. The fourth step in the Bain process is to build the organization around these decision making principles and the last step is to embed decision capabilities into the organization. Bain reports that successful companies build a foundation for effective decision making by mapping ambitious goals and involving leadership early.

The Bain approach is systematic and continuous and thus is recommended.

BUILDING A CULTURE OF SOUND DECISION MAKING

Recommendations for improving decision making are plentiful in the popular business media. The majority of these focus on tips for individuals on making better decisions. What must also be emphasized is the culture of the organization. The set of values and practices that the business advances marks its own culture. This is more than individuals making decisions, it is how groups make decisions. A culture that values sound decision making celebrates when it happens and guides toward better performance when it doesn't. Sound decision making is apparent when decisions lead to better performance. That is certain but there are more subtle ways that lead to this result too.

A culture that encourages decision making is a prerequisite. This is an idea which is abundantly given lip service but when the idea comes into practice, the "costs" of decision autonomy prevent actualization. A decision by a line employee to stop a production line is costly for a continuous throughput business such as an automobile production line. Employees need to know the consequences of stoppages and supervisors need to accept the consequences of decision empowerment by line employees. That means tolerating mistaken production shutdowns just as employees tolerate bad managerial decisions. A culture that makes room for these instances is a learning culture as in Peter Senge's book

The Fifth Discipline (Senge, 1990), because learning happens from mistakes.

The recommendation of having a decision making culture happens if good decisions are made, obviously but they will be further encouraged if they are spotlighted. Those in the organization who have made good decisions are honored and they are promoted. Those in the organization who consistently make extraordinary and correct decisions are invaluable. The business owes it to decision makers to identify what constitutes sound decision making.

The cultivation of sound decision making is another recommendation. Given the critical nature of decisions in the performance of the organization, it is clear that decision advisers can be found who are able and willing to help with decisions. This can be an informal group but not a group whose members are isolated from one another. The skills of decision making can be shared among different individuals. Motivated decision makers feed upon each other in a mutually nourishing not a cannibalistic way which would occur if one department team wins and another loses.

It is also possible to assign roles to a group decision making body. One person may be an ideas advocate and another may be a devil's advocate. This puts further rigor into the analysis of possible decisions.

A recommendation that will be needed to assure the consistency of good decisions is training in decision making. As one executive vice president told us, "Decision making gets better the more frequently you do it." Better decision makers have longer tenures in our opinion but they will not be there forever. The longevity of the firm depends on training decision makers. There are short courses and university extension courses that offer decision making. Our comment is that this skill can be learned as an apprentice to a senior decision maker.

Prioritization of decisions is a recommendation of ours. A manager could easily make their job be a series of hundreds of daily decisions if they wanted to do so. But this would leave no time for anything else. Modern management prescribes planning, organizing, leading and controlling as management duties. Deciding is part of each but the manager would be negligent if they only decided.

Most decisions can be subdivided by time. In other words, regular checkpoints can be inserted into a project which ask the question: Should we continue with this decision? Strategy theorist Charles Hofer argues that strategic management is not about making future decisions but about the futurity of present decisions. His language puts considerable weight on the quality of decisions of the day so they do not have to be reversed tomorrow. Prioritizing decisions means searching for decisions which can be sustained without the insertion of pro forma review points, which mainly are answered by staying the course and not departing from it or reversing it. A first resort in making decisions is to determine if they do need to be revisited. To establish if this is the case, a decision chronology over several weeks will reveal how many decisions are frequency-bound in terms of review points.

Another question to ask about making decisions is whether or not they are truly strategic or tactical in nature. Our interviews established that true strategic decisions were far fewer in number than tactical decisions. Sorting decisions using this screen of tactical versus strategic will go far in a prioritization decision about decisions.

Related to the prioritization issue is a timing consideration. A recommendation is to line up decisions on the basis of when they need to be made and focus on the decisions that need action the soonest. Prospective decisions will arrive from many people continuously so there should be a traffic cop kind of function in re-sorting the order of action by a strategic decision maker.

Different decisions will have different priorities as they come in for review. Normally, the functional areas of the business will have their own preference for immediate action. Marketing will have its priorities and production will have its top decision candidates. Much like a newspaper editorial board picking what goes on the front page from competing stories, the business's executives can make choices about what to decide and which department gets first attention.

A very pertinent issue is consideration of prioritization of functional area nominees for decisions to be made in the context of other origins for decisions. A major regulatory issue may enter the fray or an environmental issue. These can affect the entire business marginally at the functional level but profoundly at the total organizational level. Here again, the PESTN framework is a screening tool to entertain this possibility.

Learning from bad decisions is among our recommendations but rather than restating the blazingly apparent value of this pronouncement, we want to explore how that learning is infused into the business.

After it becomes apparent that the decision did not produce the expected outcome, there may be a tendency to personalize the outcome and blame individuals for what happened. The "solution" then is correct individual behaviors. This may be a true cause but it may also cloak a process problem, something that Deming cautioned about in observing that it is not people but processes that largely explain quality problems. Citing individuals as causes seems premature but it is natural since organizations expect individuals to be responsible for their decisions. The remedy for bad decisions, especially a series of them, can be decisive – dismissal but that prolongs a process error (which is a very common source of error compared to human error in the view of Deming). Replacing decision makers can go on for a long time, yet continued decision problems persist unless the whole system of making decisions is addressed. Even if dismissal does not occur, the errant decision maker can become gun shy and become very conservative in their decision making or even reluctant to do so.

To alleviate and isolate the individualization of performance problems from decisions generally, a culture which evaluates all major strategic decisions is a recommendation to avoid the isolation and despair of errors-only review when individuals are blamed. The Air Force Thunderbirds aerial demonstration team regularly conducted de-briefings of its practices and performances, not just when pilots did things wrong. Individual blame is reduced as a focus in routine review of important decision and again; it is a hallmark of sound business decision making to practice this.

PERSPECTIVE ON BUSINESS DECISION MAKING

A leading theorist on organizational decision making, James March (1960) provides context for making better decisions. March points out that executives face three initial problems, namely: to which of the many problems should they direct their attention, how much time, effort and expense should they invest in resolving uncertainty about that problem, and what solution to the problem should be used? Although much effort is directed to the last question, March states the first two are more important according to research. His studies found that a large share of simulated workload was spent on very routine decisions. Planning decisions lagged as workload increased.

The implication from this and the consequent recommendation is that decision makers should relinquish very routine decisions to policies and procedures about such decisions in place of individual decisions about them. It is also indicated that planning (and presumably making prospective decisions) may fall to the wayside if the workload increases.

REFERENCES

Bain & Company (2016) The Five Steps to Better Decisions, retrieved on November 28, 2016 from http://www.bain.com/publications/articles/the-five-steps-to-better-decisions.

Bolland, E. (2017) *Comprehensive Strategic Management*, Bingley, UK: Emerald Publishing.

Janis, I. and Mann, L. (1977) *Decision Making: A Psychological Analysis of Conflict, Choice and Commitment*, New York: Free Press.

March, J. (1960) Business Decision Making, *Hospital Topics*, 38(5), retrieved on January 31, 2017 from http://www.tandfonline.com/doi/pdf/10.1080/00118568.1960.9955073.

Senge, P. (1990) *The Fifth Discipline*, New York: Doubleday/Currency.

10. Deciding and performing in the future

In this final chapter, our attention is on the near future. We look at how businesses will make decisions and how performance will be measured. This will be both a projective and speculative effort, projective in that we will take what we have presented about the evolution of deciding and performing in the past and currently and use that as a basis for depicting what might happen in the near (three to about 20 years) future. It will be speculative in the sense that we will depart from purely known trends in business decisions and the measurement of performance and incorporate some new environmental forces that could dramatically alter present trends. If we were to bet on which of these might be most accurate, our answer would be the projective trend analysis. However, this approach alone is incomplete. Speculation can be more profound in the long run because it follows streams of probable events that are not apparent in pure trend analysis. As examples: take the emergence of the Internet and World Wide Web which are now almost tiresomely cited as unforeseen but revolutionary disruptions in the way business is being done.

For the projective part of our examination, we will look at the history of business from 1950 through contemporary times. Also, we will re-examine pertinent management thought, economic thought, organizational behavior and management evolution. For the speculative part, we will cast our net freely in a sea of possibilities, not certainties, to catch possible new environmental factors that might alter expectations that would be derived from trend analysis exclusively. As a final step, we will integrate what we see from the past with what is plausible in the future. No specific method is used for this other than observations of the past and informed speculation of a plausible future. The future look demands that we be reasonable but it also accommodates free form creativity which allows us to entertain far-fetched but coherent views of what could happen with businesses in the future.

This review of trends in work that may explain changes in decision making is based on a very wide-ranging literature review which includes the Bureau of Labor Statistics, the Society of Human Resource Management, popular business articles and other sources. There are some constant themes coming from the review which include technology, the changing nature of work, the composition of the workforce in the future, globalization effects and the organization of corporations. We will derive implications from each of these on business decision making. The review of these sources also touched on future scenarios which were too far-fetched in our judgment – say a workforce devoid of people. This and others were not judged to be credible in the near future and are thus not included. Flying cars and personal limitless function robots are thus not described here. What are described, in our speculative leap, are little-known science discoveries which plausibly could occur, an example being nanotechnology.

FROM THE PAST

The changes in the future mostly originate from the actuality of the past. The degree to which they do is our interest and, as such, we need to examine a few past trends to establish the degree these influence the future. Looking at the past is not a perfect indicator of the future but it does provide a vector with a force behind it. That vector is a line from which there may be directional shifts but it is less likely fundamental displacements from the direction things are going. Even less likely is that the directional vector will evaporate. If it does, that's where speculative exploration of the future can come into play.

While some of the objective conditions of businesses are hard to measure and predict such as consumer confidence, other conditions are easier. We will confine ourselves to the more objective and measurable conditions.

The first of these is in unionization of workers. One characteristic of the past has been the diminishment of unionization in businesses. In the mid-1950s, union workforce participation in manufacturing was about half the workforce while that had shrunk to about 10 percent in 2010. Are there new sources of unionization that would reverse the downward trend? Some such as Michael Harrington (1968) suggested public workers would be a source but this has not borne out. In fact, public unions have been diminished in strength as right to work laws in the U.S. have been enacted in more states and public unions have been crippled in states such as Wisconsin. As far as decision making is concerned, the influence of public unions on corporate decision making has been reduced. While some very large unions have gained membership on boards of directors such as General Motors, that does not substantially change the overall influence of unions on decisions.

The reach of unions into new labor sources of Asia and Latin America is a possibility for growth but labor power, as expressed in terms of increasing wages is not projected to grow as much as capital power in the form of the capacity to use capital to increase and concentrate capital. That is a conclusion of Thomas Piketty (2014). In his words:

> The overall conclusion of this study is that a market economy based on private property, if left to itself, contains powerful forces of convergence, associated in particular with the diffusion of knowledge and skills; but it also contains powerful forces of divergence, which are potentially threatening to democratic societies and to the values of social justice on which they are based. (Piketty, 2014, p. 571)

National economies can be directed toward either direction. Specifically, the major economic destabilizing force is that the private rate of return on capital "can be for significantly higher for long periods of time than the rate of growth of income and output" (Piketty, p. 571). This implies that wealth accumulates more rapidly than output and wages. The consequences of wealth distribution are dire according to Piketty. Wealth concentration and gains dominates wage growth. "With the average return on capital of 4–5%, it is therefore likely that the r>g (r being the rate of return on capital and g is the rate of growth of income and output) will again become the norm in the twenty-first century" (Piketty, 2014, p. 572). As far as business decisions are concerned, those decisions made which favor increasing capital could have a greater impact on wealth creation than decisions regarding wages and output.

A conclusion we draw from the diminishing of the union at work is decisions about labor contracts will be fewer in number and the relative power of unions in contract relationships will be greatly lessened.

Another objective condition is the composition of the American workforce. The composition of the American workforce has also become more diversified. In the United States, the percentage of white male entrants has shrunk considerably since 1950. In totality, there is much more gender balance now and more immigrant participation. For the impact on decisions, this puts a premium on increasing sensitivity to how corporate strategic decisions will affect workers and consumers. Even though wage gains may not happen for industrialized and post-industrialized countries, the conditions of work will need to be expanded to accommodate worker needs and expectations. Similarly, more diversified consumers mean production of a wider variety of consumer goods.

The greatest impact of an increasingly diverse workforce is and will be the increasing diversity of thought that comes with people having different backgrounds. For decisions, a greater variety of opinions emerge with a workforce with more Asian, Hispanic, African and Middle Eastern origin. Diversity of thought and opinion also occurs with four generations in full work and with more female work participation. These are the essence of diversity and they give decision makers a wider view of the consequences of decisions. It may seem that this wider view would be cumbersome. There may be a need to explain the parameters of the decision or the decision itself to people different from ourselves, but those involved in decision making can very often quickly explain the decision that is needed and what the consequences will be for anyone who needs an explanation.

The big speculative factors with the greatest possibility of affecting a change in the nature of business are already present but they may be even more pronounced in the future, among customers, competition, technology and the global environment for business. These are Gibraltar-sized topics but they are critical rocks in the systems of change. Each will be considered separately.

With customers as a speculative factor, the possibility of sudden demographic shifts in taste and preferences is less pronounced. Demographic study produces slow-moving changes in demand, not instantaneous ones. The changes in numbers of age range cohorts is predictable, which is a boon to projectors of demand. Only very drastic and worldwide conditions can alter this factor. Such possibilities arise from the passage of the horsemen of death and disease as well as natural environmental disasters that would cause death and disease.

The factor that does lead to changes in taste and preference is consumer empowerment. That is embodied in the amount of information consumers have about their decisions on purchases which is directly related to the kinds of decisions producers make about what to offer them. Consumers share this information more easily and readily through social media. As an example, social media runs restaurant reviews. Viewers can get rapid and largely honest feedback from customers. A few decades ago, information about dining experiences came from restaurant sponsored advertising or other paid advertising.

Shifts in demand can happen quite quickly. Test marketing can happen more frequently and involve better-defined target markets through social media thus reducing the costs for the producer firm. Another aspect of this empowerment of the consumer is the sharing of satisfaction with products and experiences directly with other consumers. This shared knowledge is more trusted by customers than are company-produced advertisements for reasons just cited.

The rapidity and dissemination of product and service satisfaction information means that decisions can be made more quickly by customers. It has become easier to find more up-to-date cuisine, new restaurants and availability of food services. This fact has intruded further back into the supply line as grocery stores now package food for customers ready-to-pick-up or be delivered to customer houses. The decision process and content has broadened to not only restaurant choices but to food supply choices as well. Customer power in the future is fueled by the reach of communications to them. There are almost no corners of the world any more. Amazon's acquisition of Whole Food portends the end of old habits of grocery which are inherently inefficient requiring trips to the store, selection of items, lines at check outs and bringing groceries home.

Communication technology through television and radio broadcast, satellite communications and the Internet allows for every country and most sectors in the country to have access to information about products and services. This is the emergence of consumer power at the store level where preorders can be placed and goods delivered with much more efficiency. The consumer has more choice in decisions if grocery aisles can be surveilled and filled at home, not in the aisle.

Individualization of other mass market goods as a response to consumer empowerment is also at work. Pioneered in the PC market by Dell Computers, individualization lets customers customize features on its computers. The seemingly oxymoronic mass customization became real.

A probable result of mass customization might very well be individualized clothing whereby clothing can be tailor made by taking critical body measurements. The decision function would change from how much of each size of clothing should be produced to how can we efficiently produce clothing for every size of human? For food, the customization of food provision would be what customized food packages would be cost effective to provide.

BUSINESS ANALYTICS

Several years ago, Gartner Inc., which is a technology think tank, predicted that business intelligence and analytics would be a major factor in the future. It is also a way that producer companies can keep up with empowered consumers, fight knowledge with knowledge, so to speak. The empowerment of consumers as a factor of the future is balanced by the empowerment of the producers. This has both projective and speculative dimensions. It is projective because it builds upon what is already happening, and speculative because the advances of the floodgates of information about consumers allows for even more unanticipated and inventive ways that producer companies can find out very specific things about consumers. Facebook has the capacity to build profiles of its users and make these available to commercial interests. As an example, your political persona may be built based on your comments about candidates and officeholders based on comments you posted on Facebook. In similar fashion, your spending habits including price preferences may be built into your profile. These profiles already exist. Pricing profiles of consumers already exist. Firms know what consumers are willing to pay so they adjust prices in accordance with this information. Consumers who do not know this behave as though provided prices are market-based, which would be their expectation.

This moves company decision making out of the company and into the hands of third parties who can assemble and target consumers on multiple dimensions. We see it as transfer out of the company decision making and into independent fee-for-service providers. The producing companies can avoid the costs of building their own and even more importantly the costs of maintaining individual customer profiles.

So, the advantages consumers gain by obtaining and sharing information about products and services will be countered by producers who will get more information about their customers.

Even more, the ability of corporations to put together or hire others to put together large databases eases the decisions they have to make about profiling their customers.

Our prediction is that the trend of companies getting more information about customers will lead to issues of privacy and the decisions that accompany that. What customers buy may embarrass them. They may want to buy without being known. Customers may not want information about themselves known and resold to others. It is also the case that the information about them is wrong as in many cases of consumer credit information.

The nature of the decisions on the part of the company are: how much information they need about customers, what the company will do with it, what assurances the company will provide to customers about misuse, how long the private information will be kept or if the information will be destroyed.

Something notable that emerged indirectly from the CEO interviews was the idea that decision making is not conclusive or a final state of affairs in the contemporary organization. It is more a continuous process where one decision leads to another. This is acknowledged in the feedback loop of the strategy planning process. In that process, the results of strategic decisions are the starting points for next year's decisions. The production of products is more like a continuous process. Take the example of cruise ship construction. In the past, it was done all in one dock, from the keel upward to the finished ship, but no longer. Giant cruise ships are now started in one dock as a segment of the whole ship. Other segments are built at other locations. Segment subsections are built and literally flipped over in docks so bottom sides can be wired and plumbed. Other segments are tugged in and welded together. It all becomes a process in much the same way that Airbus Industries trucks in major A 380 components from four countries and puts together the aircraft in Toulouse, France. Cruises are booked before the shakedown cruises occur for the cruise ships and A 380 commercial aircraft are started before ink dries on the order contracts. It is process, process and the acceleration of process that defines manufacturing of huge products today and in the future. Regarding decision making, this means more time constraints on the duration of decisions and the necessity of making the correct decisions initially because there is far less opportunity to reverse bad decisions when projects are underway.

If this kind of decision making is the case, then the techniques of analyzing business decisions can be done more validly by looking incrementally at the contribution of each decision to the overall stream of actions. Then, the sequence of making decisions can be analyzed as mathematical derivatives instead of discrete calculations. Such analysis would allow more focus on rates-of-change of decisions which itself make more dynamic analysis of ongoing decision impacts possible. So, instead of sampling some decisions, all decisions would be subject to analysis. Reliance would be reduced on purely historic decisions as a basis for future action.

COMPETITIVE ANALYSIS AND DECISION MAKING

The emergence of continuous and sound decision making is evident as a future trend in considering competitors and their role in business. An example of continuous decision making happens in the field of competitor analysis. Chess-like moves of competitors where one party moves and that triggers a move by a competitor are a rule of the game. In the business world, a price reduction of a product by one competitor can provoke an even greater price reduction by another competitor, or it may cause a product improvement by the competitor for a similar or same product. These chess-like moves are sequential and follow the rules of the game. In business, the moves are sequential because the reaction should not be multi-moves (since that may reveal competitor strategy). In business, the moves can be off the board by expanding the playing surface to new markets so chess has its limitations as a model for business decisions. Nevertheless, chess is a good starting point for game theory in business. More complete explanations of game theory are in *The Compleat Strategyst* by the RAND Corporation, an early but classic explication of game theory (Williams, 1954).

The speculative implications for decision making for business have to do with the new possibility of mimicking competitive moves so there is no first mover advantage which is recognized as a competitive advantage by strategy theorists. One competitor makes a small move to test another competitor and to test market receptivity. Then there is usually a small countermove by the other competitor for the same reasons. These are competitive probes where there is thrust and parry but no strikes in the direction of the competitors. These may seem back and forth moves in which no competitor gains territory but any motion by either competitor reveals nimbleness and quick decision making.

If a calculus of successive decisions can be brought in to bear on decision making in the future, then bad decisions can be revealed and corrected and good decisions can be reinforced for more gain. Old style competitive advantages like barriers to entry are lessened in knowledge-based businesses which are emerging in number.

The actual capabilities of learning quickly from decisions rest in analytic technologies not in sheer speculation but speed in decision making and analytics of the same are occurring in the present and very likely to be advanced in the near future. The field of predictive analytics is where most of the action will happen. Predictive analytics means the capacity to obtain data about customers, analyze this data and act on the results of the analysis for the betterment of the organization (Halper, 2014). Predictive analytics is important because it affects all industries, not solely technology and retail industries. Even if the buyer is one, as the Defense Department is for Defense companies, it is important for the suppliers to know as much as they can about buying procedures, habits and criteria for government buyers.

The end product of the analysis is results of course. The results can be increased revenues, more efficient processes and otherwise aid the company. The aim of the analysis is usually the creation of a model that predicts how the customer will act.

Predictive analytics is in its infancy. It has a major future ahead because there is considerable impetus to discover who customers are and how they decide what to buy. Predictive analysis is a break from usual marketing research techniques which makes judgments about larger customer populations by sampling a select group of them and using that base to predict the behaviors of the larger population. There are many ways that error can creep in to this process. Predictive analytics bases its process on examining individuals and building the model of prediction directly from them. The sampling problems are eliminated.

Fern Halper in the same TDWI source cited earlier (2014) remarks that statistical and data mining techniques are not widely found in organizations. She discusses the movement in predictive analytics to have more people doing predictive analytics and more consumption of the results by employees. Yet the expectation of managers is that these systems will be built by those who know the business, know the data and are critical thinkers. Software providers have devised and commercialized programs to do the analytics, obviating the need to write code so predicting behaviors can be more widespread among members of the organization. To assure that this more widespread analysis is done right, Halper recommends proper training occur. Not all business analysts can be top-end predictors. They must understand what is being analyzed and they need training on the tool they are using. Collaboration with data scientists is required and high-risk analysis needs to be involved in or at least guide model development.

A consequence of this for decision making is that much more decision making will be pushed down to mid-level managers. Top level managers will be alleviated of having to make all levels of decisions.

Looming over all businesses is the question of the future of artificial intelligence and how it applies to decision making. At a conceptual level, artificial intelligence has been a highly anticipated development, marked by significant consequences for the world of business. It juxtaposes humans and computers in the working environment and poses the very fundamental issue of who will make the guiding decisions in business. Will they be made by people, by computers or a combination of both?

The advancement toward this issue was hastened mainly by computer power rather than advancement in human cognitive power. It happened as computers progressed beyond pure computational roles and entered into data analysis. This occurred as computers exponentially expanded their capabilities since the 1950s. First came decision support in which data was processed for human decision making. Then came expert systems in which the human role in decisions was reduced as expert systems produced decisions themselves that would be ratified by humans. An end state for this development was theorized to be artificial intelligence. That state was envisioned as having computers or having computers embedded in machines do all the thinking about work.

The critical issue is if and when non-human decision making processes could be done better by computers and not people. The test for this would be if computer-based decision making would produce measurable and superior results compared with human-based results. It would seem reasonable that an experiment would need to be designed that would simultaneously have a human and a computer pose a decision solution then compare the results of the computer decision with the human decision in an experimental condition. What this indicates is that for experiments to be conducted there needs to be an overlap between human and computer decision making. This is not only true for experimentation but also for an actual transfer from one form to another. One can easily envision a future where there is an extended period of both human and computer decision making and not just a flip switch from one condition to another. We are in this period where humans are checking the integrity of computer decision making but the informed speculation ought to recognize that computers should be checking our decision making. That is an area we are just entering.

At the present, computers cannot make decisions better that humans can. With the rapidity of computing capability and the extension of computing into human perceptual functions like vision, hearing and touching, computers become more than computational machines. "Computers are nothing more than fast calculators," test pilot Scott Crossfield once told author Bolland (Crossfield, 1985). Crossfield was wrong in saying this in the 1980s and even more wrong in the twenty-first century. As mentioned, computers have gone far past the computational phase and are now in the turning test of: If I cannot see it, can I tell if it a human or a computer?

In the technology area, there are future developments which might mean that a device that represents a nanotechnology which can do what humans can't do is feasible. A tiny robot that can perform surgery is one example. Technology can open new universes of human operations at the micro and macro level. Coupled with the analytical abilities of networked computers exponentially raises the capabilities of micro machines and computers.

The specialness of humans is that we make decisions based on emotions and a consciousness of self. Computers have neither of these attributes but that may change too. Emotions are a function of consciousness. We blush because we are embarrassed about something and relish the sentiment when we are complimented. The reactions may surprise us, reveal something about ourselves but they originate from a consciousness of self.

Consciousness is an acutely human aspect but is it really all that unique to humanity? The physiology of consciousness shows that consciousness is a means of communication among cells in a biological organism that allows the coordination of the entire being. We see a bear in the woods and we flee due to a visual sensory path which causes our legs to run. Can't it become true that a computer with such a similar consciousness and a sensory mechanism also wants to flee if danger is near? The idea and the actualization of it may not be as far-flung as it seems.

With respect to artificial intelligence, this is a directional approach to a major change in decision making. It is consequently speculative more than it is projective because there is no agreement on when it will happen, although there is general agreement that it will happen.

PEOPLE WORKING TOGETHER

The proximity of working close to co-workers will also affect decision making. There are three components to this and they all account for decentralized decision making.

The first is that there are now more people who work at home and do not travel to and from a centralized workplace. There is definitely a trend in this direction and work circumstances have changed with the advent of flextime employment, part time employment, family leave to accommodate people being able to work at home while still participating in shared decision making activity.

The second is that the rise in shared Internet applications allows people from different work groups at different locations in the world to now make decisions over technical matters, say looking at the same circuitry on a circuit board and try different circuit paths and have other engineers from another part of the country see and understand remotely suggested designs.

The third is that third-party consultants can be involved in making decisions about problems without being an employee of the business. Third-party consultants are now much more available and can be activated for specific issue consultations when decisions have to be made. It is no longer necessary to have more extensive project contracts along with consultants being on scene most of time.

The growth in independent consultants is cited by us as one of the ways work will change. The meaning of this in decision making is that there may be less stake in the decision by an outside consultant than if the decision was made by an employee. Consultants will take issue with that and say that they do have a stake in the decision but it is less a stake than it is for continuously employed staff.

Temporary work is also changing the nature of work. It is usually thought of as being less than professional project employment which covers more than professional work but general labor as well. Consultants are affiliated with business consulting groups. Temporary workers are now a regular part of the workforce yet are rarely involved in the decision making. Still, temporary workers do have a stake in decisions because they regularly return to do repeat job in the business such as repair work, moving and clean up. In these circumstances, they may be sources of information for decisions that need to be made of how to get things done better.

The decentralization of work carries with it the promise of major changes in how decision making will happen in the future. Collaboration within teams becomes very consequential. With far-flung teams, decisions have to be made with an understanding of the issues by all members of the team wherever they are. This might require more formalization of the decision making process.

It is also very likely that the communication of decisions will change too. There will be more of a burden on existing channels of communication and messages to be delivered to audiences not always nearby. The driving force at the headwaters of this is the increasing diversity of the American workforce.

The influx of native white male workforce entrants is diminishing rapidly and it is being replaced by immigrant, minority and female entrants. To communicate decisions, a variety of ways of speaking to a more diversified workforce is needed. Not only does that mean using languages other than English, but also employment of culturally specific icons for cultures that respond to such icons and project communications that match the values of other cultures.

The formulation of decisions may not be modified as much by a diversified workforce provided that there is proportional representation of the populations in that process but it will almost certainly be the case of decision communications.

The theme increasing diversity in the workforce is carried by an article in Forbes (Schwabel, 2016). Schwabel echoes the view that a more blended workforce is in progress. This extends past 2017 as well and is an implication from the article. Other Schwabel trends in the human resource management area are: improving employee and candidate opportunities and continuous reviews of employee work.

Tenure in jobs is much shorter now than in the last decade. The Bureau of Labor Statistics put average job tenure at 3.5 years. This is a great change from the 1950s where there was much more job stability. Consider the effect of the shorter tenures on deciding. Shorter term employees may be unfamiliar with the traditions of the organization nor have as strong a commitment as do longer term employees. Shorter term employees may feel more committed to their individual goals than corporate goals.

The very pronounced shift to service jobs from production jobs introduces a third element to the production and consumption function. Services are provided and consumed at the same time. Services also vary more than products coming off the production line. Human consumers determine if decisions resulted in satisfaction.

Another idea promulgated as being a trend is generational change. For our part, we dismiss this as a trend because our own research has shown that generations share attitudes and perceptions about work more than they find differences between and among generations (Bolland and Lopes, 2014). On some 33 elements of job perceptions and motivators, no real difference was found between generations.

On another dimension, we agree with the assessment that organizational structures will become less hierarchical in the future. The reasons for this are because hierarchical organizations are less nimble in the age of a global economy. It is also the case that hierarchical organizations are less preferred by working adults.

The type of structure that a company has, or will have, will have an effect on decision making. The trend cited now from various sources is that flatter and leaner organizations are growing compared to hierarchical organizations. The strength of the hierarchical organization is that the decision is reviewed by different levels before it takes effect. The weakness is that it is a longer process. For a flatter, less hierarchical organization, decisions are often more broadly based, and more participatory in a flatter more flexible organization. The downside is that decisions are not as deliberate as they might be in a hierarchy. Hierarchical organizations appear to be the least adaptable to changes coming from technological change. This is especially true for large hierarchical organizations. When contrasted with small, flatter organizations and new venture organizations, hierarchies have more investment in moving slowly and reacting more slowly to environmental change. This may be perfect for some religious and government organizations but for most others it is an obstacle.

MORE HOMEWORKERS, MORE DECISION DECENTRALIZATION

At present, 2.5 percent of the U.S. workforce works from home (Gverstad, 2015) but another contemporary technology magazine reports a survey from the Global Leadership Summit that 34 percent of respondents said more than half of full-time work would be done by those working remotely by 2020 (Vanderkam, 2014). The 2015 data points to and projects for 2020 a very dramatic shift toward remote-based work. This will mean more challenges to decision making mainly in the form of the mechanics of doing so. Home workers could vote remotely or they could articulate their decision preferences more informally. It may be easier to decide within an intact and physically proximate group of people but deliberation and every step up to a final decision can occur with remote workers.

In all likelihood, it will not be an either/or situation – either an intact internal work group that decides or a scattered and remote group that does but a blend of both for a matter of years.

CHANGES IN DECISION MAKING AND THE NATURE OF THE DECISION

Pushing more deeply into the future of decision making, an argument can be made that the forces of change will change the meaning of decisions themselves. In what ways might this come true?

We can look at and speculate that efficiencies in making decisions will lead to having to make fewer key or strategic decisions. It can also be looked at as having the opposing effect: more continuous strategic decisions that are entwined in one and another. In other words, more decisions more frequently. The answer lies in the soundness of decisions, how many and at what frequency will sound decisions replace unsound decisions?

The single largest factor that will determine how fast the shift to continuous but consequential decision making will occur is technological. Technology is the common thread though all our projection and speculation about the future. Hence, we conclude that it is the most important factor determining the pace of business decision making.

Technology development also has the impact of creating new jobs which, in turn, makes new modes of decision making possible. New businesses such as Uber and Airbnb have come about because of new ways of providing traditional services like transportation and housing respectively by way of the Internet. Web application developers never existed a few decades ago but now their numbers abound. The jobs that have emerged from the Internet universe have their influence over work today and the future. Those who make decisions need to involve these new workers who live in the new and emerging technologies in order to make decisions that incorporate superior technological advances. Without that, the deciders can be leapfrogged easily by competitors who consult more with their temporary workers about promising new technologies.

Decisions about technologies will also happen with more frequency and more consequence than they have in the past. Companies will need to decide which technology streams of development have true commercial development and which streams will fizzle. Not all technologies will burst open from the heavens and accord prosperity on those below. Cold fusion which once looked promising dissipated quickly. The same applies to many new battery technologies.

Globalism and decision making are individually immense as topics and as such, we can only treat a few aspects of the matter.

Globalism is a shift away from national-focused economies to a more integrated and interdependent economy. It is a fact that becomes an opportunity for international businesses. Both globalism and international business are broadly encompassing of activities beyond more constricted definitions.

Globalism is an orientation. It can be said that some businesses have this orientation and some do not. Quite clearly, multinational corporations (MNCs) have this orientation. True MNCs compete throughout the world for durable goods and consumables. Business organizations at this level have already attained an upper limit of geographic presence. They are everywhere. They compete against other MNCs and nations are the mere milieu of operations, not places to conquer. Operating in another nation requires savvy, but it is not an obstacle as it might be for a company taking its first step into the international market. The MNC already has an international marketing division. It has sorted through the thousands of issues and answered thousands of questions for its employees, investors, suppliers and distributors.

International business is more than exchanges of products and services for money by businesses. Money is more than cash. It is the transfer of resources by companies that can include intellectual property, assets and liabilities in mergers and acquisitions. Licenses and letters of credit are also exchanges including certain privileges to do business in a foreign country.

Globalism has taken hold in the reality of the many products and services we see in stores today. We take the "made in. . ." sticker for granted so the effects of globalism are readily apparent. Less apparent are the financial aspects of globalism where currency exchanges, loans, investments and futures trading are happening. Also, less apparent is the vast amount of business information that is transmitted via social networking via the Internet. Yet these and other factors are making globalism more pervasive than ever.

Some convergence of consumer tastes and preferences has occurred because of globalism but there has been divergence as well. Strong international brands such as Coke and Kentucky Fried Chicken have done well in the international sphere. There is divergence as well with a preference for local sourcing in the Green movement and an outright rejection of international brands as a representation of Western dominance by Mideastern religious fundamentalism.

An issue of decision making for business organizations has to do with the concentration and distribution of wealth. This issue was prevalent but far less prominent in national economies than in an international economy. The implicit question for business entities is: What role do businesses have in the creation and distribution of wealth? Having any role whatsoever is a valid question as is the question of what businesses should do in relation to what governments should do. In the global environment, the differences in wealth concentration in terms of numbers of people affected are immense on an international scale. As workers become more equal in terms of ability to do work via shared applications, disparities in national income will have to be taken into account by businesses. Where in the world workers will be is the obvious question for businesses.

Globalism is a force that needs to be reacted to. This is consequential for small regional firms that don't consider globalism in their strategic decision making. Even if a honey producer in the Midwest sells only in the Midwest, globalism can affect it, even if there is no direct competitor from overseas. Competition might come from international distributors who can put honey in local grocery stores from bees ten thousand miles away. Or competition may come from foreign governments that subsidize their own honey producers and put honey on the shelves of Midwest grocery stores for less than the retail price of a Midwest honey supplier.

The impetus of globalism also has an effect on what and how decisions are made. Put in its most basic form, globalism means that the entire world is the arena for businesses and economies. This means that business decisions can impact actors on a world scale. Getting decisions "right" on a world scale is plainly more complex than getting them "right" in local, regional or even national markets. The decision makers must consider how far the decision will travel in an international arena. If their business, like most, aimed for growth then there are far-reaching consequences for decisions. The decisions may spread for eventual positive or negative results.

The most fundamental initial business decision is whether to enter a foreign market or not. While there are other decisions such as having components made in other countries and managing supplier relationships, the crossing of the Rubicon comes when a company decides to offer products and services in a non-domestic market. It can be the decision to export or, at the other end of commitment, the decision to relocate entirely to another country, this decision is a basic change from the way business is done.

Modes of entry to the outside world are a few well-established paths. These are the "how" of extending the enterprise outward. In order of increasing commitment, these modes are:

a) Import / Export. This could be import only, export only or a combination of import and export.
b) Licensure. This decision sells the rights to use the name of the organization in foreign businesses. It is a risk-sharing option.
c) Joint venture or partnership with another organization.
d) Company-owned division in a foreign country.
e) Wholly owned subsidiary in a country outside the country of origin
f) Wholescale transfer of the entire business to a foreign country.

In considering decision implications, each of these items requires an ascending level of risk assumption. Consequently, a country risk assessment is done before the move is done. The downside of a wrong decision is quite steep in the wholescale transfer of the business to a foreign country ends up in nationalization of that business. At the import/export level and joint venture level, the loss side of an option is shared with a partner (joint venture) or the consequences only effect single products. This may seem significant for the small business but the investment loss is not nearly as great as it is for the higher risk international movements.

Decision making for established companies which want to maintain or expand international operations can be distilled to one important dimension and that is the extent of centralization or decentralization of decision making. This is the issue faced by Alfred Sloan in deciding how to keep General Motors as a coherent unit when so many different lines of vehicles were being produced. He decided a mixed approach would be best with the major brands like Chevrolet and Buick having separate decision making but still being accountable to General Motors.

With foreign operations, it has to be determined if centralized or decentralized decision making will occur. As far as a prediction, our conclusion is that there will be more decentralization of decision making. The reason for this is the ability of producing firms to respond to varied local and regional demand. There is also the fact that regional market unions have been challenged and Western democracies have experienced nationalistic fervor over regional economic unification. A continuation of centralization of decision such as having all strategic decisions made in one national headquarters would implant more inflexibility in corporate decision making.

CULTURE AND DECISIONS

The cultures that the companies dwell in do become a modifying condition for success. A regionally based decision focal point is more responsive to regional culture. Regional decisions can be done faster.

Culture is not going away. Melting pot depictions of large scale assimilation and a uni-culture have not supplanted a mass, uniform culture within nations. Instead, cultural differences are acknowledged and celebrated in many nations. While the Internet has been a means of sharing, it is also a means of preserving cultural identity.

Culture is at the forefront when the issue of ethical business behavior is considered. What comprises good and bad business practices happens as a cultural feature. It is not an overstatement to say that where an international company touches the customer and supplier most is at the local and regional level.

CENTRALIZATION AND DECENTRALIZATION

There are positive and negative things to say about centralization and decentralization. Centralization makes for uniformity in production and the possibility of effectively reducing costs throughout the system. The drawback is slower and distant decision making. Decentralization means local and regional responsiveness but it also introduces inconsistencies in products and greater overall costs.

Seemingly, as stated before, a mix of centralization and decentralization is a possibility. The mix can have the boundary of prohibited actions on the part of local and regional agents. It is not only the prohibitions but the mandated actions that need to be stated. The needed actions can refer to the overall corporate mission and a zone of what can be done without rebuke from headquarters. There is far too much to be prescriptive at this point but regional and global activities can be coordinated in our view of the future.

In *The World is Flat*, author Thomas Friedman (2005) puts together some ten more specific global changes into three powerful and synergistic ones. The three forces are new software and the Internet (which we have discussed), the incorporation of that knowledge into business and personal communication and the market power from people from Asia and the former Soviet Union who number in the billions as emerging consumers. Friedman asserts these forces gain their own critical mass. Each of the three factors feeds the others. We can speculate this will influence decisions of production and consumption among companies embracing internationalization. Friedman says in essence that the world is flat as far as obstacles for international business are concerned. He paraphrases an Indian executive who told Friedman that "if it can be digitized, it can be outsourced." Our corollary is that if it can be digitized, the decisions can also be outsourced, meaning that not only the services themselves are spread around the world, the data needed to make the decisions can be spread as well, to New Delhi or Shanghai City. This would argue for decentralization of decision making, putting the decision making closer to suppliers and/or customers.

The Freidman thesis is quite popular but not universally held. A contrary view is offered by Pankaj Ghemawat (2001) who offers that the world is semi-globalized and multi-domestic. The Freidman view is too simplistic. This author instead advises focusing on border-to-border economic activity and the use of CAGE framework to understand country and regional differences together with distance dimensions of culture, administration, geography and economics which form the acronym for CAGE. Cultural differences of norms, beliefs and practices reduce economic exchanges of goods and services. Administrative differences which are few in the form of governmental obstacles, regulations, and trade laws encourage trade. Geography whereas distance increases, trade decreases and finally economics, which refers to differences in demographic and socio-economic factors such as GDP and per capita income. Presumably, nations and regions with similar differences are more amenable to trade than nations or regions with large differences.

Concerning decision making, the CAGE framework can be used to determine where business decisions should be made. If trade potential is very high, then local decision making should be supported instead or centralized decision making at a headquarters location. Conversely, the Ghemawat point of view suggests that border trade between two very different national or regional partners should be centralized as far as decision making is concerned. That is because the differences are profound requiring very thorough analysis and planning before advancing to active trading status.

In such situations, a framework from strategic management such as a PEST analysis can assist in the decision making. The framework is another acronym where P stands for Political and Legal factors, E stands for Economic factors, S stands for Socio-Cultural factors and T stands for Technology factors. To these factors, many add N for Natural factors. An example of the last factor might mean acres of land available for crop cultivation. Application of PEST(N) can direct decision making to factors and, very importantly, trends in trading favorability or unfavorability. If for example, all the PEST(N) show no particular historic opportunity but a rapidly accelerating improvement in all PEST(N) elements, then centralized planning could prepare the domestic corporate for entering the other nation with an appropriate entry strategy suggested earlier.

In summary of the impacts of globalism on decision making, we see the main issues as being centralization or decentralization of decision making, sourcing of supplies and customers and market entry strategies which appropriately figure risk and reward. Globalism is a direction that cannot be easily retreated from. As long as there are resource differences and wealth differences in a world dominated by nation states and as long as corporate organizations exist, opportunities are plentiful for going to the nooks and crannies of the world for profits.

As a summary of the future of decision making in general, one speculation we have is that much more decision making in business will be done by information technology systems instead of by individual humans. The decisions will also be propelled to higher levels of computing capacity so that the decisions can be faster and better.

It is as though humans will have turned over a function of their own humanity to machines. The ideas about free will can be minimized and even extinguished in such a transition. This itself is not the issue. The issue is that a reversal of computer-based decision making will make life difficult for the living. In another way of putting this, it will be tougher to fight the machine. The basis of an information technology-based decision system in business will be very difficult to challenge. If a consumer has an argument with a business about the quality of a product they purchased, the consumer's appeal may only be heard by a rule-bound machine and not a human being. Getting a machine to change its mind based on something the consumer has had a bad emotional reaction to will be very hard. Even now, business consumer complaint functions have been removed from consumer proximity. Getting the attention of a live consumer after-market representative is challenging enough. Getting a response favorable to the consumer is even more difficult since the corporate representative will not depart from the complaint procedures manual in answering the complaint. The codification of procedures easily transfers to information technology-based decision systems which obviates the need for human interactions.

It could be that there might be a human revolt against all this, the computerization of decision making, but it has not happened yet. So, if it does happen, it might be too late to reverse, as those who own the computer decision systems believe these systems are efficient ways of doing business. The revolt may be stymied by the patience of the consumer wearing out in a futile argument with a computer (for which patience is a needless emotional attribute).

Decision making will move more to computer-based systems because it can and because it is in a business organization's interest to do so. Such a move is desirable because it is cost effective, it is reliable and it is fast compared to the human decision making process.

It is entirely conceivable that terms like "strategic decision making" will be removed from the parlance of business talk in the future. Certainly, the gap between the essentially simple human tools of decision making such as SWOT analysis, decision trees and PEST analysis fall behind the computer-driven econometric models, predictive market models and risk analyses of the world of information systems.

Computer-based decision making, as we define it, means the decision to be made is mainly done through software programs that are resident in computers instead of individual humans and humans collectively. The computer-based system uses exclusively databases within the computer or databases it can access. The decision needed is inputted by humans but the process of making the decision is not influenced by humans as it is being analyzed by the computer except if instructions are needed to complete the decision. The processes used to complete the decision are transparent to humans. Modifications to the computer decision process may be made by humans only when the modifications are directed to process efficiencies, reliability and validity of decisions.

There are areas of sensitivity in how computer-based decisions will interact in the delivery of decisions. Medical patients would be highly resistive to receiving a cancer diagnosis by way of a computer. Defendants in murder trials would not want to have a judge wheel in a computer to produce a jury verdict.

The interface in these and other instances should still be the human but that human also has to be an expert in how the computer-based decision was made, at least expert enough to be able to explain the conceptual steps taken in the analysis and conclusion of the decision.

All forces in the technology realm point to the use of more computer-based decision making. Robotics anthropomorphizes computers and makes them more interactive with humans. The integration of computers with machines makes computers much more ubiquitous.

Computing power itself has leapt exponentially, meaning faster processing. Computers are being constructed to have more human-like features which means the distance between man and machine is closing. Very importantly, there is more acceptability.

THE FUTURE OF PERFORMANCE MEASUREMENT

There is a future for performance measurement. As John Reed said of the Russian Revolution, "I have seen the future and it works" (Reed, 1919). Given more contemporary history, he might have modified his evaluation but the sentiment is still appropriate because it embodies hope about the future. Our derivative saying is that we have glimpsed at the future of business and it works in different ways than could be expected or predicted.

Performance is part of that future and it is that part that happens after decisions. It is hard to see how that will change in the next few years. But performance will change. It will be more integrative of more measures and will take a step beyond financial measures.

An expectation would be that as more measurement produces more historic data, it will be possible that more accurate expectations of performance will be devised. The science analog for this effect is in meteorology. The prediction of weather and climate has become much more accurate. A mass of seventy years of gathering and analyzing past weather systems led to modeling of weather tomorrow and the days ahead. This same kind of accumulation of business performance information has been accumulated on businesses to the point where future modeling of business performance can be done with reasonable accuracy. The business sector deals with more variables than weather variables (temperature, humidity, location, wind etc.) and it will probably take longer for business performance models to become accurate but some usable form of business performance modeling is coming. Why? Because there is a strong incentive to accomplish this by investors and also because business analytical techniques are advancing independently toward making this happen.

Within our crystal ball of prediction, we also see in the clouds a merger of the function of decision making and performance measurement. This is a natural development from the science side of business. It is a fundamental question to ask: "If we do this, what happens?" That is what experimentation in science does. In business, we also want to know as quickly and accurately as possible what results have been achieved by decisions.

What we expect as a result is measurements of current performance and not just cumulative performance at set intervals. Current performance measurement takes in very small time increments that can be compared to cumulative measurement. This measurement could go so far as instantaneous measurement under a calculus-type of approach to measurement mentioned earlier in the chapter, but that is not likely an immediate breakthrough.

Our speculation is that decision results will be isolated and delivered to software programs that produce partial results of the decisions as they are happening. The inputted results will be calculated to the extent they can be calculated based on incomplete information. What would also happen would be a comparison between expected and actual results at points in time. Put another way, for every stage of decision implementation, the corporate executives and others concerned would see the needle change on the results gauge.

Both decision making and performance measurement will change radically in the future. Of the two, changes will be most consequential in decision making. Performance that stems from decisions is a consequence but not an instigator of performance. So it is the decision making that we see as most susceptible to the forces affecting it. We would put technology as a leading force in this.

The fusion of decisions and performance, a prediction we arrive at by noting that decisions can be implemented more quickly than ever before and performance linked to decisions can be reported almost instantly, leads us to advance the idea that there will be a shift in the character of industry. That shift is the replacement of discrete product production to more continuous process-based functions. Think flow not form; a river not molecules of water. The move to mass customization to satisfy higher order customer demand is a driver for this. As a consequence, process industries such as electric utilities, natural gas producers and water utilities have an advantage over the traditional assembly line. The process industries have always been this way and they have practices in place to instantly react to changes in demand, whereas such changes require changeovers on the assembly line.

The way this shift will emerge starts with the capacity to merge decision making with performance measurement. This will come from technology. The capacity does not mean the result is deterministic though. The conduit will be consumer expectation for more, better, and faster and cheaper from producers. While producing forms may respond with "pick three of the four," it will be the producers who need to choose the three from the mix knowing all four are desirable but not ordinarily achievable. This shift will change the nature of decision making.

The acceleration of the ordering process is another prospect for the future. Shipbuilding is an example of this. Cruise ships take years to build and there is a contest on who can build the largest ships to handle larger numbers of passengers as described earlier. The more passengers, the more profits, but more passengers mean more cabins and more nautical challenges with the potential for capsizing as decks are piled on top of one another. The race to haul more passengers, now at 7,000 and more, translates into longer shipbuilding timetables. In these circumstances, the decisions need to be made earlier than ever before for many major capital projects like building a cruise ship. The same is true of most other businesses and this demonstrates the viability of early and sound decision making in present and future businesses. From this follows desired performance.

REFERENCES

Bolland, E. and Lopes, C. (2014) *Generations and Work*, New York: Palgrave Macmillan.
Crossfield, S. (1985) Private conversation with Eric Bolland, May 15.
Friedman, T. (2003) *The World is Flat*, New York: Farrar, Straus and Giroux.
Ghemawat, P. (2001) Distance Still Matters. The Hard Reality of Global Expansion. *Harvard Business Review*, 79(8), 137–147.
Gverstad, E. (2015) *PC Magazine*. December retrieved February 7, 2015.
Halper, F. (2014) *Predictive Analytics: Revolutionizing Business Decision Making*, October TDWI eBook.
Harrington, M. (1968) *Toward a Democratic Left*, New York: MacMillan Company.

Piketty, T. (2014) *Capital in the Twenty-First Century*, Cambridge, MA: Harvard University Press.

Reed, J. (1919) *Ten Days That Shook the World*, New York: Penguin Classics.

Schwabel, D. (2016) Ten Workplace Trends You'll See in 2017, *Forbes*, November 1, retrieved on February 7, 2017 from http://www.forbes.com/sites/danschawbel/2016/11/01/.

Vanderkam, L. (2014) Will Half of People be Working Remotely by 2020? *Fast Company*, August 14, retrieved on February 6, 2017 from https://www.fastcompany.com.

Williams, J. (1954) *The Compleat Strategyst*, Rand Series, New York: McGraw-Hill.

Index

Printed and bound by CPI Group (UK) Ltd, Croydon, CR0 4YY

23/04/2025

14660979-0002